THEMES OF THE BIBLE

Fides Publishers Association

THEMES

OF THE

BIBLE

by

JACQUES GUILLET

Translated by ALBERT J. LAMOTHE, JR.

NOTRE DAME, INDIANA

LIBRARY OF CONGRESS CATALOG CARD NUMBER: 61–9867

NIHIL OBSTAT:

James T. Burtchaell, C.S.C., S.T.L.

IMPRIMATUR:

Leo A. Pursley, D.D.

Bishop of Fort Wayne—South Bend

COPYRIGHT:

Fides Publishers Association

Notre Dame, Indiana, 1960

Published originally in France by F. Aubier, Éditions Montaigne,
13, Quai de Conti, Paris, 1954, under the title *Thèmes Bibliques*.

MANUFACTURED IN THE UNITED STATES OF AMERICA BY

BOOK CRAFTSMEN ASSOCIATES, INC., NEW YORK

Dedicated to

FATHER VICTOR FONTOYNONT

Contents

These few themes do not cover the entire Bible. They perhaps do not even represent its main outlines. Other themes might be vaster in scope, perhaps more important. These were chosen to open up certain perspectives in various directions. That is to say, this work is fragmentary. It is also an attempt, rather than a finished work; an attempt to study the religious vocabulary of the Bible; to grasp, through the history of a few words and a few images, the richness of the religion of Israel and the movement which led it to Jesus Christ. Desirous above all of taking in this movement in its entirety, I have had to leave aside a great many details, to go a bit fast at times. There are a certain number of hypotheses in these pages. Perhaps there is, above all, the fatal risk of trying to reconstruct the nuances of a mentality from which one is separated by thousands of years.

Nevertheless, one fact justifies this boldness. As far removed from the Hebrews as we are today, we live by the same Revelation. This work proposes to study the origins of this Revelation. These origins seem at times to be lost in the domain of primitive and naturalistic religions. This is an illusion. To conclude from certain contacts to religious dependence is to misunderstand the religion of the Bible. While it does borrow certain images from the surrounding religions, and even more from the religious substratum common to all mankind, it does so only in order to orient these immediately in its own way. This transformation in expression corresponds to the conversion of heart necessary for adhering to the true God. Just as conversion requires the grace of God, so too the foundation of the religious language proper to Yahwism owes its origins to God's Revelation.

The subsequent progress of this language is also that of Revelation. Because it is sometimes the work of exceptional people, or seems to be the fruit of a destiny without precedent, one is tempted to see in it the result of a natural process of refinement. These pages, on the contrary, seek to highlight the supernatural nature of this progress. The experiences which constantly give new wealth and depth to the religious language of Israel are the work of the Spirit of God and the revelation of His Word. In its most diverse forms, whether in the great work of a Moses, in the vibrant heart of a poet, in the wise man's daily effort at being faithful to the Law, in the message of the prophets, God was blazing His paths.

Until we have emerged from the Old Testament, this supernatural character remains obscure. It is revealed in its full splendor when Jesus Christ appears. Then is manifested the profound convergence of many diverse paths, then is discovered the full meaning of the boldest formulas. Revelation bursts forth in a definitive manner. Everything seems new and, yet, everything was already well-known. *Vetus Testamentum in Novo patet*, "The Old Testament stands revealed in the New." Thus, on his last night, the faithful servant, upon opening the door to his Lord, sees revealed, in the look of Jesus, the ultimate meaning of his existence, by discovering that it was entirely the work of His love.

I wish to thank my two Scripture teachers, Fathers Raymond Pautrel and André Lefèvre, for their help and advice. I cannot calculate the extent of my debt to Father Victor Fontoynont. I know only that the best of what is in these pages comes from him. May he accept the homage of this dedication.

The transcription of the Hebrew alphabet is that of the *Revue Biblique*, except for a few details: *aleph* noted by an apostrophe ', the aspirate *p* by *ph*, and *shin* written *sh*.

FOREWORD TO THE SECOND EDITION

With the exception of certain formulas concerning the notion of justice, modified in Chapter II, certain footnotes corrected or added, and inaccurate references corrected, this second edition is identical with the first.

TRANSLATOR'S NOTE

In rendering the Biblical references encountered in *Themes of the Bible*, I have used, wherever possible, the Confraternity of Christian Doctrine translation. Where that was not available —and, in a few cases, where I judged the Douay version to fit the context better—I used the Douay. In a few instances, where there were differences in the numbering of chapter and verse between the English translations referred to above and the French translation used by the author, I have followed the numbering of the particular English version used.

In the course of tracing the evolution of certain words and concepts, the author quotes extensively from the Bible, and the references contain the word or phrase he is explaining. Occasionally, especially in Chapters II and III, the English version of the same biblical reference does not contain the word or phrase in question. As this would obviously make the references meaningless for the English reader, I have taken the liberty of making a direct translation from the French version used by the author, of the words or phrases in question.

THEMES OF THE BIBLE

Chapter I

THEMES OF THE EXODUS—THE
MARCH THROUGH THE DESERT

The Exodus is the decisive event in the history of Israel. In the consciousness of the people, the march through the desert, between the miracle of the Red Sea and the miracle of the Jordan, holds the place which is occupied in the Christian consciousness by the life of Jesus. Many features attest to the exceptional importance of this period in the Hebrew religion.

It is, first of all—and almost exclusively—the time of miracles. Next to it, only the period of Elias and Eliseus shows a series of miracles, and, even in these, the memory of the Exodus appears in the multiplication of food, the march through the desert, the vision of Horeb. The Exodus remains the exemplary period of the miracle, of a miracle prolonged for forty years, of an existence raised entirely to the level of the miraculous. Of course, among the accounts found in the Pentateuch, a certain number allow us to get a rather different picture of the end of this period, a picture that was one of the common facts about the desert—the migration of sheep-herding tribes already living off the resources of the land and on the point of giving up the nomadic life.[1] Still, the lasting impression which Israel has of this era is that of a forty-year-long segment during which God suspended, in favor of His people, the normal conditions

1

of life. He alone saw to its needs, He became its guide and defender. Daily life did not start up again until after the first Passover celebrated in Palestine, after the crossing of the Jordan, when the manna ceased falling.[2]

Another indication of its place in the religious memory of the people is that the Exodus transformed the Hebrew liturgy into a memorial. The most ancient Hebrew code, the one called the Code of the Covenant,[3] prescribes the celebration of three annual feasts: the feast of the unleavened bread, that of the planting, and that of the harvest.[4] All three are agrarian feasts, celebrating, in succession: spring, with the beginning of the barley planting, summer, with the end of the wheat planting, autumn, with the grape-gathering. They are seasonal feasts, three feasts of a peasant religion, sensitive to the forces which give life to nature, forces that are universal symbols of the divine power.[5]

These feasts all tend to be transformed into historical anniversaries. Pentecost is to become, in later Judaism, the feast of the Law, promulgated on Sinai fifty days after the crossing of the Red Sea.[6] After Leviticus, the autumn feast of the Tabernacles is no longer only the harvest festival, but the remembrance of the leafy huts of the desert march.[7] For the Passover, the transformation goes back to the most ancient texts.[8] The Code of the Covenant links it explicitly with the feast of the unleavened bread and the departure from Egypt.[9]

Thus, the God to whom Israel offers the first-fruits of its flocks and its harvests is no longer the faceless divinity whence spring the obscure forces of life; He is Yahweh, the God of its fathers, the God who freed it from Pharaoh's tyranny. By becoming an historical commemoration, the liturgy imposes the personal traits of God. Conversely, by penetrating into the sphere of worship, the historical memory of the Exodus ceases to be an exhilarating remembrance of the past and becomes charged with the religious emotion aroused by the rites; it be-

2

comes, each year, the supreme moment when Israel renews its communion with its God.[10]

If it had been present only in the cult, the event of the Exodus would have not succeeded in coming out of the past, no matter how profound Israel's religious sentiments had been. The cult would have remained the commemoration of an historical fact without precedent, but also without future. The prophets, totally intent upon the realization of God's designs and on the doing of His will by men, made the Exodus into a moment destined to be renewed in the future. In this way, they gave to the liturgical celebrations their efficacious value of actual communion with a God whose past action guaranteed His unfailing presence in the history of the world. They made the Exodus into a permanent act of God.

Although it is difficult to regain contact, through the obscurity of documents and the distance between mentalities, with the religious forces which animated the liturgy of Israel, the words of the prophets impose themselves upon us still, in their warmth and light. They, above all, permit us to pursue, throughout history, the themes of the Exodus.

Amid the multiple recollections of the Exodus, the prophets show little attachment to the great dates solemnized by the liturgy—the sacrifice of the Pasch, the concluding of the covenant, the crossing of the Jordan. One grand image absorbs them all, the march through the desert, the forty years during which the people lived under God's direct guidance.

For Amos, these forty years are the exemplary period of the history of Israel, to which one has to turn to find the authentic ideal of Yahwism, away from the failures and deviations of the present:

Did you offer victims and sacrifices to me in the desert for forty years, O house of Israel?[11]

For Osee, the vision of the desert evokes the freshness of first love, the blessed moments of the wedding day, when the faith-

fulness of Israel responded to Yahweh's tenderness.[12] Despite
the people's treason, these moments will return. Yahweh's love
can remake the adulterous spouse into the virgin who gives
herself in the purity of her first giving:

> Therefore, behold I will allure her and will lead her into the wilderness:
> and I will speak to her heart.
> And I will give her vinedressers out of the same place, and the valley of
> Achor for an opening of hope; and she shall sing there according to the days
> of her youth, and according to the days of her coming up out of the land of
> Egypt.[13]

The conversion of Israel must literally be a second Exodus.

In Isaias, the recollections of the Exodus seem, even more so
than in all the other prophets, linked with liturgical ceremo-
nies and formulas. The hostility of Assyria threatens to plunge
the people back under the tyranny of Egypt,[14] but the "Lord
of hosts shall raise up a scourge against him according to the
slaughter of Madian in the rock of Oreb."[15] This past has more
than just the value of an example. It repeats itself. The flood
that will destroy Assyria will mark a new Passover night. Just
as on the day when He came down into Egypt to kill all the
first-born of the land, sparing those of His people, passing over
the latter without touching them,

> . . . so shall the Lord of hosts come down to fight upon mount Sion and
> upon the hill thereof.[16]

He will repeat the Passover action:

> . . . so will the Lord of hosts protect Jerusalem, protecting and delivering,
> passing over and saving.[17]

And while He "shall show the terror of his arm," and Assyria
will feel Yahweh's fury falling upon it, the night, "the festive
night,"[18] the paschal night, will ring with the sound of the "tim-
brels and harps," and the dances of consecration,[19] just as the
women of Israel, led by Miriam, had accompanied with dancing
Yahweh's triumph over Pharaoh.[20] The liturgy which com-

4

memorated the ancient miracle will therefore serve to celebrate the coming deliverance.

The prophecies addressed to the exiles sing especially of a new world:[21]

> Remember not former things, and look not on things of old.
> Behold I do new things, and now they shall spring forth, verily, you shall know them.[22]

Again, to describe this new exploit of God's, the poet takes up the memories of the Exodus, enlarging upon them as he does so. Here is the flight out of the condemned country:

> Depart, depart, go ye out from thence, touch no unclean thing. Go out of the midst of her, be ye clean, you that carry the vessels of the Lord.
> For you shall not go out in a tumult, neither shall you make haste by flight.[23]

the miracle of the protecting cloud:

> For the Lord will go before you, and the God of Israel will gather you together.[24]

the crossing of the sea on dry ground:

> Thus saith the Lord, who made a way in the sea, and a path in the mighty waters.[25]

the water flowing from the rock:

> The Lord hath redeemed his servant Jacob.
> They thirsted not in the desert, when he led them out. He brought forth water out of the rock for them, and he clove the rock, and the waters gushed out.[26]

At the passing of the people, the desert will become a garden:

> I will make a way in the wilderness, and rivers in the desert.
> . . . to give drink to my people, to my chosen.
> This people have I formed for myself, they shall show forth my praise.[27]

The people that God will guide in this way is no longer characterized by its blood, but by its divine mission. It is charged with singing the praises of Yahweh. The itinerary which it fol-

lows is not only strewn with prodigies, but also consecrated
to God:

And a path and a way shall be there, and it shall be called the holy way:
the unclean shall not pass over it.[28]

Along with the unclean, fools are eliminated from the ret-
inue.[29] That is to say that the scene, although inspired by the
visions of the return from exile, takes place in sapiential horizons. The caravan of the redeemed is no longer the little group
that Zorobabel brought back from Babylon to Jerusalem, but
the mass of the Hebrews faithful to Wisdom, faithful to the
Law.

The famous poem which describes the descent into Sheol of
the King of Babylon, seems to link, in a single liberation, the
deliverance effected by Noe, by Moses, and by Cyrus:

And it shall come to pass in that day, that when God shall give thee rest
from thy labor, and from thy vexation, and from the hard bondage, where-
with thou didst serve before,
Thou shalt take up this parable against the king of Babylon. . . .[30]

The rest from the fatigue arising from working under a
cursed sun, had been the blessing which Noe had won for the
earth,[31] and the hard bondage was that which Israel had known
at the time of the forced labor in Egypt,[32] so that the curse of
the earth after Adam's sin, the oppression of Egypt, and the
Captivity, merge into one picture, the archetype of all servitude. The liberation of the Exodus, which had given Israel its
homeland, becomes by analogy the archetype of the liberation
we are eternally hoping for.

With the same frequency as the prophets, the psalms take up
the theme of the march through the desert. At times they see
in it the supreme gesture of God's power laughing at the elements, as in the psalm *In exitu*:

Before the face of the Lord, tremble, O earth,
    before the face of the God of Jacob,
Who turned the rock into pools of water,
    the flint into flowing springs.[33]

Most of the time, the march in the desert is described as the wandering of a flock led by its shepherd. Reflection upon the Exodus is one of the sources of the theme of the Shepherd.[34] In Osee, the departure from Egypt already evokes the care bestowed upon a flock,[35] but Yahweh's attentiveness to His own is so full of human tenderness that His actions are no longer those of a shepherd toward his sheep, but rather those of a father, and of a mother with her child. The vision of Yahweh bringing His people back to Palestine recalls that of Jacob bringing his flocks back from Laban's country, his concern for the weakest animals. Again, it is the Exodus which calls forth the image of Yahweh's flock:

Where is he that brought them up out of the sea, with the shepherds of his flock?

He that led them out through the deep, as a horse in the wilderness that stumbleth not.

As a beast that goeth down in the field. The spirit of the Lord was their leader.[36]

The picture returns in the great psalms which review the history of Israel:

But his people he led forth like sheep
and guided them like a herd in the desert.[37]

It is also linked with the Exodus in the hymns of praise, where the historical recollections are normally much less frequent:

Come, let us bow down in worship;
let us kneel before the LORD who made us.
For he is our God,
and we are the people he shepherds, the flock he guides.
Oh, that today you would hear his voice:
"Harden not your hearts as at Meriba,
as in the day of Massa in the desert,
Where your fathers tempted me;
they tested me though they had seen my works."[38]

In the prayers, the petitioner nourishes his confidence with the remembrance of the exalted deeds of Yahweh, that is, of the Exodus:

7

Through the sea was your way,
    and your path through the deep waters,
    though your footsteps were not seen.
You led your people like a flock
    under the care of Moses and Aaron.[39]

Thus the psalms, the liturgical canticles, give to the liturgy of Israel its meaning. Centered on the divine presence of the sanctuary, it perpetuates the presence and the action of God in the midst of the people. Yahweh is not only the shepherd who led the ancients into the desert; He is today the shepherd of Israel, and the latter can now say: "We are the people of thy pasture." And so the faithful find again the situation of their fathers. They too have their Exodus. While the prophets, who tend toward the future, invoke the second Exodus, the final liberation, the psalms, expressing the actual interior life of the community, see the drama of the Exodus being renewed every day in each Israelite.[40] External circumstances lose some of their importance. The emphasis is on the parallelism of the situations. The events of the past become types of an interior order.

Here the vocabulary adds to its marks. Of the characteristic words of the Exodus, it is noteworthy that the psalms have retained those whose sense is purely interior, those of the temptation. The Pentateuch accounts were already partly constructed on this theme. The words of the root to tempt, *nasah,* come up time and again like a refrain. The Jews are scarcely out of Egypt when the episode of Mara recalls the first instance when Yahweh "tempted" Israel.[41] The manna is a way for God to "tempt" His people,[42] as is the descent of Yahweh on the mountain in clouds of fire.[43] Deuteronomy reproduces these interpretations[44] and generalizes them by summing up the forty years as one single test or temptation:

For forty years now the LORD, your God, has directed all your journeying in the desert, so as to test you by affliction. . . .[45]

The people succumbed to this temptation by Yahweh, and their fault lay in "tempting God" in their turn. The same words,

8

the verb *nasah,* the noun *massah,* express the two temptations and place them in the same episodes. At the waters of Mara, Yahweh tempts His people; at the waters of Massa, it is the people which tempts Yahweh.[46] The murmurings and the revolt of the people of the desert are just so many temptations of God.[47] Deuteronomy sums up fidelity to the Law in a formula:

You shall not put the Lord, your God, to the test, as you did at Massa.[48]

The psalms too, have stressed this word. For them also, the Exodus was the moment when Israel tempted God.[49] And, since the Exodus takes place forever, it is still, even today, a question of not tempting God:

> Harden not your hearts as at Meriba,
>   as in the day of Massa in the desert,
> Where your fathers tempted me.[50]

The Epistle to the Hebrews noted the ever-present nature of the appeal: "While it is still Today."[51] It would be possible to see in his reasoning only an argument of rabbinical fabrication, based on some surprising detail of the text requiring an explanation. It is possible that such was indeed the conscious intent of the author. But in fact, what he finds himself expressing is the profound thought of the psalmist for whom Yahweh's call never ceases echoing "today."

Another expression, "the ways of Yahweh," takes on an interior meaning in the recollections of the Exodus in the psalms. Actually, the expression does not belong to the proper vocabulary of the Exodus as do those concerning temptation. The word *derek,* from a root which signifies walking and, more particularly, the movement of the foot being set down, primarily designates the road, the path outlined by the impression of repeated steps. Transferred to the moral sphere, it is equally used to designate a habit, the repetition of the same actions. Not, however, common habits, but rather those which are properly characteristic of an individual or of a community; *derek* is almost always followed by a personal suffix or by a deter-

9

minative. It is someone's personal "way." The well-known phrase, "My ways are not your ways,"[52] admirably states this individual characteristic: everyone follows his own path, accord to his own pace, or, as we would say today, his style. And it is altogether natural that God, too, should have His personal styles, His "ways." Of itself, the expression has only a general meaning, even if the primitive image remains very concrete. But the psalms insert it on several occasions in a context of the Exodus which gives it a singular evocative power:

> Forty years I loathed that generation,
>   and I said: They are a people of erring heart,
>   and they know not my ways.[53]
> I, the Lord, am your God
>   who led you forth from the land of Egypt;
> If only my people would hear me,
>   and Israel walk in my way.[54]

In this historical context, God's ways are not merely His general intentions. At one point in history, Yahweh revealed in a dramatic light what His ways were: during forty years, He led His people according to His own itinerary. Without the ever-living memory of this march in the paths of his God, the Israelite, in speaking of the "ways of God," would only have evoked mere human constructions and abstractions. God's ways might have been the interior aspirations of his conscience, or the imperatives dictated by his social environment. Perhaps they would not have lacked grandeur. But they would always have remained the ways of man. Because his ancestors really did follow God's ways, because the Yahweh of the Exodus continues to be the Shepherd of Israel, the Israelite can no longer think about God's ways without having some historical experience—more or less consciously—give this word a touch of authentic reality, nor can he any longer dissociate his personal conduct from the revelation of God in history.

In the recollections of the Exodus, the motifs of water and manna are often joined to the themes of the Shepherd and of

His ways. Deuteronomy gives manna a spiritual significance:

He therefore let you be afflicted with hunger, and then fed you with manna, a food unknown to you and your fathers, in order to show you that not by bread alone does man live, but by every word that comes forth from the mouth of the LORD.[55]

These words signify first of all that God has other means of nourishing man than with natural products, and that He has at His disposal food unavailable to man. Nevertheless, the remark, "every word that comes forth from the mouth of the Lord," points in a higher direction. For, if from the mouth of God proceeds the breath which gives life to all living things,[56] this breath is above all the bearer of His word and of His will, so that the formula at least intimates an immaterial food.

Psalm 80 sees, in the miraculous nourishment of the desert, the sign of the good things with which God wants to shower His people once they are established on their land:

> I, the LORD am your God
>   who led you forth from the land of Egypt;
>   open wide your mouth, and I will fill it.
> If only my people would hear me,
>   and Israel walk in my ways,
> . . . Israel I would feed with the best of wheat,
>   and with honey from the rock I would fill them.[57]

This exquisite food given by God to His children is none other than the prosperity promised by Yahweh for the faithful keeping of His commandments, and this entire Psalm 80 is interwoven with allusions to Deuteronomy.[58] In any event, it establishes a continuity between the miraculous food of the desert and the fertile harvests with which the land of Palestine is to reward the faithfulness of Israel. Once again, the daily life of the Hebrew takes its meaning by reference to the sacred period of the beginning: it must reproduce this period.

Psalm 22 seems to push the symbolism of the motifs of the Exodus to the point of voiding all history:

11

> The LORD is my shepherd; I shall not want.
> In verdant pastures he gives me repose;
> Beside restful waters he leads me;
> he refreshes my soul.[59]

Is the poet still thinking of God bringing His flock up out of Egypt? Undoubtedly, the word "repose" evokes the theme of Josue leading the people into the repose of the Promised Land,[60] and belongs to the ordinary vocabulary of the Exodus.[61] To be sure, we must point out that the image of Yahweh "preparing a table" for His faithful one is found elsewhere, where it designates the miracle of the manna. Still, the expression, borrowed from daily life, was common enough, so that it would be useless to conjecture about some literary reminiscence.[62] The association of the table and the cup[63] is also commonplace. These are the inevitable actions of the host receiving his guests. Psalm 22 might therefore contain no reference to the Exodus and be merely a description of God's generosity to His creation which He invites to His own table. But it remains that, without the Exodus, this beautiful image would only be a poetic parable, unverifiable. But the parable *had* been lived. The images of Yahweh shepherding His people, giving it its food in the midst of its enemies, receiving it, so to speak, at His table, remained facts of experience in the consciousness of Israel. Faith rested upon history.

The Book of Wisdom, the latest book of the Old Testament, shows how far the Israelite's reflections on his history could lead, and at the same time sets the limits that could not be exceeded. Along the lines of Deuteronomy and Psalm 80, it sees in the miracle of the manna an invitation to penetrate into the real meaning of creation, entirely docile to the divine intentions, transparent to the eye of faith which can discover, beneath the most natural, the most impersonal, phenomena, God's love, concerned with feeding His children and teaching them that:

> . . . it is not the various kinds of fruits that nourish man,
> but it is your word that preserves those who believe you![64]

12

Pushing this reflection further, Wisdom discovers, beyond the divine actions, the heart of their author. It tastes with pleasure, in the exquisite flavor of the manna, God's own savor, "your sweetness toward your children."[65] This look which traverses history in order to fix itself upon the sweetness of God, represents the supreme effort of the Old Testament, an effort which would, without the New Testament, end in failure, in a sublime contemplation doomed to remain isolated. To do away with this isolation, to substitute for this soliloquy the revelation of a presence, the response of a person, the Word of God became incarnate in Jesus Christ. In this meeting, the world is transformed. Alone, Jesus Christ suffices to replace all of Scripture.

Still, Scripture remains necessary. Not alongside Jesus, but in order to explain Him. What meaning can Christians attach to the unique event which has turned their lives inside out? There is no other way to interpret the Christian fact but through the Old Testament. Though it seems no more than a groping in the dark, it is still a journey under the guidance of God. With love, Christians tie themselves to this history in order to understand their own experience. Amid this world of images, those which evoke the Exodus and the march in the desert hold a privileged place. Here, more than anywhere else, God Himself had acted.

In St. Paul, the interpretation is already complete. He formulates it in an apparently baffling symbolic arrangement which, however, actually reveals a most profound understanding of the biblical facts. For if, in order to give meaning and names to their experience, Christians draw upon biblical history, if, for example, they call it redemption or expiation, referring to the liberation from Egypt or the annual solemnity of expiation, they find themselves at the same time throwing light upon their own experience, and attaining to the most profound essence of the events of the history of Israel. St. Paul gives the clearest example of this procedure at work.

13

According to St. Paul, the Hebrews underwent a Baptism in crossing the Red Sea; not merely because they went across the water, but because they were under the cloud, because they had a truly supernatural experience. They were, in effect, "baptized in Moses in the cloud and in the sea,"[66] that is, they were associated with the new community founded by Moses. The use of unleavened bread[67] is the sign of this renewal, which, since Judaism, has been the essential feature of Passover. All these details had their importance: They happened "as a type, and were written for our correction, upon whom the final age of the world has come."[68] The crossing of the Red Sea was the figure of Christian Baptism; the manna and the water from the rock, the symbols of the Eucharist. The Exodus is the type of the two fundamental sacraments.

What do we mean when we say "type"? Is it not an abuse of a simple external resemblance—passing through water—to say that the Red Sea is a Baptism? Is that not the usual method of St. Paul, who is accustomed to taking the liberties of a son of the family with the heritage which he knows to be his?[69] Certainly, there are some disconcerting procedures in these Pauline exegeses.[70] St. Paul makes use of the rabbinical methods of argumentation of his time. But he is infinitely more than a rabbi. He is constructing a theology. He is formulating the meaning of the event which has just transformed the world: the life, death, and resurrection of Jesus. And he is formulating this meaning in Old Testament terms. His genius consists in having isolated from the great mass of rabbinical theories their guiding lines, those which express both the structure of Israel's religion and the essential data of the religious consciousness: the role of the law and of faith, the hope of justice, the forgiveness of sins, the knowledge of God. While he attaches to external similarities the conclusive value of a sign, which nowadays astonishes us, still, in his own eyes, that is not the essential part. The essential part is that, in leaving Egypt on the word of Moses in order to bury itself in the desert under the direct guidance of Yahweh, the Hebrew people accomplished a religious effort analogous to that of the Christian who renounces the pagan world and places his existence in God's hands.

The march through the desert, finally, holds an important place in the Gospels, absolutely independent of the theological reflections of St. Paul. The account of the temptation of Jesus in the desert, during the forty days of fasting, is an obvious recalling of the forty years of the Exodus. But the parallelism is not limited to the number forty. It extends to the very substance of those forty years, which consisted of a temptation. Just as Israel, after having been chosen by Yahweh as His son,[71] was led into the desert by a column of fire, that is, according to a consecrated interpretation in Israel, by the holy spirit of Yahweh,[72] in order to be tempted for forty years,[73] so too is Jesus, the well-beloved Son of God,[74] impelled into the desert by the Spirit who has just revealed Himself at the Jordan, in order to undergo His temptation.[75] His temptation is that of His people: to look for His nourishment to the earth and not to God alone,[76] to demand signs for His imagination, to tempt God,[77] and finally, the supreme trial, to adore another than God.[78] If Jesus answers Satan with scriptural texts, it is not only in order to rebuff the dangerous suggestion by an unanswerable argument, even less because of some magical virtue in the inspired words themselves. It is because He has been placed by the devil in the situations in which Israel had fallen, by demanding meat on the day of the quail,[79] by demanding a sign at Massa,[80] by renouncing Yahweh in front of the Golden Calf.[81] Of course, there are some rather appreciable differences: while the conduct of Yahweh had been revealed in the Exodus by a series of striking miracles, Jesus must find it here in the refusal of any outward sign. Still, the continuity with Israel far exceeds the external framework; similar situations are involved. In re-crossing Egypt, the Jordan, or the desert, Jesus is doing something quite different from pious pilgrimages over the footprints left by His people. He is remaking, on His own account, the people's spiritual journey. Triumphing over the trial in the desert, He reveals Himself to be, alone, the faithful people, the authentic Israel, the Son of God.

The temptation in the desert is itself but the type of the decisive temptation. Like the entire public life, it remains partially prophetic. "The devil," rebuffed, "departed from Him for a while,"[82] until His hour should come, the hour of the power of darkness.[83] Until His hour has come, Jesus has not truly completed His Exodus.[84] This hour is called by Jesus Himself His Baptism,[85] the hour of the chalice which He must drink.[86] Like St. Paul, Jesus interprets His Passion in a vocabulary which will later become that of the two great Christian sacraments, but which also links up with that of the Exodus.

These verbal connections are the sign of profound contacts. Between the way in which Jesus accomplishes the Exodus of His people, and the way in which He establishes His sacraments, there is a kind of symmetry. Every year, the Hebrew people relived its Exodus in its liturgy. Jesus relived it, first in His heart, then in His flesh and in His blood. This act definitively fulfilled and made forever vain the entire liturgy of Israel, which was directed toward a memory. At the same time it inaugurated a new era. From now on, the Exodus of this era must be in turn relived by Christians. Such is the role of their liturgy and their sacraments, which are not the evocation of a bygone past, but the gift of a living presence.

For if Jesus relives in His existence the history of His people, it is not only because He is its representative: it is also because He is the perfect man. He takes unto Himself the experience of mankind. In order to be able to baptize His own, He must first be plunged into His own Baptism; in order to distribute to them the chalice of His table, He must first drink His own chalice. But, once the chalice had been consumed, once He had been immersed even to the death, in the deep waters of suffering, once the horror of the world abandoned by God and given over to Satan had been crossed, Jesus rose again. From that moment, He could become "our Passover."[87] Without Christ, man would pursue all alone his religious journey, would experience all alone the great realities which make up his life: evil, work, love, death. He would live in a monologue, imprisoned within the bounds of his own consciousness. Jesus has broken down these barriers by making the destiny of man His destiny, and by transfiguring it. The aspiring to conversion, to the search for God, such as man naturally experiences it, is fulfilled in this aspiration as Jesus Christ experienced it, strongly enough to make Him pass through death. The spontaneous disgust with sin is transformed on contact with Jesus' infinite horror of evil.

NOTES

[1] Cf. Num. 32: 1–15.
[2] Jos. 5: 10–12; Ex. 16:35.
[3] Ex. 20: 1; 24, 8.
[4] Ex. 23: 14–16.
[5] The three feasts of the Code of the Covenant already presuppose agrarian rites. They are the feasts of farmers who are at least semi-sedentary. Nevertheless, the feasts of the Azymes is also, according to the code of Ex. 34: 18–26, and also Ex. 23: 14–19, a feast of sheep-herders, and the two rites will continue to be associated (Lev. 23: 10–12). It is difficult to specify whence this association arises, but it is quite natural. Spring brings both the first-fruits of the earth and of the flock (cf. R. Dussaud, *Les origines cananéennes du sacrifice israélite*, 2e edition, Paris, 1941, p. 209). According to W. Eichrodt (*Theologie des A.T.*, 3e Aufl. Berlin, 1948, I, p. 52), the tribes of the north, engaged in agriculture, celebrated the agrarian rites, while the tribes of the south, specializing in sheep-raising, sacrificed the first-born of their flocks during the "Paschal festival."
[6] Cf. Ex. 19: 1.
[7] Lev. 23: 43.
[8] Ex. 23:15. A critical historian, A. Lods, pushes this transformation back to "before the eighth Century." (*Israel, des origines au VIIIe siècle*, Paris, 1930, p. 505.)
[9] M. H. Cazelles, in his *Études sur le Code de l'Alliance*, Paris, 1946, indicated the extent to which the content of the Code justified the tradition that associates it with Moses. In turn, the upheaval which transformed into historical anniversaries festivals which their own laws assigned to perpetuating the eternal return of the natural cycles, confirms the historical nature of the traditions concerning the Exodus.
[10] W. Eichrodt has brought to light the actual contact, the evocation of the divine presence brought about by the liturgy. Cf. op. cit., pp. 39–40, 69–70.
[11] Amos 5: 25; cf. 2: 10.
[12] Os. 2: 17; 9: 10; 11: 1; 13: 4–5.

[13] Os. 2: 14–15; cf. 12: 10.

[14] Is. 10: 24.

[15] Is. 10: 26.

[16] Is. 31: 4.

[17] Is. 31: 5. The reference to the account of Ex. 12: 21–33 seems indisputable.

[18] Is. 30: 29.

[19] Is. 30: 32, according to the generally accepted correction of *milhamot* to *meholot*. O. Procksch (*Jesaia I*, Leipzig, 1930, pp. 402–403) notes that these *meholot tenuphah* recall the rites in which the first-fruits offered for the Pasch were balanced (*nuph*) before Yahweh.

[20] Ex. 15: 20.

[21] Cf. the return of the word *bara'*, the word of the divine creations.

[22] Is. 43: 18–19.

[23] Is. 52: 11–12. It is very likely that "in a tumult" (*hippazon*), is a reference to the haste in which the Hebrews had to eat the Pasch (Ex. 12: 11; Deut. 16: 13).

[24] Is. 52: 12.

[25] Is. 43: 16.

[26] Is. 42: 20–21.

[27] Is. 43: 19, 20, 21.

[28] Is. 35: 8.

[29] *Ibid.* The end of the verse is hopelessly corrupted. But it is certain that the fools disappear, that they are converted or are reproved. The word *'awil* is typically sapiential.

[30] Is. 14: 3.

[31] Gen. 5: 29, where the verb *nuh* and the noun *'isbon* seem to have been the inspiration for the compound *nuh 'oseb* in Is. 14: 3.

[32] Ex. 1: 14; 6: 9. *'abdah qachah* are found again in Is. 14: 3.

[33] Ps. 113A: 7–8.

[34] The other, or at least one of the others, is the motif of the Shepherd-King, perhaps common to all oriental cultures. (Cf. L. Durr, *Ursprung und Ausbau der israelitischen-jüdischen Heilandserwartung*, Berlin, 1925, pp. 116–117.) In Israel, at any rate, it is given new life by the image of David held by the people (cf. 1 Kings 16: 11; Ps. 77: 70–72), and becomes in Jeremias 23: 1–4, Ezechiel 34: 1–31; 37: 24, and Zacharias 10: 3; 11: 4–17, a messianic motif.

[35] Os. 11: 1–4.

[36] Is. 63: 11, 13, 14.

[37] Ps. 77: 52.

[38] Ps. 94: 6–9.

[39] Ps. 76: 20–21.

[40] Cf. Ps. 94: 7.

[41] Ex. 15: 25.

[42] Ex. 16:4.

[43] Ex. 20: 20.

[44] Deut. 8: 3, 16.

[45] Deut. 8: 2. It is probable also that the "great temptations" which Israel witnessed in seeing the miracles accomplished on Pharaoh, his people, and his army (Deut. 4: 34; 7: 19; 29: 2) are temptations intended for Israel, not for the Egyptians. They are signs analogous to those of the desert, and, while the Old Testament is aware of the visitations of God coming to punish the heathen peoples, temptation is a privilege of the chosen people.

[46] Ex. 17: 2, 7.

[47] Cf. Num. 14: 22.

[48] Deut. 6: 16.

[49] Ps. 77: 18, 41; 94: 8–9; 105: 14, always with the verb *nasah*.

[50] Ps. 94: 8–9.

[51] Heb. 3: 13.

[52] Is. 55: 8.

[53] Ps. 94: 10.

[54] Ps. 80: 11, 14; cf. 76: 14.

[55] Deut. 8: 3.

[56] Ps. 103: 29.

[57] Ps. 80: 11, 14, 17.

[58] Especially the motif "Hear, O Israel." Cf. Deut. 5: 1–7.

[59] Ps. 22: 1–2.

[60] Jos. 1: 13–15.

[61] Is. 63: 14; Ps. 94: 11.

[62] Is. 21: 5; Ex. 23: 41; Prov. 9: 2.

[63] Ps. 22: 5.

[64] Wis. 16: 26.

[65] Wis. 16: 21.

[66] 1 Cor. 10: 2.

[67] Cf. 1 Cor. 5: 7–8.

[68] 1 Cor. 10: 11.

[69] Cf. J. Bonsirven, *Exégèse rabbinique et exégèse paulinienne,* Paris, 1938, p. 338.

[70] Cf. J. Bonsirven, *op. cit.,* pp. 327–330.

[71] Ex. 4: 22.

[72] Is. 63: 11, 14.

[73] Deut. 8: 2.

[74] Matt. 3: 17.

[75] Mark 1: 12; Luke 4: 1.

[76] Matt. 4: 4; Deut. 8: 3.

[77] Matt. 4: 7; Deut. 6: 16.

[78] Matt. 4: 10; Deut. 6: 13.

[79] Num. 11: 33.

[80] Ex. 17: 2, 7.

[81] Ex. 32: 1–35.

[82] Luke 4: 13.

[83] Luke 22: 53.

[84] Luke 9: 31. Rendel Harris ("The Early Interpretation of the Passover," *The Expository Times,* Nov. 1926, p. 90) maintains that it is certain that the quotation which begins the Last Supper in John: "Jesus, knowing that the hour had come for him to pass out of this world to the Father" (John 13: 1), is a reference to the new Passover. It can be seen, at any rate, that, for all the evangelists, the Passion had a paschal sense.

[85] Mark 10: 38–39; Luke 12: 50. The sweat mingled with blood which bathed Jesus in the garden is perhaps for Luke the sign of this Baptism.

[86] Mark 10: 38–39; 14: 36; John 18: 11.

[87] 1 Cor. 5: 7.

Chapter II

GRACE, JUSTICE, AND TRUTH—THE BASIC VOCABULARY

1. GRACE

If there is one reality which characterizes the Christian religion and distinguishes it from the Old Dispensation, it is surely grace. St. Paul opposes the reign of grace to that of the Law: "You are not under the Law but under grace."[1] St. John, in his prologue, takes up the theme of this opposition in almost identical terms: "The Law was given by Moses; grace and truth came through Jesus Christ."[2]

To designate a reality without precedent, Christianity adopted a word which, neither by itself, nor by its previous usages in the language of the Septuagint, had any distinctive religious significance. The word χάρις, translated in Latin by *gratia,* is one of the typical words of the Greek spirit. Originally, it designated the charm of beauty, so attractive to the Greeks; then, by a natural transposition among these people who never distinguished between the good and the beautiful, it came to mean "favor"—the radiance of a generous heart. This favor is manifested in good deeds, and from this meaning derives the definition of thanksgiving, gratitude. Χάρις, in the Septuagint, generally translates the Hebrew *hen.* The semantic evolution of *hen* is about the reverse of that of the Greek word. The verb *hanan* seems originally to have meant: to look while leaning, to lower one's look; the primitive idea of *hen* would seem to be "favor," the regard of a powerful personage who looks benignly upon some privileged one whom he has chosen. It is a word of court language. It is naturally applied to God in a world such as that of the Semitic religions, where God is called upon as a powerful sovereign, toward whom one bows as to one's Lord.[3] By a process of derivation, *hen*, recapturing the original meaning of the Greek χάρις, finally comes to mean that principle in the object itself which draws the regard and holds the favor, namely, the beauty, or more precisely, that which renders it precious and delightful, namely, charm. It is possible to speak of a "beautiful and charming" woman, literally, "beautiful with grace," *tobat hen*,[4] and also of a "stone of charm,"[5] that is to say, no doubt, a magical stone, a good-luck piece. Nevertheless, while the Greek retains primarily the objective value of the attractive object or of the gift granted, the Hebrew is primarily attached to the personal gesture of the giver.

One essential aspect of the word *hen* is gratuitousness; to the greed of the wicked man is opposed the attitude of the just man, who is "kindly and gives," *honen wenoten*.[6] The adverb *hinnam*, from the same root, also suggests this quality of gratuitousness. Like the Latin *gratis*, it designates actions done without finding a like return, such as the years spent by Jacob in the service of Laban,[7] or, possibly, the "useless service" which God asks of His own and which will not know any recompense except to go without payment.[8] On the other hand, here on earth, "woe to him who . . . will oppress his friend . . . and will not pay him his wages."[9] Sold to the Assyrians without their having paid anything for the acquisition,[10] Israel will be liberated without paying a ransom.[11]

The word χάρις rarely appears in the Gospels. Completely

missing from St. Matthew and St. Mark, it is still rare in St. Luke. There it keeps its customary meaning from the Septuagint, where it corresponds to the Hebrew *hen* and designates the favor of God. Still, when this favor rests on two privileged beings like Jesus and Mary, it is charged with unfathomable riches. When Gabriel announces to the young girl "full of grace"[12] that she has "found grace with God,"[13] he is only using a common Hebraism,[14] but the exceptional privilege of Mary gives us to understand something quite other than just attention from God. The grace which characterizes in so remarkable a way the growth of Jesus obviously means, in this instance, unique intimacy with the Father.[15]

Outside of these examples, all taken from the accounts of the childhood, in which imitation of the Septuagint is so consciously sought, it does not appear that St. Luke, in his Gospel, gave any special meaning to the word χάρις.[16] On the other hand, it becomes frequent in the Acts. There it takes on at times a frankly Pauline sense; thus, in the formula which concludes Peter's discourse in the "Council of Jerusalem": "We believe that we are saved through the grace of the Lord Jesus."[17] Most of the time, χάρις retains a rather particular meaning, which might be called proper to the Acts. It designates in a general way the work which God has just accomplished in the world, and which manifests His generosity and His power. Even when the association of χάρις and δύναμις is not formal,[18] the context gives to the word a very pointed note of power.[19] So much so that χάρις finally comes to mean simply the Gospel itself, the new religion,[20] the supreme witness of God's unlimited generosity.

Even more central is the place occupied by χάρις in the epistles of St. Paul. It is he who gave grace its place in Christian dogma. For the ordinary greeting of the Greeks, χαῖρε, χαίρειν, he substitutes the typically Christian formula χάρις και εἰρήνη, by which, at the beginning of each letter, he calls down upon his correspondents the gifts of God, summed up in that of grace. And he takes leave of them also by entrusting them to the grace of God.[21] These are mere epistolary formulas, of course, but if the victory of Christ has really transformed the world, the most insignificant gestures take on a new value. Grace is, for St. Paul, one of the words which express the sense of the event of which he was made an Apostle, one of those which sum up Christianity. If he adopts it with so much fervor, it is because it symbolizes, in his eyes, this free gift of salvation which he defends with all his passion. Grace is, for him, the word which destroys all human pretensions to justification by works. If he combats the latter so furiously, it is because the entire history of the world comes to a head under the reign of grace.[22]

Whether it be St. Paul himself who introduced the word grace into the Christian vocabulary, or whether, even before his first writings, the Christian communities had adopted this word without a religious past in order to translate an experience unique in history, it is clear that it expresses the feeling, so powerful in the infant Church, of being submerged in a sudden overflowing of the infinite generosity of God. The word is new, because it was necessary to find an expression to convey this feeling of absolute newness. It is, from its very origins, theological, that is, born of reflection and intended to give exact expression to an experience. It necessarily postdates that experience, and it is a good sign of the veracity of the evangelists that the term is absent from the Gospels. But while it does not belong to the evangelical message properly so-called, that is, to the preaching which aims to bring faith to birth through a confrontation with Christ, still it does belong essentially to the Christian faith the moment the believer, once he has come into contact with Christ, wants to give a name to the transformation that God has wrought in him.

A new word, bearer of a new experience, the word "grace" is, nonetheless, often associated in the New Testament with other

23

words that have a very rich past in the Old Testament. In St. Paul, the recurring link is that between grace and justice. He uses the word grace to characterize the justice received from God:

All have sinned and . . . are justified freely by his grace, through the redemption which is in Christ Jesus.[23]

God's gift to the world is called "the abundance of the grace and of the gift of justice,"[24] a formula which seems to indicate the equivalence of grace and justice. It is "by justice" that God establishes the reign of grace.[25] Grace and justice are inseparable for St. Paul; they will remain so in the Christian tradition. The decree of the Council of Trent on justification constantly uses these words interchangeably.[26] While the word grace is a Christian creation, the word justice, on the other hand, fills the Old Testament. St. Paul himself affirms it: "the Law and the Prophets" give testimony to the justice of God which Jesus Christ has manifested.[27]

St. John also opposes grace, as the supreme and total gift, to the Law, as the provisional and limited gift. Grace is Jesus Christ's own gift, entrance into intimacy with God. Still, since the word alone did not suffice to express all these riches, John does not say grace by itself, but "grace and truth."[28] Truth is also a biblical term. For John as for Paul, the grace of Christ is a new reality, but only reveals its full import by reference to the Old Testament.

2. JUSTICE AND JUDGMENT

Two words, frequently associated, fill the Old Testament: justice and judgment, $\delta\iota\chi\alpha\iota\sigma\dot{\upsilon}\nu\eta$ and $\chi\rho\dot{\iota}\sigma\iota\varsigma$ (or $\chi\rho\dot{\iota}\mu\alpha$), sedeq and michpat. Often set alongside one another, they seem interchangeable. Still, they designate quite different things.

In all the Semitic tongues in which it appears, the root SDQ means moral rectitude. This rectitude—which the Greeks, with their artistic temperament, define as the perfection of a being—suggests, in Hebrew, fullness and peace, the state of him who responds exactly to what the situation calls for. Hence its juridical aspect. Reference is made to true weights,[29] to "scales of justice."[30] Justice is justness. It is something more: justness recognized by a tribunal. He is just who is declared such, he who is "justified"; he is unjust who is proclaimed guilty and is condemned.[31]

The idea of justice holds a larger place in Hebrew than in the occidental languages. It is this term which expresses essentially moral perfection. The Hebrew combination *tob-raʿ* does not have as immediate a moral aspect as the English combination good-evil. Whereas *raʿ* spontaneously means moral evil, the root *tob* maintains for a long time its original meaning—which is clearly physical and palpable—and only takes on secondarily the meaning of moral goodness. In English however, the movement from physical to moral good is immediate. While we speak of the "good man" and the "wicked man," this judgment is expressed in Hebrew by the opposition of the just to the guilty, *saddiq* to *rachaʿ*.[32]

This opposition of the just and the guilty, as spontaneous as our opposition of the good man and the wicked man, translates a different mentality. The *saddiq* is not precisely what we call the good man, the type of our moral ideal. He is the just man, and even more accurately, the innocent man. The fact is, that for the Hebrews, the life of man is forever exposed to the view of God. The good man in this perspective is the one who can support this judgment. Such were Noe[33] and Abraham.[34]

Certainly, the idea of a judgment reserved to man is not the privilege of Israel. From the time of the ancient Egyptian Empire, in the third millenium, the sun god Ra of Heliopolis is a god of justice, who examines as to their justice the actions of the Pharaoh who has just died, before admitting him to regain his sovereignty in the celestial kingdom.[35] Under the Middle

Empire, these ideas progressively win over the nobles, then the entire Egyptian people.[36] Among the Greeks, Pindarus knows "him who judges beneath the earth,"[37] and Aeschylus evokes "the implacable justice of Hades."[38] The Hebrews hardly think about any judgment after death. Such thought only makes its appearance in the last centuries of their history, as the prelude to the resurrection.[39] But, starting with this life, and at every moment, the Hebrews are undergoing the judgment of God, the God whose essential activity is to be the "judge of all the earth."[40] There is no mythological stage setting, no special moment set aside for this judgment. Instead, there is the profound conviction that men live under the eyes of God, from which arises a directly religious attitude. To be just, it is not enough to be a good man, to realize, like the Greeks, a human ideal, but rather it is to be judged by an infallible look.

Thus, justice is at once a moral, a juridical, and a religious notion, and we cannot isolate any one of these complementary aspects. However, it is necessary to add that, in the ancient texts, justice is not conceived of as a quality or a virtue, or even as an ideal. Not that the conscience of Israel had not, even at that time, perceived the imperatives which are imposed on every man, and whose violation calls down chastisement upon the generation of the Deluge or on the people of Sodom;[41] but still, justice is not defined by the contents of an ideal. It is always defined by reference to immediate and concrete exigencies, to a duty which is imposed at the moment. It is not the rigorous observance of a sovereign law. It is the fidelity, constantly on trial and unceasingly renewed, of the man who is capable of responding, at every instant, to the requirements with which he must deal. This gives justice its personal aspect. In the ancient passages, the nouns *sedeq* and *sedaqah* are never employed without determinatives—they always designate the justice of someone.

So little is justice an abstract notion that it takes a plural.

Three ancient texts speak (in the Hebrew) of the "justices of Yahweh," which He has "accomplished in favor of Israel."[42]

What meaning are we to give to this expression? Grammatically, the explanation is simple enough. This plural simply refers to various manifestations of the same quality.[43] But in what does this quality precisely consist? One fact is certain right at the outset: in the three cases, it is a question of benefits granted, and, more specifically, of enemies put to flight, of liberations. Must we thenceforth identify justice and salvation, as the prophets did? Such identification is natural at the end of a long history during which the word justice has been spoken anew by all the prophets and filled with a rich meaning, but it is scarcely likely in a literature which is still primitive. Still, it is necessary to retain, out of this attempted explanation, the fact that, starting with these texts, there was a suggestion of movement from the idea of justice to that of salvation. Is it then necessary to see in these justices, according to another recurrent association, that of justice and fidelity, the fulfilment by Yahweh of the promises made to His people?[44] Is it not an anachronism to assume, at the time of Debora, an expression which seems rather to have come later? Or is it enough to translate simply "the judgments of Yahweh," which, in sum, would correspond perfectly to the given situations? That, however, is to give *sedaqah* the sense of *michpat*, which, as we shall see, is quite different. It is clear that, despite everything, these passages are the beginning of the identification which in the end will blend these two words into one.

It is likely that we must, in effect, see in these "justices" of Yahweh the outlines of all later meanings. But perhaps it is not impossible, even so, to find therein a meaning more in keeping with the primitive idea. Two of these texts, that of the Book of Kings and that of Micheas, picture an explanation between Yahweh and His people, a hearing. The prophet announces it solemnly:

Let the mountains hear the judgment of the Lord, and the strong foundations of the earth, for the Lord will enter into judgment with his people,
and he will plead against Israel.[45]

Yahweh then indicates all that He has done for His people.
These are the first reproaches:

O my people, what have I done to thee or in what have I molested thee?
Answer thou me.[46]

The plea ends with these words:

That thou mightest know the justices of the Lord.[47]

Here, perhaps, the word finds its true meaning. The justices of
Yahweh are no doubt the facts which the defendant—since
God is not a judge here, but the party constrained to defend
Himself—adduces in his defense. In the Book of Kings, it is
once again a question of a plea: Samuel calls the people "in
judgment" to set before its eye "all the kindness of the Lord,
which he hath shown to you, and to your fathers."[48] The Canticle of Debora, however, does not involve this juridical frame
of reference, and *sidqot* cannot mean strictly "the justifications." Whereas the victory of Israel manifests to the world the
greatness of Yahweh, and justifies Him in the eyes of men, it
reveals above all to Israel that its God is the God of "justices,"
He who assures its peace by delivering it from injustices.

Justice, expressed by the root SDQ and its derivations, is therefore a complex notion, at once juridical, since it designates innocence recognized by a judgment; moral, because this innocence
is not merely the absence of guilt, but the perfection of someone
who is what he is supposed to be; and finally, religious, because
it is God who pronounces the judgment. This justice, therefore,
takes precedence over every human determination; it expresses
the natural law, it is imposed in an absolute way, like truth.
When Jeremias renews the promise of Yahweh to David:

Behold the days come, saith the Lord, and I will raise up to David a
just branch. . . .[49]

he is apparently prophesying a reign of justice, but he intends first of all to signify a legitimate son, an authentic heir.

The word *michpat*, constantly associated with *sedeq*, has quite a different origin. It is generally translated as judgment, frequently, also, as law. It belongs, in effect, to the positive and customary law, to the law which depends on circumstances and is generally born of formal prescription. *Michpat* is derived from the verb *chaphat*. This verb has two characteristic usages, both very frequent. It means to govern[50] and to judge.[51] Accustomed to making a clear distinction between the executive power and the judiciary power, we are tempted to see therein two different activities. A Hebrew did not recognize this distinction. For him, the chief is the judge. One of his essential functions is to adjudicate the lawsuits arising among his people or coming from beyond borders, to maintain the political and social equilibrium. It is therefore not a question of two associated meanings, but of one single meaning which we can no longer translate except by using two different words.[52] Since the idea is basically Semitic, it is not very easy to elucidate. There has been an attempt to rediscover the original meaning in certain, more typical, expressions. The remark of the Sodomites to Lot, who refuses to hand over his guests: "This fellow came in as a stranger, and he would play the judge!"[53] seems to mean: "He tries to impose his will upon us."[54] An analogous meaning can be found in the reply of the two Hebrews whom Moses tries to separate: "Who has appointed you ruler and judge over us?"[55]

These two examples testify to a will which attempts to impose its decision. This would seem to be the original meaning of the verb *chaphat*, and it is found in the action of the judges as well as in that of the chief. But these two examples bring to light another, equally important aspect of this verb: its moral character. Lot and Moses are not merely attempting to impose their will: they want to give a lesson to others, to lecture them, though their position does not give them the authority to do so. The role of ruler-judge is not so much to impose orders as to insure the carrying out of a just order.

However, this moral characteristic is not of an interior nature, a search for a kind of perfection. It is essentially juridical, and corresponds to a concrete case. The common translation of *michpat* as judgment is generally awkward and inadequate, but it is on the whole correct, in that it always evokes a positive decision. In order to be exact, the translations of this word have to be more diverse: sentence, trial, justice, law, decision, privilege, right, attribute, custom, habit. One common feature is that the *michpat* is always oriented to a specific case. It may be a general law, but its object is always to regulate a concrete situation. The *michpatim* correspond to the different articles of our codes, and try to anticipate all possible cases.[56] But each case is individual, and the role of the judge is precisely to take into account the facts proper to each case, and to pronounce a *michpat*. The true *michpat* is that which is imposed without reply, because it decisively settles the debate. Such is the famous judgment of Solomon,[57] such is the arbitration of David regarding the division of booty among the combatants and the rear-area service troops, which was so perfect a solution to the case that it subsequently became law in Israel.[58]

Each case, each individual has its own law, its particular *michpat*. Quite frequently, the word is followed by a personal suffix or by a determinative object. There is, for example, the king's *michpat*, which Samuel details with a bitter deference to the people seduced by monarchical dreams.[59] The natural translation is the "right of the king," and it is indeed a list of the rights of the sovereign over his subjects that Samuel unfolds. But this right is at the same time that which characterizes the king as such, and distinguishes him from the Judges, his predecessors. The right expresses, if we may say so, the essence of the individual possessing it. From this example we may learn how

30

michpat can often signify habit. This habit is not the simple repetition of an ordinary action. It is the typical habit, the one which reveals the proper nature of a man, because he puts himself entirely into it.[60] It is the word *michpat*, for instance, which indicates the line of conduct adopted by David during his sojourn at the court of the King of Achis. It is the term which Ochozias uses to ask his messengers who, without recognizing him, had met Elias: "What manner of man was he who met you?" And the description by the servants: "A hairy man with a girdle of leather about his loins," suffices for the king to understand that: "It is Elias the Thesbite." The apparel guaranteed the prophet.[61]

As the need for justice grew in Israel, the word *michpat* saw its usages multiplied, but the proper nuance which characterizes it can almost always be perceived. Justice consists in giving every man "according to his *michpat*," according to his right. Every man has his own right, which results from his situation. The poor have theirs,[62] the afflicted also.[63] The guilty, the murderers, the adulterers, also have theirs which is due them.[64] Israel in exile has hers—her misery.[65] It even happens that *michpat* seems to signify simply justice, as in the prayer of Solomon asking of God "an understanding heart, to judge thy people, and discern between good and evil."[66] whom God praises "because thou hast asked . . . wisdom to discern judgment."[67] But we see that, although it requires a sensitive discernment, this justice is not a universal and general ideal. It is the solution, the only solution, which is specifically required in any circumstance.

Different as their origins might be, *sedeq* and *michpat* are very frequently associated, and the expression comes ultimately to designate simply justice, goodness.[68] Many causes favored this association. On the one hand, the insistence of the prophets upon respect for justice tended to bring out, among all laws that are imposed on the conscience, the obligation to render to each his due; on the other hand, moral innocence was, from

the very beginning, sanctioned by God's judgment. The juridical aspect of the moral sense, and the moral exigencies of law,
contributed to the establishing of justice at the very core of the
morality of Israel.

But the best-established formulas never succeed in completely
eliminating the nuances proper to these two ideas. Job, for instance, speaks now of his right, now of his justice, and these are
two different things:

> I am innocent, [*sadaqti*] but God has taken what is my due [*michpati*].[69]

The justice of Job is that he is irreproachable; his right is to
obtain from God the proclamation of his justice. In this vein,
where he says: "My justice I maintain and I will not relinquish
it,"[70] he means, according to the very words of the parallel verse
which precedes it: "Till I die I will not renounce my innocence."[71] On the other hand, when he complains about the Lord
"who withholds my deserts,"[72] while he intends at all times to
present his own defense, the point of view is different: God refuses to recognize his situation.

3. TRUTH AND FIDELITY

The Old Testament often connects truth, *'emet,* to justice,
sedeq.[73] What does this connection signify? It is not the spontaneous product of everyday language; it is the prophets who
consecrated it. In order to understand it, it is necessary first
to study what truth is for an Israelite.

The Septuagint, generally speaking, translated a certain number of Hebrew words derived from the root 'MN, by ἀλήθεια
and parallel words. But they translated other derivations of the
same root by Greek words designating confidence, πίστις, and
its corresponding words. This is an indication that the Greek
and Hebriac notions overlap only imperfectly. In fact, 'MN
expresses a typically Hebraic concept.[74]

It is quite difficult to express precisely its original sense. It

32

seems clear that it was material, since the material usages of certain derivations are too precise to have come from metaphorical extensions of a primitive psychological meaning. The best-characterized of these uses is that of carrying a suckling child.[75] Then, the probable meaning of doorposts, for the *'omnot* of the Temple of Jerusalem,[76] suggests a material sense akin to erecting, raising up. However, it must be admitted that the traces of the material sense are weak and that, in related languages, in Arabic, Aramean, Ethiopian, the moral meaning of fidelity, security, shows a development similar to the Hebrew. It is therefore probable that this moral aspect is very ancient.

The material meaning of carrying a suckling child, moreover, involves a very clear-cut distinction. The resting child depends as much on an attentive protectiveness as on the strength of the arms which hold him. There is the same combination of the two meanings in the expression which describes the prayer of Moses during the battle against the Amalechites:

. . . Aaron and Hur supported his hands, one on one side and one on the other, so that his hands remained steady till sunset.[77]

The word indicates the firmness of the outstretched arms as much as it does the perseverance of the prayer.

In its two habitual forms, the *nifal* and the *hifil*, the verb *'aman* easily takes on a religious sense. In the *nifal*, it designates that which is solid, that which, when put to the test, endures.[78] The participle *ne'eman* easily qualifies the exceptional servants of Yahweh, those who have deserved His confidence. Their number is small. There is Abraham, "faithful of heart,"[79] Moses, to whom God speaks face to face because he has been tried and proven: "Throughout my house he bears my trust,"[80] and perhaps also Samuel;[81] David himself, though he is sometimes called "my servant"[82] by Yahweh, is never termed "faithful servant."

The association of *ne'eman* with servant indicates the kind of faithfulness to which it refers. It is not directly the attachment of the heart: it is the solidity of a dependable man, on whom

33

one can depend without a second thought. Conversely, if God reproaches the generation of the Exodus because of its infidelity, it is because this generation "kept not its heart steadfast."[83]

To the faithfulness of man corresponds the faithfulness of God. The latter is expressed in His covenant. *Ne'eman* is one of the typical words of the covenant.[84] It does not, in general, express God's attitude, but it characterizes the solidity of the works which God engages Himself to perform, and, above all, the perpetuity of the dynasty of David.[85] Isaias renews the traditional image by restoring to it its concrete vigorousness:

> And I will fasten him as a peg in a sure place.[86]

To the passive sense of the *nifal* form corresponds the active sense of the *hifil*. It may be freely translated by "to believe," and that is accurate, provided it is clearly understood that faith, for a Hebrew, consists in depending on someone of whom one is sure. Besides, it can be, and even more frequently, it is, the adherence of the intellect to the announcement of a fact,[87] but such adherence is commanded by the absolute confidence deserved by the one who speaks. Also, faith ultimately is placed directly in God, in whom one believes.[88] A play on words by Isaias sets forth clearly the solidity on which faith always depends:

> If you will not believe, you shall not continue.[89]

He who hesitates in entrusting himself to God feels the ground shaking beneath his feet. Night and day he trembles, no longer sure of his life.[90]

The nouns derived from the root 'MN, *'emet* and *'emunah*, evoke the same idea of tested stability. Often interchangeable, they nevertheless are largely distinct. *'Emunah* has a more pronounced psychological character, and can almost always be translated as "faithfulness"; *'emet* designates something more profound: the very sources of the faithfulness, the essential solidity of a being. The Septuagint generally renders it ἀλήθεια,

which is accurate in that, most of the time, *'emet* characterizes a formula which is found to be true, and thus corresponds
to our word "truth." But a Hebrew does not see in truth exactly
what a Greek or a Latin sees there. For a Greek, awed by luminous perfection, truth is what is unveiled, freed from shadows
and obscurity; for a Latin, enamored of juridical principles,
truth is that which is authentic, of guaranteed origins. Truth,
for a Hebrew, is that which has been put to the test and has
revealed itself to be solid. The words of Joseph to his brothers
are almost a definition of truth:

Send one of your number to bring your brother while you others remain
in bonds. Thus shall your statements be tested for their truth.[91]

For a Hebrew, truth is not opposed to error, but to the lie
and to what he calls vanity, that is, that which lacks consistency
and solidity.

While the false Gods are in his eyes "idols," vain images without power, Israel calls his God "the God of truth,"[92] the "living
and True God,"[93] on whom one can always count.[94]

'Emet also goes far beyond our current notion of truth, and
designates at the same time, sincerity, loyalty, and, above all,
that basic quality which makes men reliable. It is sometimes
easy to fail to recognize this wealth.[95] Thus, in the fable told
by Joatham to the people of Sichem, about the declaration of
the thorn bush to the trees:

If you wish to anoint me king over you in good faith . . .[96]

seems to us to mean only: "If in reality. . . ." But, what follows
shows the complete meaning of this simple word "in reality."
For *'emet* has a parallel, *tamim*, which means the absence of
duplicity, that is, sincerity. The phrase therefore comes to
express something different:

. . . if you have acted in good faith and honorably in appointing Abimelech
your King. . . .[97]

'Emet can even, finally, no longer describe a word or an action,

35

but a man, with all that this involves, and can point him out as someone of confidence, capable of bearing the most serious responsibilities. Such are the chiefs whom Moses, on the advice of Jethro, has to choose to lead the people,[98] such is Hanania, to whom Nehemias entrusts the defense of Jerusalem.[99]

This fundamental aspect of moral solidity destined *'emet* to enter into the vocabulary of the covenant, among those words commonly associated with the promises of God. The prayer of David for his dynasty calls on this unshakeable firmness of the divine promises:

And now, O Lord God, thou art God, and thy words shall be true.[100]

This was so from the moment that:

The LORD swore to David
a firm promise from which he will not withdraw.[101]

To this firmness, the psalmist abandons himself in his distress:

Into your hands I commend my spirit;
you will redeem me, O LORD, O faithful God.[102]

You will know how to assume the deposit which I am confiding to you, and which I can no longer defend.[103]

4. TRUTH AND GOODNESS

By itself, the word *'emet* was not sufficient to characterize the attitude of the God of the Covenant. The Covenant is indeed more than a promise involving fidelity. It establishes between God and His people a real community, personal relationships. The proper word of the Covenant is the word *hesed*,[104] so much so that in many texts it is the equivalent of the technical term designating the Covenant, *berith*. The parallelism between these two words is so close that they become interchangeable.[105]

From its origins, *hesed* designates the attitude which is in order among people united by some bond.[106] Abraham demands

36

it of his wife Sara;[107] Abimelech exacts it as a promise from his guest Abraham;[108] Eleazer expects it from the God of his master Abraham.[109] This is the attitude which David wants to take toward the survivors of the house of Saul, in remembrance of the pact of friendship which bound him to Jonathan;[110] it is the same attitude which he asks Solomon to show toward the sons of Berzellai, in gratitude for the generosity of their father during the dark hours of the revolt of Absalom.[111] It is the attitude of Yahweh Himself toward His servant David.[112] It is not necessary that there be an explicit pact in order for the obligation of evidencing *hesed* to exist, but there is always a real obligation nonetheless. A bond of blood, a debt of justice, of gratitude or of friendship—it is always a real duty,[113] a duty which imposes effective actions. *Hesed* is not a sentiment, and the customary Septuagint translation, ἔλεος, nearly creates this illusion. It is never a question of feeling *hesed* toward or for someone: the word is almost always accompanied by the verb "to do." Still, it is not a matter of any specific measures, but of a complex behavior pattern composed of respect, benevolence, generosity and fidelity. The common translation "goodness" is often most felicitous, because this word is vague enough to cover just about all the diverse aspects of *hesed*, but it does not indicate sufficiently that it is a goodness imposed by some human bond. The Latin *pietas*, which has been perpetuated in an attenuated form in our "filial piety," would be a more exact translation of this profound fidelity to the family, to the nation, to friendship.[114] The Latin word is perhaps more directly religious, more narrowly linked to social frames of reference. The most elementary bonds of humanity can oblige one to *hesed*.

A complex notion, with varied shades of meaning, *hesed* is difficult to analyze. It represents one of the fundamental aspects of Israelite morality, expressing the ensemble of acts and attitudes on which the social life rests, that atmosphere of confidence and loyalty without which life among men would become impossible.

The Book of Ruth, an account permeated with the most popular and the purest Israelite ideal, is entirely built up on the theme of *hesed*. It is their *hesed* toward deceased husbands which keeps her two daughters-in-law by Naomi's side.[115] When Naomi, powerless to help them, wants to give them their freedom, she entrusts these two women who are without support to the *hesed* of Yahweh.[116] When Ruth informs her mother-in-law of the attentions of Booz toward her, Naomi recognizes in this sign the nobility of a well-born heart, of a man "who is ever merciful to the living and to the dead,"[117] who knows how to treat men like men. When Booz finally discovers, in Ruth's act of lying at his feet, not the ardor of a desire "eager among young people" but the fidelity of a woman who has given herself to a family and does not want to leave it, it is this attachment which captures his imagination:

May the Lord bless you, my daughter! You have been even more loyal now than before. . . .[118]

"Love" is doubtless not the exact word for this feeling. In any case, the love which the Book of Ruth extols is not the inebriating and blooming passion of the Canticle of Canticles; it is a fidelity which has given itself for better or for worse, and knows no turning back. This calm and profound attachment of a loyal heart is the human perfection of *hesed*.

The word *'emet* is frequently associated with the word *hesed*. This association is not a literary creation; it is an expression common in the everyday language. It is found in the accounts of the popular type, such as the episodes of Eliazer and of Rebecca,[119] or of the spies of Josue at Rahab's house in Jericho.[120] The uniting of these two words is quite natural. To the loyal devotion in human and social relations as expressed by *hesed*, *'emet* adds its own nuance, that of solid faithfulness. At all times, it is a question of a fidelity distinguished by actions,

38

for the complete expression is *'asah hesed we'emet,* literally: "to do goodness and truth." No formula in English coincides exactly with all these meanings that the Hebrew expression can take, according to the various situations in which it presents itself. The general idea which it evokes is that of an attachment which nothing can destroy.

Even more directly than each of its components, the compound *hesed we'emet* is a formula of promise and covenant. The episode of Eliazer, in which the words, either isolated or connected, return as refrain, has as its entire purpose to show the fidelity of Yahweh in bringing the mission of Abraham's servant to a successful conclusion, a sign of His fidelity to the commitment He has made to the patriarch. And the fidelity which Eliazer invokes to ask Rebecca's parents to unite their daughter to Isaac, is probably the remembrance of the blood bond which joins the two families and which this marriage is to renew.[121] The prayer of Jacob:

I am not worthy of all the kindnesses and the constant solicitude which you have shown your servant,[122]

evokes the promises received from the "God of my father Abraham, and God of my father Isaac."[123] Jacob, feeling death approaching, asks Joseph to make the solemn promise to "act kindly and faithfully" and not to leave his body in the land of Egypt.[124] Josue's spies, according to the same formula, bind themselves upon their lives to protect Rahab and her family.[125] When David wants to recommend to Yahweh's protection the people of Jabes, or his officer, Ethai of Geth, he expresses the wish that "Now the Lord surely will render you mercy and truth."[126] The nobility of soul which he admires in men is for David one of the essential traits of the God he serves.

This nobility, this chivalrous fidelity, is certainly one of the qualities which has made the memory of David dear to the tradition of Israel. The latter has gathered with love the episodes in which the spontaneous reactions of the father, the friend, the patriot, naturally triumphed, as it were, over the suggestions of resentment or of ambition. The attitude of David toward Absalom, toward Jonathan, and toward Saul, these various manifestations of a fundamental virtue, is perhaps the best illustration of the profoundly Hebraic ideal: "to do truth and goodness."

The God of Israel, the God of the Covenant, who swore to David that He would never withdraw His fidelity from his descendants,[127] is therefore the God who fully embodies this generous and loyal solidity, truth.

5. GOODNESS AND TENDERNESS

To *hesed* is easily joined *rahamim*[128]—to good will manifested in actions, the interior sentiment which is its source.

To designate this sentiment, the Hebrew, according to a common procedure,[129] utilizes the plural of a concrete noun, *rehem*. *Rehem* means the maternal womb, the uterus.[130] This organ, "for the Hebrews as for the Akkadians, is naturally the seat of the mother's pity for her children."[131] The denominative verbs formed from the noun, the Hebrew *piel riham* and the Akkadian *remu*, express primarily this maternal reaction. This original meaning appears again in the word of the prophet:

Can a woman forget her infant, so as not to have pity on the son of her womb?[132]

Then the meaning is extended and designates every sort of pity. *Remu* in Akkadian, in Hebrew the plural *rahamim*, have this rather general meaning.[133] Nevertheless, the meaning of pity, even if it becomes the most frequent one, never completely obliterates the original image of the root, this emotion which derives from the physiological depths, and reveals a bond of nature among beings. It is the voice of the blood which stuns Joseph when he finds himself in the presence of his brethren and feels "his bowels moved."[134] It is this authentic maternal

40

reflex which Solomon was able to set in motion in order to decide the famous case.[135]

Also, and quite as much as pity, *rahamim* signifies love.[136] Only it is a love which has "bowels." Our word "tenderness" is no doubt the one which best translates the vulnerable nature of this love. The usual Greek translation, οἰχτείρω οἰχτιρμός, has the drawback of insisting too much on the sorrowful aspect of this love, of transforming it into compassion.[137] That is not exactly the meaning of the Hebrew word. Even the Latin word *misericordia*, while it has the advantage of expressing, better than the Greek term, the positive and practical aspect of a love which transcends sentiment and is carried out in effective actions,[138] still evokes too much of an atmosphere of distress, By themselves, *rehem* and its derivatives do not connote suffering, but rather warmth and intimacy. The New Testament texts most faithful to the line are the two passages in which the Hebraism "the bowels of mercy" appears as the echo of the combination *hesed werahamim*. In the canticle of the Benedictus, St. Luke sings of the salvation which John the Baptist is to announce:

> Because of the loving-kindness of our God,
> wherewith the Orient from on high has visited us.[139]

And St. Paul recommends to the Colossians to "put on the bowels of mercy."[140] In these two texts, mercy has its place, for the salvation of God consists in the forgiveness of sins,[141] in the shining forth of the Rising Sun "on those who sit in the darkness and in the shadow of death,"[142] and also, Paul exhorts the Christians at Colossae to "forgive one another."[143] But this mercy is much more than the reflex action of a heart seized with pity in the face of suffering; it is the expression of an essential bond between men and God, of a family oneness more intimate than that of blood, a manifestation which was only made possible by the revelation of the love of Jesus for His Father and for His own. Still, many centuries before Christ, a proper name such as *Jerahme'el* already bears witness to the feeling that, between God and His creatures, there ought to exist a union so close that the tenderness of a mother toward the child whom she has borne would only prefigure it.[144]

NOTES

[1] Rom. 6: 14–15.

[2] John 1: 17.

[3] Cf. Foerster, article κύριος, in *Theol. Wörterbuch,* Kittel, II, pp. 1045–1048.

[4] Nahum 3: 4.

[5] Prov. 17: 8.

[6] Ps. 36: 21.

[7] Gen. 29: 15.

[8] Luke 17: 10.

[9] Jer. 22: 13.

[10] Is. 52: 3.

[11] Is. 52: 5.

[12] Luke 1: 28.

[13] Luke 1: 30.

[14] Cf. Gen. 30: 27; 32: 6; Ruth 2: 10, 13, etc.

[15] Luke 2: 40, 52.

[16] While he did substitute the expression "What merit have you?" (Luke 6: 32) for the simpler formula of St. Matthew, "If you love those that love you, what reward shall you have?" (Matt. 5: 46), it is perhaps not necessary to see traces of Pauline influence in this (cf. Holtzmann, *Handkommentar zum Neuen Testament,* 3 Aufl. 1901, I, p. 341), but simply a desire to express the idea in a purer Greek.

[17] Acts 15: 11.

[18] As in Acts 4: 33; 6: 8.

[19] Acts 11: 23; 14: 3, 25; 15: 40; 20: 32.

[20] Acts 13: 43; 20: 24.

[21] 1 Thess. 1: 1; 5: 28; 2 Thess. 1: 2; 3: 18; 1 Cor. 1: 3; 16: 23; 2 Cor. 1: 2; 13: 13; Gal. 1: 3; 6: 18; Rom. 1: 7; 16: 20, 24; Col. 1: 2; 4: 18; Eph. 1: 2; 6: 24; Phil. 1: 2; 4: 23; 1 Tim. 1: 2; 6: 21; 2 Tim. 1: 2; 6: 22; Tit. 1: 4; 3: 15. Christian in content, this formula signifies at the same time the fusion of Semitic and Hellenic cultures, since it unites the Greek desire for joy to the Jewish desire for peace.

[22] Rom. 5: 21.

[23] Rom. 3: 23, 24.

[24] Rom. 5: 17.

[25] Rom. 5: 21.

[26] Cf. Denzinger, Nos. 795, 797, 798, 799, 801, 811, 821.

[27] Rom. 3: 21–22.

[28] John 1: 14, 17.

[29] Lev. 19: 36.

[30] Job 31: 6.

[31] As is indicated in the expression: "it was reputed to him unto justice" (1 Mac. 2: 52; Gen. 15: 6; Ps. 105: 31); "just in my [i.e. God's] sight" (Gen. 7: 1).

[32] True, *racha'* is often translated as "impious." From the time of Ezechiel and the exile, this word designates that class of the people of Israel who were unfaithful to their religion, while the just are characterized above all by the "fear of God," their piety. But

it is quite apparent that this meaning is secondary. If it becomes rather frequent after the exile, it is because the sapiential literature, at least from the time of Ezechiel on, and a goodly portion of the psalms, are based on the opposition between these two categories; but the opposition between the *saddiq* and the *racha'* seems to antedate by far this particular situation. In an ancient account such as the dialogue between Yahweh and Abraham before Sodom, the opposition is already very marked. It is a question of knowing whether, among all the guilty, some just men could be found. Even if these verses (Gen. 18: 22–23) represented, as Gunkel (*Die Genesis*, Göttingen, 1917, p. 203) and Eissefeldt (*Einleitung in das alte Testament*, Tübingen, 1934, p. 239) would have it, an expanding of a primitive story—which has not been proved (cf. J. Chaine, *Le Livre de la Genèse*, Paris, 1948, p. 240)—passages, certainly quite ancient, such as Gen. 7: 1 or Gen. 20: 4, while not involving the word *racha'*, do have the same idea of the *saddiq* as the former verses. There is the same opposition between *saddiq* and *racha'* in Is. 5:23 and Deut. 9:4, in a very general and in no way pietistic, sense.

[33] Gen. 7: 1.

[34] Gen. 15: 6.

[35] Cf. J. H. Breasted, *Development of Religion and Thought in Ancient Egypt*, London, 1912, p. 171, p. 251.

[36] Cf. J. H. Breasted, *op. cit.*, pp. 238–249; E. Drioton and J. Vandier, *Les Peuple de l'Orient méditerranéen, II, Egypt*, Paris, 1938, pp. 100–101 and 125–127.

[37] *Olymp.* II, 65.

[38] *Eumenides*, 273.

[39] 2 Mac. 7: 14; Wis. 4: 20 to 5: 13.

[40] Gen. 18: 25.

[41] Gen. 6: 5; 18: 20.

[42] Judg. 5: 11; 1 Kings 12: 7; Mich. 6: 5.

[43] Thus the plural of *geburah*, power, signifies the actions that manifest this power, these exploits. The *geburoth yhwh* are the great deeds of Yahweh (Ps. 19:7; 70: 16; 105: 2; 144: 4, 12; 150: 2; Deut. 3: 24; Is. 63: 15).

[44] This is the interpretation of C. F. Burney, *The Book of Judges*, London, 1920, p. 129.

[45] Mich. 6: 2.

[46] Mich. 6: 3.

[47] Mich. 6: 5.

[48] 1 Kings 12: 7.

[49] Jer. 23: 5; 33: 15.

[50] Judg. 3: 10; 4: 4; 10: 2, 3; 12: 7, 9, 11, 14; 15: 20; 16: 31; 1 Kings 4: 18; 8: 5; 4 Kings 23: 22; Ruth 1: 1; Dan. 9: 12.

[51] Gen. 16: 5; 31: 53; Ex. 18: 16; Deut. 1: 16; Judg. 11: 27; 1 Kings 24: 13, 16; Is. 2: 4; 5: 3; Mich. 4: 3; Ex. 34: 20, 22.

[52] The Assyrian has the same duality of meaning as the Hebrew. Cf. Herntrich, art. χρίνω, in Kittel, *Theol. Wörterbuch*, III, p. 923.

[53] Gen. 19: 9, *wayyichpot chaphot*.

[54] Cf. H. W. Hertzberg, "Die Entwicklung des Begriffes michpat im A. T.," *Zeitschrift für die altestamentliche Wissenschaft*, 1922, p. 259.

[55] Ex. 2: 14; cf. Hertzberg, *op. cit.*, p. 258.

[56] Ex. 21:1, 31.

[57] 3 Kings 3: 28.

[58] 1 Kings 30: 25.

[59] 1 Kings 8: 9, 11; 10: 25.

[60] Cf. Pedersen, *Israel, Its Life and Culture*, I–II, London—Copenhagen, 1926, pp. 350–351.

[61] 4 Kings 1: 7–8. Cf. Judg. 18: 7; 3 Kings 18: 28; 4 Kings 17: 33.

[62] Ex. 23: 6; Jer. 5: 28.

[63] Is. 10: 2; Job 36: 6.

[64] Ezech. 23: 45.

[65] Is. 40: 27; 49: 4. Even God has His *michpat* which He defends: Jer. 1: 14.

[66] 3 Kings 3: 9.

[67] 3 Kings 3: 11.

[68] Gen. 18: 19; 2 Kings 8: 15; 3 Kings 10: 9. Beginning with the prophets, the examples are more frequent.

[69] Job 34: 5.

[70] Job 27: 6.

[71] Job 27: 5.

[72] Job 27: 2.

[73] Deut. 32: 4; Is. 1: 21, 26; 11: 5; 16: 5; 42: 3; 59: 4, 15; Jer. 4: 2; 5: 1; 7: 28; Hab. 2: 4; Ezech. 18: 8; Zach. 7: 9; 8: 8, 16; Is. 26: 2; Ps. 14: 2; 44: 5; 95: 13; 97: 2, 3; 110: 7; 118: 138, 142, 160.

[74] Cf. R. Bultmann, "Untersuchungen zum Johannesevangelium," *Zeitschrift für die neutestamentliche Wissenschaft*, 1928, pp. 113–117.

[75] Num. 11: 12; 2 Kings 4: 4; Ruth 4: 16; Is. 49: 23; 60: 4. Cf. 4 Kings 10: 1, 5.

[76] 4 Kings 18: 16. The *'omman* of Cant. 7: 2, doubtless means artisan. The relationship of this meaning to the root is impossible to trace.

[77] Ex. 17: 12. The Hebrew has the apparently unusual expression: "remained fidelity" (*'emunah*). The Septuagint simply translated it by the participle.

[78] Cf. Gen. 42: 20.

[79] 2 Esd. 9: 8.

[80] Num. 12: 7–8.

[81] If 1 Kings 3: 20 means not only that Samuel had a prophet's status in Israel, but also that God Himself confirmed this status. In any event, it is a matter of shades of meaning.

[82] 2 Kings 3: 18; 7: 5, 8.

[83] Ps. 77: 8, 37.

[84] Cf. Deut. 7: 9; Ps. 77: 37; 2 Esd. 9: 8.

[85] 1 King 25: 28; 2 Kings 7: 16; 3 Kings 11: 38; Ps. 88: 29, 38.

[86] Is. 22: 23.

[87] Gen. 15: 6; 45: 26; Ex. 4: 1, 5, 8; Deut. 9: 23; Jer. 40: 14; Hab. 1: 5; Is. 43: 10; 53: 1; 2 Par. 9: 6.

[88] Gen. 15: 6; Ex. 14: 31; Num. 14: 11; Deut. 1: 32; 9: 23; Is. 43: 10.

[89] Is. 7: 9. Cf. 2 Par. 20: 20.

[90] Deut. 28: 66. Cf. Job 24: 22.

[91] Gen. 42: 16. Cf. Deut. 13: 15; 17: 4; 22: 20; 3 Kings 10: 6; 17: 24.

[92] Ps. 30: 6.

[93] 1 Thess. 1: 9.

[94] Still, it is the Greek word that ultimately expresses the idea.

[95] For *'emet* and ἀλήθεια sometimes seem to overlap perfectly. The fact is that a language which is true in the Greek sense, that is, one which is an exact translation of the reality of things, is at the same time worthy of all confidence in the Hebrew sense. Cf. C. H. Dodd, *The Bible and the Greeks*, London, 1935, p. 71.

[96] Judg. 9: 15.

[97] Judg. 9: 16. The same expression is in Jos. 24: 14: "Fear the Lord and serve him completely and sincerely [*tamin, 'emet*]."

[98] Ex. 18: 21.

[99] 2 Esd. 7: 2.

[100] 2 Kings 7: 28.

[101] Ps. 131: 11.

[102] Ps. 30: 6.

[103] From the root *'mn* comes the word "Amen," whose entire original force we have allowed to be lost. *'amen* is rather rarely used in the Old Testament, and always in a very strong sense, to designate a positive and specific commitment.

It is used as a formula of oath. Thus in Num. 5: 22, the woman suspected of adultery must, in drinking the water mingled with dust, respond to the threats of curse made by the priest. Thus, in Deut. 27: 15 to 26, the whole people takes upon itself the solemn curses pronounced against violators of the Law. Likewise in 2 Esd. 5: 13. On the other hand, in 2 Esd. 8: 6, the people ratifies by a twofold collective Amen the blessing of the Levites, but this is once again on the occasion of the reading of the Law, and certainly for the purpose of manifesting adherence to it. In Jer. 11: 5, the prophet also ratifies by an Amen the curse pronounced by God against the unfaithful people. In Jer. 28: 6, the Amen with which he concludes the false prophecy of Ananias announcing the ruin of Babylon is no doubt ironic, but with an irony dripping with divine wrath.

The double Amen also ratifies the formula of blessing which concludes the first four groups of psalms: Ps. 50: 14; 71: 19; 88: 53; 105: 48. It also concludes the psalm of the consecration of the Temple in 1 Par. 16: 36. These are therefore always very solemn uses.

Less solemn in outlook, the Amen of Banaias to David, at the time of the improvised anointing of Solomon (3 Kings 1: 36), is no less decisive. It entrusts to Yahweh the whole future of the dynasty. Finally, the text of Is. 65: 16, is obscure on the "God of the Amen," but it suffices to show the sacred character of this formula.

In recalling it in the Christian liturgy, St. Paul was still aware of its force. For him it evoked the Amen that Jesus had come to give to all the promises of God, accomplishing them completely (2 Cor. 1: 20). The same idea is found in Apoc. 3: 14, where St. John calls Jesus "the Amen, the faithful and true witness," the divine confirmation of all the promises.

The Amens which, in the Gospels, are put into the mouth of Jesus, are therefore quite different from stylistic formulations. They have the value of solemn affirmations. Joined to declarations made by Jesus in the first person, in His own name, they attest that His words need not appeal to the guarantee of divine authority, but possess and express this authority.

[104] Cf. N. Glueck, *Das Wort hesed im alttestamentalichen Sprachgebrauche*, 1927, p. 13.

[105] 2 Kings 7: 15; 3 Kings 8: 23; Deut. 7: 9, 12; Is. 54: 10; 55: 3; 2 Esd. 1: 5; 9: 32; Dan. 9: 4; Ps. 88: 29; 105: 45.

[106] In contrast, *hen* is the gratuitous favor, that which imposes no obligations. Cf. W. F. Lofthouse, "Hen and Hesed in the Old Testament," in *Zeitschrift für die alttestamentliche Wissenschaft*, 1933, p. 29.

[107] Gen. 20: 13.

[108] Gen. 21: 23.

[109] Gen. 24: 12, 14.

[110] 2 Kings 9: 2–3.

[111] 3 Kings 2: 7.

[112] 3 Kings 3: 6.

[113] "It is benevolence based on the spontaneous sense of the right," Ouell, in Kittel, *Theologisches Wörterbuch*, II, p. 177, no. 3.

[114] Cf. C. H. Dodd, *The Bible and the Greeks*, London, 1935, p. 61.

[115] Ruth 1: 8.

[116] *Ibid.*

[117] Ruth 2: 20.

[118] Ruth 3: 10.

[119] Gen. 24: 27, 48.

[120] Jos. 2: 14.

[121] Gen. 24: 12, 14, 27, 48.

[122] Gen. 32: 11.

[123] Gen. 32: 10.

[124] Gen. 47: 29.

[125] Jos. 2: 14.

[126] 2 Kings 2: 6; 15: 20.

[127] 2 Kings 7: 15.

[128] Os. 2: 21; Is. 54: 8; Lam. 3: 32; Zach. 7: 9; Dan. 1: 9; Ps. 50: 3; 102: 4.

[129] P. Joüon, *Grammaire de l'hébreu biblique*, Rome, 1923, par. 136 g. According to Mayer Lambert, *Traité de grammaire hébraique*, Paris, 1932, p. 85, it would be an ancient form of the feminine singular, confused with a plural, and having the same common ending in *im*.

[130] Cf. Jer. 1: 5: "Before thou camest forth out of the womb, I sanctified thee."

[131] P. Dhorme, *L'emploi métaphorique des noms de partie du corps en hébreu et en accadien*, Paris, 1923, p. 134.

[132] Is. 49: 15.

[133] P. Dhorme, *op. cit.*, p. 135.

[134] Gen. 43: 30 (heart=bowels). In this example, we see to what extent the Hebrew is unable to distinguish between the idea and the image. For a Hebrew, our distinction between "his bowels were moved," and his "tenderness was moved," is incomprehensible.

[135] 3 Kings 3: 26.

[136] R. Bultmann, in G. Kittel, *Theologisches Wörterbuch*, II, p. 477.

[137] οἰχτείρω can designate pure sorrow (Sophocles, *Ajax*, 652); the derivatives of the root RHM never have such a meaning.

[138] Cf. R. Bultmann, *loc. cit.*

[139] Luke 1: 78.

[140] Col. 3: 12.

[141] Luke 1: 77.

[142] Luke 1: 79.

[143] Col. 3: 13.

[144] 1 Kings 27: 10; 30: 29; Jer. 36: 26.

Chapter III

GRACE, JUSTICE, AND TRUTH—EVOLUTION OF THE VOCABULARY

Justice, truth, fidelity, tenderness—these words which denote fundamental attitudes of the Israelitic ideal were foreordained to furnish valuable themes for the preaching of the prophets and the prayers of the psalmists. Unceasingly, the preoccupations proper to each age, the personal experiences of each writer, enriched these words with new resonances. It is impossible to analyze each text, but it is possible to point out certain lines of development that are fairly clear.

1. AMOS AND MICHEAS

Amos and Micheas are almost exclusively prophets of justice. Amos, who never names the covenant of Yahweh,[1] also never uses the words of fidelity, *hesed, 'emet, rahamim*. On the other hand, he links justice with right, *sedeq* and *michpat*, according to a strict parallelism which abolishes all distinction between the two terms.[2] In this formula, literarily abstract and colorless, he apparently encloses the ideal which he sees being violated every day by the greed of the nation's business men,[3] the scandalous luxury of the rich,[4] but for which he struggles without a let-up. If the formula, in his writings, is ready-to-hand, it is not that

47

he lacks conviction, but, on the contrary, it is because he usually sums up in a simple expression the substance of his preaching.

Nevertheless, there are cases where the words resume their original meanings. When Amos asks that justice be restored to the gate of the city, that is, in the assemblies of the elders charged with the resolving of disputes, he is speaking of "restoring *michpat*," which is entirely in order. It is necessary that everyone should see his rights recognized.

Micheas is also unaware of the expression "covenant of Yahweh." He too stigmatizes injustice, in line with Amos. But he ignores the formula "right and justice." When he wants to decry the injustices of which he is a witness, when he sees "the women of my people" cast out "from their houses,"[5] he calls this "despoiling them of their *michpat*," that is, depriving them of their essential rights, in the most common acceptance of the word. Likewise, when he accuses those whom, because of their function, it behoves to "know the right," that is to say, the "princes of Jacob and . . . chiefs of the house of Israel," saying that they "abhor judgment and pervert all that is right,"[6] he is using *michpat* in its correct original meaning. To know the right is not to be capable of reciting entire pages of the code; it is to be capable of rendering to each his due.

Alongside these common usages, the prophet needs to create new formulas in order to interpret exceptional experiences. In order to characterize his mission and to express his opposition to the illusions which the false prophets are spreading, Micheas uses the word *michpat* in a sense which is difficult to state precisely, because it denotes a unique position:

But yet I am filled with the strength of the spirit of the Lord, with judgment [*michpat*], and power, to declare unto Jacob his wickedness, and to Israel his sin.[7]

Properly speaking, the role of the prophet is not to judge, and that is why the meaning proposed by Van Hoonacker,[8] the "authority to judge," does not seem quite applicable, especially since, joined as it is to some very positive virtues, the word here must denote an interior quality rather than a function. It might even be translated as "filled with conscience." Conscience, that loyalty which lets man face up to his responsibilities, which forces him to look at things and people in their true light, to respond exactly to their needs, doubtless expresses one of the aspects of this fluid word. The moral accent, very much in evidence, underscores one of the aspects of the original meaning: exact response to a given situation.

The justice that Micheas preaches is always called *michpat*. The word *sedaqah* only appears in the last two chapters of the Book of Micheas.[9] Once it is in the singular, another time in the plural, but in both cases it is associated with Yahweh. It refers to the justice or justices of Yahweh.[10]

> Rejoice not, thou, my enemy, over me, because I am fallen. I shall arise. When I sit in darkness, the Lord is my light.
> I will bear the wrath of the Lord, because I have sinned against him, until he judge my cause and execute judgment for me. He will bring me forth into the light: I shall behold his justice.[11]

Michpat here has its original meaning: Jerusalem, in its misfortune, waits for the judge to render justice in its case. But *sedaqah* has an altogether new meaning. It refers to the justice of Yahweh. There is no basis for thinking that it is a question, as in Chapter VI, of a justification which would make its innocence shine forth. For this justice does not concern God himself, but Israel. It is therefore not an attribute of God, and it would be a serious error to read in the formula "I shall behold his justice," contemplation of the Platonic type, the vision of an ideal quality of which God would be the perfection. Moreover, throughout the Bible, God never reveals Himself except through His actions. To contemplate the justice of God is, if we wish to be faithful to the text, to come forth out of the ruins, to see day again, to be reborn to life. It is a restoration, but it is much more than a human deliverance, the simple return to a previous order: it is a divine act whose effects transcend earth.

Without abandoning himself to any vision of a marvelous renewal, the prophet goes right to the essentials. He sees God Himself introducing His people into a new light, uncovering for them the splendors of His own justice. The justice of Yahweh is therefore, in this case, a divine reality, because God alone can introduce it, but it is also a transformation of the world, a new condition of the people.

Can we rediscover here the persistence of the original meaning of upright fidelity in fulfilling everything one must fulfill? At first glance, the distance to be covered seems too great to be bridged. The point of transition is perhaps the idea of judgment. The justice of man must be proclaimed by the judgment of God. But here, there *is* a judgment of God. This judgment is, of course, not achieved by a declaration of innocence. However, it is not its own innocence that Israel wants recognized. Israel is waiting for God to take onto Himself this right, a right which, however, is not that of innocence: rather, it is that of the unfortunate one. Israel is guilty and acknowledges it: "I will bear the wrath of the Lord." In the treatment to which its enemies subject it, it sees its punishment. Still, its faults do not justify the crimes of its oppressors, and the day will come when Yahweh will become aware of this situation. That will be the day of justice, the day of terror for tyrants, the day of light for the liberated people. While justice is not as yet an eschatological grandeur because its coming does not presuppose the destruction of the world itself, it is already the accomplishing of salvation, the inaugural of a new age. The final chapters of the Book of Isaias are dimly foreshadowed.

It is also the last two chapters of the Book of Micheas that propose the ideal of goodness, or mercy, and fidelity. Missing from the first five chapters, *hesed* and *'emet* make their appearance at the end of the book. *Hesed*, which no doubt aims at the duties of mankind toward others, is associated with *michpat*, the practice of a justice which renders to every man his due:

I will show thee, O man, what is good and what the Lord requireth of thee: verily, to do judgment [*michpat*] and to love mercy [*hesed*], and to walk solicitous with thy God.[12]

This ideal of human goodness is also one of the essential traits of God:

Who is a God like to thee, who takest away iniquity and passest by the sin of the remnant of thy inheritance? He will send his fury in no more, because he delighteth in mercy [*hesed*].[13]

This proper trait of *hesed* as the mercy which forgives will be found also in Jeremias.

The Book of Micheas ends with the recalling of the ancient promises, of the covenant of Yahweh with the patriarchs. The tone is simple, almost prosaic, the formula seems almost fixed by tradition:[14]

Thou wilt perform the truth [*'emet*] to Jacob, the mercy [*hesed*] to Abraham, which thou hast sworn to our fathers from the days of old.[15]

The expression *'asah hesed we'emet* was common in the everyday language, where it formed a whole. The combination is broken up here. It is undoubtedly a creation of poetic style, but the laws of parallelism continue to give to the two words, even separated, an overall meaning which fuses their own proper nuances.

2. OSEE

Osee does not ignore the requirements of justice. Yet the words *sedeq* and *michpat* do not occur frequently in his book, and they are never used alone. By themselves, they would not suffice to express the prophet's ideal. They are always joined to Osee's characteristic word, *hesed*:

. . . keep mercy [*hesed*] and judgment [*michpat*].[16]

While mercy, more than justice, or judgment, seems to constitute the essential part of his message, it is not because he is indifferent to the injustices he finds; it is rather that he is less sensitive to the objective disorder in this injustice than to the affront to human relations. For him, justice is less a state of order and of peace than it is an interior condition of hearts:

> Sow for yourselves in justice [*sedaqah*] and reap in the mouth of mercy [*hesed*], break up your fallow ground: but the time to seek the Lord is, when he shall come that shall teach you justice [*sedaqah*].[17]

Justice is attained only by an interior effort, analogous to the patient labor of the peasant. Still, it is not a human grandeur. Like the rain which comes down from heaven, justice is "spread" from on high, it is a divine outpouring. The formula "when he shall come" gives us to understand that this gift of justice is to mark a new moment in the world, the transformation of the people.

It is *hesed*, far more than *sedeq*, which characterizes Osee's ideal. It is this word which defines the essential requirement of God:

> For I desired mercy [*hesed*] and not sacrifice.[18]

The second part of the verse—"And the knowledge of God more than holocausts"—would seem to indicate that *hesed* is directed toward God, that it is authentic piety, the fidelity of man in his relations with God.[19] Yet it seems, taking the book as a whole, that *hesed* primarily denotes an attitude to be maintained toward men. One text, which presents the same parallelism with the knowledge of God, seems clear enough:

> Hear the word of the Lord, ye children of Israel: for the Lord shall enter into judgment with the inhabitants of the land. For there is no truth ['*emet*], and there is no mercy [*hesed*], and there is no knowledge of God in the land.
> Cursing and lying and killing and theft and adultery have overflowed.[20]

It is quite possible that Osee here is recalling the Decalogue. The sins which he stigmatizes seem to correspond closely to the prescriptions which precede the Code of the Covenant.[21] But it does not seem that we can isolate the first verses, which envisage the service of God, from the final ones, which condemn the sins committeed against one's neighbor. It is much more in accordance with the normal sense of the expression *'emet we hesed*, and with the general thought of Osee, to see in this violation of truth and goodness the basic sin, of which the faults that follow are but the detailed manifestations. In an overall view, all the more remarkable because he is really referring to a code, Osee goes back to the source of all these sins, the lack of *hesed*. To the extent that it is possible for us to transpose into a modern vocabulary the ideal so violated, it seems that it denotes an atmosphere of sincerity and of benevolence among men, of respect for the ties which bind them, the end of hatreds —we would say today, a fraternal world. However, for Osee, this mercy toward men is inseparable from fidelity to God, from what he calls the knowledge of Yahweh. The knowledge of Yahweh is something quite different from an abstract representation, something, according to the very concrete force of the Hebrew word, [22] that is an intimate and personal contact. Also, by violation of *hesed*, it is Yahweh Himself who is affronted:

What shall I do to thee, O Ephraim? What shall I do to thee, O Juda? Your mercy is as a morning cloud and as the dew that goeth away in the morning.[23]

While *hesed* essentially denotes that which God expects from man, fidelity to the bonds which attach him to his brethren and to God, the word *rahamim* is, in Osee, reserved for God.[24] He introduces us to a new world, the world of love. For Osee, the entire history of Israel is the adventure of a love, the love of God.[25] This love is at one time the love of a husband,[26] at another time the love of a father.[27] There is nothing capricious, whether of the head or of the heart, in this love. It is a love of the entire being. The words which describe it are properly borrowed from the root RHM; they are words referring to the maternal breast, words of the most profound tenderness, which "turn the heart."[28]

A text which is one of the major ones of the Old Testament condenses Osee's message. It interprets the hopes of Israel in the vocabulary of love:

> And I will espouse thee to me forever: and I will espouse thee to me in justice [*sedeq*] and judgment [*michpat*] and in mercy [*hesed*] and in commiserations [*rahamim*].
> And I will espouse thee to me in faith [*'emunah*]: and thou shalt know that I am the Lord.[29]

By a remarkable coincidence, all the words we are concerned with are together here. The eternal laws of justice and the infinitely varied requirements of the most concrete situations, the dreams of a brotherhood among men and the anticipated tenderness of the heart of God, the unshakeable solidity of God, the foundation of His union with His people—all these converge in this one formula. It encompasses at one and the same time the relations of men among themselves and their situation before God; the movement of the creature which aspires to meeting its Creator, and the generosity of Him who loves His creatures dearly; the renewal of hearts and the coming of a new world.

The fulness of this promise does not come solely from the riches gathered together by the grouping of so many evocative words. The syntax of the phrase is perhaps even more significant. The preposition "in" probably signifies "at the price of."[30] it would seem to designate the price which, according to the custom of the time, the fiancé had to pay to the family of his betrothed.[31] Thus, in the union of God and His people, Israel has nothing to offer to the husband who comes to take it. All its riches are but gifts. This is not yet grace in the sense of St. Paul, for the secret of the promised gift remains impossible even to guess at. Already, however, it is the purest Christian attitude, the expectation, in faith, of the free gift of God.

3. ISAIAS

Isaias is the great prophet of justice. Not that he condemned social injustice more vigorously than an Amos or a Micheas. His frankness had but to imitate their courage. But, for him, justice is no longer just an ideal trodden underfoot: it becomes a messianic hope, a more-than-human grandeur. The essential function of the Davidic Messias is, for Isaias, the establishment of justice:

> For a CHILD IS BORN to us, and a son is given to us, and the government is upon his shoulder: and his name shall be called, Wonderful, Counsellor, God the Mighty, the Father of the world to come, the Prince of Peace.
> His empire shall be multiplied, and there shall be no end of peace. He shall sit upon the throne of David, and upon his kingdom: to establish it and strengthen it with right and with justice. . . .[32]

This prophecy seems very much like another promise:

> And a throne shall be prepared in mercy [*hesed*]: and one shall sit upon it in truth [*'emet*] in the tabernacle of David, judging and seeking right, and quickly rendering that which is just.[33]

The combination mercy-truth is here associated with the combination right-justice. It appears but rarely in Isaias. Is it simply the equivalent of the words of justice? It does not seem so. The two prophecies seem to be linked with the promise made by God to the dynasty of David.[34] This promise of Yahweh's was founded on His mercy (*hesed*); it was a covenant. No doubt it is this context of covenant which determined the appearance of the compound word *hesed-'emet*. These words did not denote qualities of the promised ruler, but divine qualities, the fidelity of God to His commitment. Still, they are found alongside right and justice, which certainly do characterize the government of the Messias. We are here at the boundary between two worlds. Right and justice, distinctive marks of the messianic reign, are human grandeurs, determining a terrestrial order. But they are also gifts from on high. Only the power of God can bring to the world the establishment of justice. There is, from this point on, a continuity between the fidelity of God who strengthens the throne of the Messias and the fidelity of the sovereign fulfilling his duty to be just.

Not to "judge according to the sight of the eyes, nor reprove according to the hearing of the ears . . . [to] judge the poor with justice, and . . . reprove with equity for the meek of the earth. And . . . (to) strike the earth with the rod of his mouth: and with the breath of his lips . . . slay the wicked. And justice shall be the girdle of his loins: and faithful ['emunah] the girdle of his reins": this ideal—the ideal of Isaias—cannot be carried out by man alone. The consecration of the "spirit of the Lord,"[35] is required.

Almost always, the expression right-justice, whether in this simple form or in a more developed one, denotes the essential aspect of the messianic era.[36] At times it characterizes the appearance of Yahweh Himself making His glory burst forth in "right and justice."[37] One is tempted to see in this manifestation the revelation of an attribute of God. That would not be accurate except on condition that it be remembered that this revelation is, at the same time, a transfiguration of the world:

The Lord is magnified, for he hath dwelt on high: He hath filled Sion with right and justice.[38]

If this expression assumes, in this manner, in Isaias, a consecrated and directly religious force—one might even say theological, for it marks a clearly-defined aspect of the divine action —it is obviously because it responds, for him as for Amos, to an ideal need. It is this ideal which animates the struggle of the prophet against his people, which serves as his norm in describing the moral state of Israel:

For the vineyard of the Lord of hosts is the house of Israel: and the man of Juda, his pleasant plant. And I looked that he should do judgment, and, behold, iniquity: and do justice, and, behold, a cry.[39]

Not only do *michpat* and *sedeq*, now interchangeable, lose their proper meanings here, but they now denote only a unique grandeur, an ideal. At these heights, human words lose their force. They can no longer encompass realities of which earth offers no examples, but can only suggest them.

Still, the moment they are used by themselves, *michpat* and *sedeq* regain their proper value. To call forth the concrete details of the sin of injustice, to denote the particular rights violated by the lying magistrates and the prevaricating functionaries, who

oppress the poor in judgment and do violence to the cause of the humble of my people.[40]

michpat, with its individual aspect, is well-suited. It is this word also which is in order to denote the properly juridical activity of the tribunals:

Seek judgment. Relieve the oppressed. Judge for the fatherless. Defend the widow.[41]

When Isaias, sketching the grand tableau of the regenerated city of messianic times, wants to indicate precise features, he does not call upon the general formula "right and justice" but on *michpat* in its determinate sense:

In that day, the Lord of hosts shall be a crown of glory and a garland of joy to the residue of his people:
And a spirit of judgment to him that sitteth in judgment, and strength to them that return out of the battle to the gate.[42]

The soldier and the judge each have their proper function, the one on the ramparts, the other at the city gates, that is, in the public forum. In the new city, both receive from the spirit of God a superhuman strength, but it is in order that they might fulfill their missions.

Similarly, *sedeq* and its compounds retain the original meaning of the root in concrete descriptions:

Woe to you. . . .
That justify the wicked for gifts, and take away the justice of the just from him.[43]

57

While they have thus retained, when isolated, their original force, it is clear that, when joined together, the two words continue to evoke vivid images. The composite formula which expresses the ideal of Isaias may perhaps be less abstract than it would seem. It is of course difficult to determine its precise meaning, because it is a question of an artificial construction. But it is possible, amid the overall richness, to rediscover what each component contributes. Along with right, that which Isaias stresses about the messianic age is the establishment of social justice, the elimination of scandals—in one very biblical word, peace.[44] Justice adds to these perspectives which are still exterior the vision of a new purity, a fulness of innocence, a world in which everyone would accomplish to perfection what God expects of him. Significantly, the promise of regeneration—

After this, thou shalt be called the city of the just, a faithful city,[45]

is preceded by a twofold act of God; an act first of all interior,

I will turn my hand to thee, and I will clean purge away thy dross, and I will take away all thy impure metal.

This purifying action, which makes "sins, though they be scarlet, as white as snow," is reflected exteriorly by a transformation in political morality:

And I will restore thy judges as they were before and thy counsellors as of old.[46]

This coming of justice does not seem attainable, in the eyes of Isaias, except by means of an exceptional trial. Almost all the prophets announce in this way, to the people, the imminence of a severe crisis.[47] This is generally called the judgment, but it is much more than a judgment in the ordinary sense of the word. It is the intervention of the Lord. Often, it is true, this intervention concludes a process of law entered into between God and His people. Ever since the departure from Egypt, since the birth of Israel, Yahweh was at law with His people.

58

The episode of Meriba was the first in time of these trials, *rib*. This is one of the favorite themes of Osee, and, after him, of Jeremias. Micheas also makes use of it. Isaias likewise is aware of it.[48] But this lawsuit is only the first act. It is the explanation between the two partners. It invariably leads to the confusion of the people, convinced of its guilt. Never is a sentence of absolution pronounced. Or rather, it is always Yahweh who comes out justified. He is the just one. However, His justice cannot be satisfied with a platonic recognition of His right. The suit once begun can only terminate in the annihilation of the guilty parties. The debate which opposes Yahweh to His vine:

Judge between me and my vineyard,

ends with this pitiless declaration:

And I will make it desolate. It shall not be pruned and it shall not be digged: but briers and thorns shall come up. And I will command the clouds to rain no rain upon it.

These are threats which do not remain merely as words in the air. The sinner must perish:

Therefore hath hell enlarged her soul and opened her mouth without any bounds: and their strong ones and their people and their high and glorious ones shall go down into it.

But the annihilation of the sinner is still not justice; it is only the necessary preamble for the appearance, in the final vision, of the very justice of God, along with the revelation of His holiness:

And man shall be brought down, and man shall be humbled, and the eyes of the lofty shall be brought low. And the Lord of hosts shall be exalted in judgment: and the holy God shall be sanctified in justice.[49]

This revelation of the justice of God, while it destroys the sinner and confounds all human grandeur, also marks the coming of a new world. In place of the city buried in hell there arises a regenerated Sion. The justice of God becomes the justice of the transformed people:

And it shall come to pass, that every one that shall be left in Sion, and that shall remain in Jerusalem, shall be called holy: every one that is written in life in Jerusalem.

If the Lord shall wash away the filth of the daughters of Sion, and shall wash away the blood of Jerusalem out of the midst thereof, by the spirit of judgment [*michpat*] and by the spirit of burning.

And the Lord will create, upon every place of mount Sion and where he is called upon, a cloud by day and a smoke and the brightness of a flaming fire in the night.[50]

Thus does Isaias accomplish the fusion of the two great themes which inspire him. The holiness of God is revealed in establishing justice in Jerusalem. Coming from on high, this justice is first of all, in God, the fulness of perfection and of "innocence," contact with which suffices to burn away all impurity; it is also a new state of man. The action of the seraphim bringing the divine fire to the lips of the prophet will be renewed by the Lord for His people, by His own hand. While He prepares for His people a terrible chastisement—

Ah! I will comfort myself over my adversaries, and I will be revenged of my enemies,[51]

the purpose of this destructive torrent is to make the "consumption abridged . . . overflow with justice."[52] In fact, the threat concludes with a promise:

And I will turn my hand to thee, and will clean purge away thy dross, and I will take away all thy impure metal. And I will restore thy judges as they were before and thy counsellors as of old. After this, thou shalt be called the city of the just [*sedeq*], a faithful [*ne'eman*] city.

Sion shall be redeemed in judgment [*michpat*]: and they shall bring her back in justice [*sedaqah*].[53]

Caught up as he is by his ideal of justice, Isaias does not ignore other important aspects of the moral life. He also preaches fidelity. The foregoing text, which interprets his profound aspirations, specifically identifies the "city of the just" and the "faithful city," and alongside these two principal words, *sedeq* and *michpat*, we see, on several occasions, some derivatives of the root 'MN:

How is the faithful [*ne'eman*] city, that was full of judgment [*michpat*], become a harlot? Justice [*sedeq*] dwelt in it. . . .[54]

Here again, fidelity is no doubt recalled less directly by the idea of justice than by the image of the prostitute. But the vision of the Messias-King establishes an absolute parallel:

And justice [*sedeq*] shall be the girdle of his loins: and faith [*'emunah*] the girdle of his reins.[55]

Nevertheless, it is always the words of justice which set the tone. Fidelity, for Isaias, is a quality of justice. It marks, above all, the solidity of justice, which is as inaccessible to seduction as to threats.

Still, for Isaias, there is something more essential than justice itself: there is faith. Faith is the ultimate foundation on which everything rests. The substance of the message of Isaias is contained in the words which he hurls at the head of King Achaz, who is terrified at the strength of his adversaries:

If you will not believe [*ta'aminu*], you shall not continue [*te'amenu*].[56]

To believe, to attach oneself to the unshakeable solidity of God, is to assure oneself of the same solidity. He who believes attains "when the overflowing scourge shall pass,"[57] the only foundation which endures, the stone placed by God, the "tried stone, a cornerstone, a precious stone, founded in the foundation. He that believeth, he will not waver."[58] Moreover, he shall see the monument built by God arise, the city where justice reigns:

And I will set judgment in weight, and justice in measure.[59]

Faith placed in God, justice done to men, these are the two poles of the religious life.

The prophecies addressed to the exiles propose, along with familiar horizons, several new vistas.

The distinction between the themes of justice and those of fidelity is clearer than ever. The vocabularies are not confused. That of justice is by and large dominant. But fidelity also has its place, in chapters 54 and 55;[60] *hesed* remains a word of covenant. The association is explicit:

> Incline your ear and come to me. Hear and your soul shall live. And I will make an everlasting covenant [*berit*] with you, the faithful mercies [*hasde*, in the plural] of David.[61]

Likewise, in the preceding chapter:

> For the mountains shall be moved, and the hills shall tremble: but my mercy [*hesed*] shall not depart from thee, and the covenant of my peace [*berit*] shall not be moved, said the Lord that hath mercy [*merahamek*, root RHM] on thee.[62]

According to the common association, goodness called forth tenderness. So, two verses later:

> In a moment of indignation I have hid my face a little while from thee: but with everlasting kindness [*hesed*] have I had mercy [*rihamti*, root RHM] on thee.[63]

These are all themes of fidelity. But they only hold a modest place in these chapters. On the other hand, justice plays a large role and takes on some new meanings.

In a first series of texts, it is, conforming to its original meaning, a state of innocence and of perfection acknowledged before God's tribunal. This proclamation is made at the end of a long argument. However, it is not the justification of the past. Never is there any question of going back to the past, except to declare it abolished. One event alone fills these pages: the intervention of Yahweh who will transform all things—"Behold I do new things."[64] This work is to cause the justice of His people to triumph. At the conclusion of a long pleading, the sentence is pronounced:

> For every knee shall be bowed to me: and every tongue shall swear.
> Therefore shall he say: In the Lord are my justices [*sedaqoth*] and empire, they shall come to him, and all that resist him shall be confounded.
> In the Lord shall all the seed of Israel be justified [*yisdequ*] and praised.[65]

In order to understand what justification is meant in this case, it is necessary to see who Yahweh had opposed in His pleading.

His adversaries are first of all the false gods, who have seduced Israel and have plunged it into sin. But behind these idols of wood, of stone, or of gold, behind the "powerful" and the "judges of the earth,"[66] the enemy which confounds the revelation of Yahweh is the forces of sin, so that justice becomes the triumph of the Lord over evil. But this triumph is not accomplished in an ideal world. The battle has taken place around the chosen people. God and His rivals have fought over Israel, and God was the stronger; His people have nothing more to fear:

No weapon that is formed against thee shall prosper: and every tongue that resisteth thee in judgment, thou shalt condemn. This is the inheritance of the servants of the Lord and their justice with me, saith the Lord.[67]

This justice is obviously divine, the exclusive work of God's power, but it is also human, because it is a new condition for Israel. The Hebrew text has, literally, "Their justice which is from me." This justice goes infinitely beyond the juridical framework, although the struggle of which it marks the final stage is described as a debate before a tribunal. It is a question, in fact, of a total renovation of the people, of the establishment of a new order, of a world marvelous beyond all dreams:

And I will make thy bulwarks of jasper, and thy gates of graven stones, and all thy borders of desirable stones.[68]

This state marks the perfection of justice. On the one hand, sin having been expelled, the people is at peace with God, carrying out to the full the requirements of the divine order; and, on the other hand, evil has no more hold over the people:

All thy children shall be taught of the Lord: and great shall be the peace of thy children.
And thou shalt be founded in justice [sedaqah]. Depart far from oppression, for thou shalt not fear: and from terror, for it shall not come near thee.[69]

Justice is now the innocence of a new world. In short, it maintains its original meaning, but the eschatological perspectives, the expectation of an intervention by God coming to inaugurate a new era, also transform justice into an innocence of paradise-like fulness.

A second series of texts gives justice a more individualized meaning. These are the solemn proclamations by which Yahweh announces and authenticates the mission of His representatives. The formula is repeated three times, almost identically. Once it refers to Cyrus:

I have raised him up to justice [*sedeq*], and I will direct all his ways.[70]

Another time, to Yahweh's servant:[71]

I, the Lord, have called thee in justice [*sedeq*] and taken thee by the hand, and preserved thee. And I have given thee for a covenant of the people, for a light of the Gentiles.[72]

The third time, it is unclear whether the reference is to Cyrus, to Israel, or to one of his ancestors:

Who hath raised him up from the East? Who, in justice [*sedeq*], hath called him to follow?[73]

What meaning is to be attached to this expression "to call in justice"? First of all, it must be noted that the text never says "in *my* justice." The idea must nevertheless be very nearly that, because a text in the same series, without using the identical formula, states:

But thou Israel, art my servant, Jacob whom I have chosen, the seed of Abraham my friend. Fear not, for I am with thee: turn not aside, for I am thy God. I have strengthened thee and have helped thee: and the right hand of my justice hath upheld thee.[74]

The justice in question is therefore a divine reality. Could it be a divine attribute? Would it not be one of God's essential qualities to be just? That would seem to be entirely natural. The "right hand of my justice" is a Hebraism which corresponds to the English "my just right hand."[75] Still, it must be remembered that never until now has justice appeared as a quality attributed to God; we must keep in mind the original meaning of the word. Justice is as much a situation as it is a quality. It is the official recognition of innocence and integrity. Normally, it is up to God to proclaim the justice of men. But who would then be equal to the task of recognizing the justice of God? Only Yahweh can make it shine forth before the face of the world. Such is the purpose of the pleas which fill these chapters and of which God Himself is the source.[76]

These pleas are not mere rhetoric: they are the remembrance of indisputable actions, and the announcement of the decisive event which is to mark the supreme defeat of the powers of evil, and the triumph of Yahweh and of His justice. This event is the liberation of Israel from the hand of its enemies. Now that the punishment for its sins has been visited upon it, now that Jerusalem has "drunk at the hand of the Lord the cup of his wrath" and that it has "drunk even to the bottom of the cup of dead sleep,"[77] God Himself comes, "who will fight for his people"[78] and bring down upon the heads of its oppressors the evil which they forced it to undergo.[79] It is the hour of God's justice. This revelation of justice has two aspects which are inseparable. It is the annihilation of God's adversaries, but it is also the establishment of the chosen people in a new state of innocence. In truth, these two moments are but one. God reveals His justice in expelling from the world the sin which seemed to be its master. The return from the exile is to be the external sign of this, but the real triumph will be the coming of God into the hearts of men. It is necessary to remember all these various aspects in order to keep for justice its true face. It is at once "God's justice,"[80] "justice which comes from God"[81] unto men and, consequently, "the inheritance of the servants of the Lord,"[82] as well as an historic event, the triumph of God over the oppressors of His people. At the same time, it is a transformation of the world and of hearts which seems to demand the end of history.

In this way is explained the very characteristic association between justice and salvation, between *sedeq* and *yecha‘*.

One might believe that salvation is a justice rendered to

Israel after its tribulation. That would be a serious misreading. Israel has no right to claim any such justice. From the time of the ancient texts, we have seen that the "justices of the Lord," while denoting the exalted actions of God on behalf of His people, are not justices that He was obliged to render, but rather actions through which He made its cause triumphant.[83] The only right that Israel can invoke,[84] the only one to which the Servant of Yahweh Himself has recourse, is that of its distress.[85] The notion of right, moreover, is almost totally absent from these chapters. The word *michpat* is rare, and is never associated with *sedeq*.[86] The liberation of the people is not the recognition of any right: it is the act of establishing the people in justice, that is to say, in a state of innocence and perfection. There is nothing natural about this state. It surpasses the most audacious dreams and cannot be established except at the price of a radical upheaval. The combination "justice-salvation" has an eschatological aspect. It is awaited as an apparition:

My just one is near at hand; my savior is gone forth. . . .[87]
I have brought my justice near: it shall not be afar off, and my salvation shall not tarry.[88]

This is the vocabulary of imminence. It is also nature transfigured in the service of the divine work:

Drop down dew, ye heavens, from above: and let the clouds rain the just [justice]. Let the earth be opened and bud forth a savior: and let justice spring up. . . .[89]

This union of justice and salvation takes on, according to the context, different aspects. At one time the emphasis is placed on the divine aspect of justice, the gift of the just God. At another time it has a bearing on the hope for this justice among men. In God, justice appears as the supreme example. God saves because He is just:

A just God [*saddiq*] and a savior [*mochia'*], there is *none besides me*.[90]

Salvation is never due to fidelity, to mercy. It is all the more remarkable to realize that all the words referring to the Covenant are not here, when their presence would seem to be indicated. In reality, in these debates with His adversaries, God does not call upon His fidelity but upon His truthfulness. God saves us because He has said so, and His justice shines forth in that no one has ever been able to convict Him of lying:

The word of justice shall go out of my mouth and shall not return.[91]

We could say, with equal accuracy, "justness" instead of "justice." The original meaning is still very close. The justice of God consists in being capable of justifying in actual facts the words which He pronounces, and which, in the mouth of false gods, are only words, lies.

Other passages stress the human side of this justice. It is called forth by the hope of men, or, on the contrary, spurned by their indifference.[92] It is translated into a new attitude: docility to God. To seek justice is also to "seek the Lord,"[93] and, even more specifically, to "have my law [torah] in your heart."[94] Thus, God's answer to this expectation is the gift of this doctrine. The promise,

My just one [i.e. justice] is near at hand, my savior is gone forth, and my arms shall judge the people,[95]

is the equivalent of the one in the preceding verse:

For a law [torah] shall go forth from me, and my judgment [michpat] shall be . . . a light of the nations.[96]

Through this identification between justice and the practice of the Law, the original meaning again reappears. Israel will not only be justified in the face of its enemies, but it will really be just before God—it will rediscover its innocence in obedience to Yahweh. This, however, will no longer be its natural innocence. Its justice will be a gift from God, a justice of God. Forever, it will be inseparable from salvation, from that action by which Yahweh snatched His people from sin:

For the heavens shall vanish like smoke, and the earth shall be worn away like a garment, and the inhabitants thereof shall perish in like manner. But my salvation [*yechua*] shall be for ever: and my justice [*sedaqah*] shall not fail.[97]

Reading this text rapidly, one may see only one common area: the reworked theme of the contrast between the ephemeral world and the unchangeable solidity of God. That theme is there, in point of fact, but in an original form. Salvation and justice do not, by themselves, form part of the group of qualities which forcibly evoke the thought of Yahweh—mercy, truth, tenderness, holiness. These are human realities; associating them in combination signifies, for the prophet, the decisive event of history, the transfiguration of Israel, and with it, of all the nations. It is a new state of the world. However, since it is the exclusive work of God, it is also a divine reality, and just as it is His triumph over His adversaries, it is also a major revelation of His person.

The last prophecies clearly remain in line with the preceding chapters. There is the same almost complete absence of the Covenant,[98] the same predominance of justice, the same identification of justice and salvation. Still, some differences do appear.

The sharpest is the return of the old formula "right and justice."[99] Moral preaching reappears here. Nevertheless, even in this traditional expression, one perceives the influence of new ideas. Justice in this instance is not only respect for the rights of others. It is practicing the will of Yahweh, the Law.[100] Thus, the formula "to render justice and judgment," takes on an extremely broad meaning, that of fulfilling God's will, of being faithful to His law.

This insistence on the moral and human aspect of justice denotes an innovation with respect to the preceding chapters. On the other hand, the eschatological announcement of justice, the foundation of a new world, is precisely along the same lines. Justice is born of this new growth which is to bloom in the

Messias, and which here begins the springtime of a renewed earth:

> For as the earth bringeth forth her bud and as the garden causeth her seed to shoot forth: so shall the Lord God make justice [*sedaqah*] to spring forth and praise before all the nations.[101]

The parallelism with glory points up the eschatological nature of this justice. It returns a bit later, bringing completely to light the transfiguration of Israel under the influence of this justice:

> And the Gentiles shall see thy just one [justice=*sedeq*] and all kings thy glorious one [glory=*kabod*].[102]

The connection between justice and peace is also an eschatological theme:

> And the work of justice shall be peace: and the service of justice quietness and security for ever.[103]

It is called forth in the vision of the new Jerusalem:

> For brass I will bring gold, and for iron I will bring silver . . . I will make thy visitation peace, and thy overseers justice.[104]

The association of justice and salvation, so characteristic of the preceding chapters, is also found here. It is even commonplace enough to form an allegorical motif. The image of Israel adorned for its wedding—

> For he hath clothed me with the garments of salvation and with the robe of justice he hath covered me,[105]

or that of Yahweh coming to judge the nations—

> He put on justice as a breastplate, and a helmet of salvation upon his head,[106]

prove that this is an expression common enough to be adapted to diverse contexts, but whose dominant note is still to evoke the awaited new age.[107]

Still, these examples are rare. Most of the time, even when associated with salvation, justice keeps its own proper meaning.

The fact is that it is one of the major ideas of the last prophecies. It inspires one of their original themes, the encounter between justice of man and that of God. For the new world to appear, for the justice of God to be revealed, there has to be a prior condition, namely, that Israel be faithful to God's requirements:

Thus saith the Lord: keep ye right [*michpat*] and do justice [*sedaqah*], for my salvation is near to come and my justice to be revealed.[108]

However, an obstacle looms in the way of this revelation:

We shall roar all of us like bears and shall lament as mournful doves: We have looked for right [*michpat*]; and there is none: for salvation; and it is far from us.[109]

It is to be noted that right has been substituted for justice, the normal counterpart of salvation. The transition is quite natural: the viewpoint here is that of the people, which is concerned with its own situation, which it spontaneously refers to as its right. Justice would be God's point of view. He is always ready to give it:

Behold the hand of the Lord is not shortened that it cannot save: neither is his ear heavy that it cannot hear. But your iniquities have divided between you and your God.[110]

Because man refuses to do his part; because "judgment is turned away backward and justice hath stood far off,"[111] God cannot in turn play His role and establish justice:

Therefore is judgment far from us and justice shall not overtake us.[112]

The parallelism between the two formulas is perfect. It expresses beautifully an essential feature of God's justice: that it is the transfiguration of man's activity. There is no grace without moral life, says Christian theology, but the moral life has no value without grace. It can only be the expectation of grace. The Hebrew prophet could not find these formulas. He could not know what "the grace of God through Jesus Christ our Lord"[113] means, but he was already deeply aware that

70

We are all become as one unclean: and all our justices as the rag of a menstruous woman.[114]

Therefore, he awaited a justice capable of regenerating us. More than the flowery descriptions of a paradise-world, this humble avowal bears testimony to what the expectations of God's justice could be in Israel.

4. JEREMIAS.

In many respects, Jeremias is the heir of Osee. He, too, is the prophet of the New Covenant,[115] of the God in love with His people,[116] shaken with emotion in the face of His guilty son.[117] He, too, has as his religious ideal the knowledge of the Lord.[118] Jeremias, however, is in no way an imitator. He is too obsessed by the faults and the misfortunes of his people to repeat formulas. He apparently knows the expression "justice and judgment"[119] which was already common in Amos. He preaches like all his predecessors, the loyal practice of *michpat*, and that is, for him as for them, respect for human justice, that which renders to every man his rights,[120] which guarantees, in particular, the most threatened of rights, that of misery.[121] This justice must be the rule of all tribunals,[122] but also of all ministering, for it goes beyond juridical norms and embraces all human relationships.[123]

Like Isaias, Jeremias sees in the Davidic Messias the King who is to carry out this ideal:

Behold the days come, saith the Lord, and I will raise up to David a just branch. And a king shall reign, and shall be wise, and shall execute judgment and justice in the earth.[124]

The vision of this blessed reign determines the association which fills the second half of the Book of Isaias, that of justice and salvation:

In those days shall Juda be saved and Israel shall dwell confidently: and this is the name that they shall call him: the Lord, Our Just One [justice].[125]

71

Surrounded on all sides by the vision of ruins and disasters, the prophet naturally conceives the messianic future as a liberation, but he does not lose sight of the fact that it must first of all be the coming of justice.

While new circumstances bring with them new relationships, the words generally maintain, in Jeremias, their ordinary meaning. Still, there are certain peculiarities. Thus the word *michpat* seems at times to take on a very broad meaning:

> Go about through the streets of Jerusalem, and see and consider, and seek in the broad places thereof, if you can find a man that executeth judgment [*michpat*] and seeketh faith ['*emunah*]: and I will be merciful unto it.[126]

According to the context, what is dealt with here are all the faults which upset the social order, injustices properly so-called, but also lies, adultery, violence. In all such cases, the personal right of the neighbor is violated, and the meaning of *michpat* is perfectly natural. But Jeremias also catalogues sins which seem not to fall into these categories, the faults of idolatry:

Thy children have forsaken me and swear by them that are not gods.[127]

How can we still speak of *michpat?* Is it solely because the prophet must not only struggle, as had Isaias, against social injustice, but also against pagan seductions, that he extends to the new ideal which he defends, the term commonly used by his predecessors? Does *michpat* finally become simply goodness, duty?

There is no doubt an evolution of the word toward a more general meaning. But it does not seem that, with this, it loses its own meaning. In the same passage, *michpat* is applied to God:

. . . These are poor and foolish, that know not the way of the Lord, the judgment [*michpat*] of their God.[128]

Apparently, *michpat* here denotes the will of God in a very general sense, and this sense is but the natural development of a primitive meaning of the word. It is the decision taken by one

72

who possesses authority, who is in a position to judge (*chaphat*). However, this is no longer a question of a particular decree, but of the total will of God, embracing all of life. In this way, *michpat* will parallel the Torah and be the equivalent of the Law of Israel.[129] Here, however, even if the meaning is very broad and certainly includes all of God's prescriptions, it is still close to the original images. The parallelism of *michpat* and *derek* is very noticeable. *Derek* signifies someone's own "way," his personal "style."[130] *Michpat*, therefore, quite naturally has the very personal sense that it had from the beginning. God's *michpat* is not only the promulgation of His will, it is the manifestation of His essential desire, of His most profound originality, in short, of His very nature. The scandal is precisely that the people of Yahweh should have strayed so far from Him that it can no longer recognize the traits of its own God:

> The kite in the air hath known her time: the turtle and the swallow and the stork have observed the time of their coming: but my people have not known the judgment [*michpat*] of the Lord.[131]

To scorn God's law, is to fail to know His face.

If Jeremias has so clearly brought to light the personal aspect of *michpat*, it is because, in his solitude,[132] he is the man who looks into the depths of hearts. He has been set by the Lord in the midst of his people as a "strong trier" who "shalt know, and prove their way."[133] To try, from the root BHN, is one of the key words in Jeremias. The God of Jeremias is He who "triest the reins and the hearts."[134] It is in this vision, ultimately, which reaches to the very roots of being, that the judgment of God consists. The punishment of the wicked man is but the consequence of this look which projects justice:

> But thou, O Lord of Sabaoth, who judgest justly and triest the reins and the hearts, let me see thy revenge on them: for to thee have I revealed my cause.[135]

What this scrutinizing look is searching for in man is the essential solidity, truth. *'Emunah*, and especially *'emet* hold an important place in Jeremias.[136] Surely, the solidity which these words evoke is one of the most profound aspirations of the Hebrew soul,[137] but in Jeremias it takes on a very pronounced interior tone. Isaias already saw, in the rediscovered moral solidity of the messianic age, the basis of the new city, of the "city of the just"[138] founded on faith.[139] Jeremias ignores these images from architecture and politics. He shows scant interest in anything other than hearts. But he finds there only lies and vanity —we would say today, frivolity and duplicity. It is his constant lament:

> This is a nation which hath not hearkened to the voice of the Lord their God nor received instruction. Faith ['emunah] is lost and is taken away out of their mouth.[140]

Jeremias here seems to be indicting that incurable superficiality which is impervious to all trials. But this lack of foundation, of seriousness, is revealed in contacts with others. The solidity which the prophet demands is, equally, fidelity in human relations and fidelity to God:

> And they have bent their tongue, as a bow, for lies and not for truth . . . they have proceeded from evil to evil, and me they have not known, saith the Lord.[141]

This truth, which permits men to have confidence in one another, is the great requirement of God:

> O Lord, thy eyes are upon truth.[142]

Always those eyes, that look which asks questions and wants true hearts in which to confide.

This truth, Jeremias' own ideal, gives its particular coloration to the common ideal of the prophets—right and justice. It is the interior aspect of the latter. He whose heart is not accessible to temptations practices justice.

This whole wealth of meaning blossoms forth in the image of the vine:

> Yet I planted thee a chosen vineyard, all true seed; how then art thou turned unto me into that which is good for nothing, O strange vineyard?[143]

74

God had placed His hope in His people. He had done every-thing to have a "true" people who would respond to their history, to so much effort. For an answer He gets only "lying." Jesus alone is to be the true "vine" and is to fulfill the expecta-tions of the Father.[144]

The God of Jeremias who probes men in order to test their authentic basis, their truth, is Himself, it seems, never described in terms of this truth.[145] The proper attribute of God, accord-ing to Jeremias, is *hesed*. With one near exception,[146] the term is always applied to God. The parallels with love:

I have loved thee with an everlasting love: therefore have I drawn thee, taking pity [*hesed*] on thee,[147]

with tenderness:

I have taken away my peace from this people, saith the Lord, my mercy [*hesed*] and my commiserations [*rahamim*],[148]

with right and justice:

I am the Lord that exercise mercy [*hesed*] and judgment and justice in the earth,[149]

give *hesed* various shades of meaning, but all these texts have a common factor. They are all, explicitly or not, formulas of the Covenant. In them, God is always referring to the commit-ment He has made to His people; *hesed* remains what it has been from the beginning: loyal and generous respect for a personal bond. Osee, who anxiously watched this sentiment all around him, used to see it melt away in the first heat, "As a morning cloud, and as the dew that goeth away in the morning."[150] Jeremias, on the other hand, sees it in God as a non-returnable gift:

For the Lord is good and his mercy [*hesed*] endureth forever.[151]

This fidelity is given in full measure in the face of man's betrayals. In almost all cases, Jeremias opposes God's *hesed* to the infidelity of the sinner. The common translation "mercy," adopted by the Septuagint in the word ἔλεος, is certainly close to the text. It seems to be indicated in statements like this one:

Thou showest mercy [*hesed*] unto thousands and returnest the iniquity of the fathers into the bosom of their children after them.[152]

Moreover, it presents an opportunity to highlight the idea of forgiveness which is manifest in all these texts. Its bad feature is that it implies that this forgiveness is more or less the sign of some indulgence, of the weakness of a heart which lets itself be mollified. This ingredient, of course, is not lacking in God's pardon. But it is the presence of *rahamim* that brings it out. On the other hand, *hesed*, much more frequent, manifests the generosity of a heart large enough to forget all meannesses and to triumph over all infidelities.

It is this mixture of grandeur and of tenderness which characterizes the God of the Covenant. One formula, quite similar to that of Jeremias, remained particularly popular in Israel for recalling God's pardon. It seems to go back farther still, to an ancient passage in the Book of Exodus. In any event, it relates one of the most solemn scenes of the march of Israel through the desert. It is the forgiveness granted by God at Moses' request, after the apostasy of the people before the Golden Calf. This pardon is, at the same time, a theophany: in forgiving, Yahweh reveals His inmost nature. In the presence of Moses, He expresses and pronounces the formula through which He defines Himself:

The LORD, the LORD, a merciful [*rahum*] and gracious [*hannun*] God, slow to anger and rich in kindness [*hesed*] and fidelity [*'emet*], continuing his kindness [*hesed*] for a thousand generations.[153]

Whether because of its solemn context or because of its fulness, the expression remained. It is found on many occasions, more or less intact, in the Bible.[154]

5. THE VOCABULARY OF THE PSALMS

The psalms bring us into a different world. Many of them are in the first person and translate the feelings of the individual. These sentiments are often the spontaneous sentiments of man in the face of the divine power. Cries of distress hold an important place, we are tempted to say even a disproportionate place; victims of the prejudice according to which the Bible, an "edifying" book, must contain only the purest manifestations of religion, we forget that it is the Book of a whole people, and that it is within its province to gather, under forms quite free of illusions, but not of human reactions, all the truly religious attitudes of man in the presence of God, from the basest to the most heroic. The psalms cover the complete gamut of prayer, and the simplest appeal of primitive man, as soon as it becomes an authentic prayer, finds its place therein.[155]

Man's appeal to God is instinctively an appeal to His grace. God is a power whose favor men seek to gain. Many of the psalms seem to have no other object. They are supplications, as the words *tehinnah* or *tahanun,* the two derivatives of *hen,* which occur frequently, clearly show.[156] Their purpose is to call down the favor (*hen*) of God upon the faithful person. They express the human heart's innate need to find, behind the impersonal mechanisms of the world and the blind fatalities which crush him, an attentive will, a look. There is anthropomorphism here, to be sure, but also, in this childish need, the authentic foreshadowing of the true face of God. If they were ignorant of that face, could the psalms still interpret all of man's prayer?

As a matter of fact, they are not ignorant of it, they even correct its image. These supplications, whose natural origin is to be appeals for favors, are specifically unaware of the word favor. *Hen* appears only twice in the Psalter, and not once in the prayer of the psalmist is God's favor called for.[157] This absence is remarkable. It does not stem from the fact that the word *hen* would not be applicable to God. The expression "to find grace" often has God as its object in the Bible.[158] In God it sees the powerful sovereign. More powerful than other forces, He nevertheless belongs to the same order as they. This God is also the God of the pagans, of those who have not truly known God.[159] But this God is not the God of the psalms. The God of the psalms is the God of the prophets. In his most individual prayer, the Israelite finds himself face to face with the God who revealed Himself to his fathers, Abraham, Isaac and Jacob, the God of the Covenant. This God does not wear the impersonal mask of the pagan divinities; He has some well-defined features. He does not grant favors, but He is the God of judgment and justice, of truth and salvation, goodness and tenderness. These are the words which run through the psalms, and sometimes through each verse. Such are, if we may say so, the chords which Yahweh's faithful one tries to touch when misery or despair assail him.

Apparently, all these words are interchangeable in the psalms, and this realization is not at all astonishing. In these collective chants, made fatally trite by long liturgical usage, the part played by convention, by mechanism, in the interplay of associations, is stronger than in the prophetic compositions. The themes, too, are often confused. It seems impossible to distinguish the motifs of salvation, those of the covenant, those of justice. But, what is the use of distinguishing between points of view in seeking to act upon Yahweh? On the contrary, it is necessary to make use of all advantages. Everything is good in attaining to Him. Often, too, the usual themes, isolated in the prophets, are added:

> O LORD, your kindness [hesed] reaches heaven;
>   your faithfulness ['emunah] to the clouds.
> Your justice [sedeq] is like the mountains of God;
>   your judgments [michpat] like the mighty deep;
>   man and beast you save [yacha], O LORD.
> How precious is your kindness [hesed].
> . . . .
> Keep up your kindness [hesed] toward your friends,
>   your just defense [sedaqah] of the upright of heart.[160]

However, even placed alongside one another, the words often

keep their original meaning: the currents join without becoming confused. Thus Psalm 102 seems to join indiscriminately both goodness and justice:

> But the kindness [*hesed*] of the LORD is from eternity
> to eternity toward those who fear him,
> And his justice [*sedaqah*] toward children's children
> among those who keep his covenant.[161]

Still, it continues giving each of them its own proper role. God's justice bursts forth in His spontaneous gestures, which save His people and transform the world:

> The LORD secures justice [*sedaqot*]
> and the rights [*michpatim*] of all the oppressed.
> He has made known his ways to Moses,
> and his deeds to the children of Israel.[162]

The work of His goodness is different: it is the forgiveness of sins, the supreme testimony to the faithfulness of a love that can never be taken back:

> Merciful [*rahum*] and gracious [*hannun*] is the LORD,
> slow to anger and abounding in kindness [*hesed*].
> . . . .
> For as the heavens are high above the earth,
> so surpassing is his kindness [*hesed*] toward those who fear him.
> As far as the east is from the west,
> so far has he put our transgressions from us.
> As a father has compassion [*rahem*] on his children,
> so the LORD has compassion [*riham*] on those who fear him.[163]

These characteristics proper to each theme are not rare in the Psalter. In a general way, the justice of God is not shown as a quality which He possessed in a permanent way. It is rather the act, of which God alone is capable, which restores the disturbed order. It is also invoked when there is an appeal to the judgment of God:

> Awake, and be vigilant in my defense;
> in my cause [*michpat*], my God and my Lord;
> Do me justice, because you are just, O LORD;
> my God, let them not rejoice over me.[164]

It is also something objective that one can look for and obtain:

> He whose hands are sinless, whose heart is clean,
>   who desires not what is vain,
>   nor swears deceitfully to his neighbor.
> He shall receive a blessing from the LORD,
>   a reward from God his savior.[165]

In certain respects, it is also possible to distinguish it from the God who gives it. One can write:

> Of justice your right hand is full,[166]

because it is a good which God distributes over the world. But the same could not be said of His goodness, which is incommunicable. One bold image seems to show the goodness and kindness of God come down upon the earth:

> He pardons all your iniquities,
>   he heals all your ills.
> He redeems your life from destruction,
>   he crowns you with kindness [*hesed*]
>   and compassion [*rahamim*].[167]

In reality, this goodness and this kindness never really leave God. They accomplish their function toward man, which is to guard him,[168] to surround him with the divine presence, but they do not enter into him in order to transform him.

Purely divine grandeurs, the goodness and the fidelity of God are also as ancient as He, eternal,[169] and one can ask Yahweh to "remember them,"[170] to return to His most profound nature. If the same thing is never said about His justice, it is undoubtedly because this is almost always placed at some time in the future. It preserves, even in the psalms, a noticeable eschatological accent, an eschatology which, if we may say so, is at times reduced to the dimensions of individual destiny. The justice which the supplicant implores is not the renovation of the world, it is above all a change in his own existence. Certain psalms, however, have kept for justice all of its eschatological greatness. Thus, the theophany of Psalm 49:

80

God the LORD has spoken and summoned the earth,
   from the rising of the sun to its setting.
. . . .
May our God come and not be deaf to us!
   Before him is a devouring fire;
   around him is a raging storm.
. . . .
And the heavens proclaim his justice;
   for God himself is the judge.[171]

The imprecations of Psalm 68, one of the psalms recalled in the accounts of the Passion, call down upon wicked men the vengeance of God:

Pour out your wrath upon them;
   let the fury of your anger overtake them.
Heap guilt upon their guilt,
   and let them not attain to your reward.
May they be erased from the book of the living,
   and not be recorded with the just![172]

After the experience of the most profound despair comes the expectation of the justice of God, not as the hope of a complete happiness, but as the final extermination of the wicked, the entrance into the world reserved to the chosen ones of God. "To enter into the justice of God"—the very image anticipates the evangelical parables, the doors opened upon the joy of the feast. Justice is already the kingdom.

Right up to the last pages of the Old Testament, the justice and God remains the object of expectation. The First Book of Machabees, when describing Hebrews faithful to the religion of Israel, speaks of "many that sought after judgment and justice."[173] The formula is perfectly stereotyped: it is simply the equivalent of our no less stereotyped expression "religion." But it is all the more remarkable to see, in an association fixed by usage, justice linked to the verb "to seek." It is at all times the object of expectation.

God's fidelity, on the other hand, is not the object of any hope. Men await only for it to be made manifest. But it already exists, in God Himself, and the purest prayers know how to enjoy its presence:

> Thus have I gazed toward you in the sanctuary
> to see your power and your glory,
> For your kindness is a greater good than life;
> my lips shall glorify you.[174]

Likewise, the perfection of man is to conform his behavior to this divine ideal:

> For your kindness is before my eyes,
> and I walk in your truth.[175]

The old Israelite ideal was the faithful practice of "goodness and truth," *hesed we'emet.* For Osee, it was the means of reaching the Lord, of knowing Him. Here, fidelity to the human virtues is not merely the practice of a moral ideal, no matter how exalted; this fidelity seems to be fixed on the divine model itself. Is this not already the Gospel's theme?

6. THE NEW TESTAMENT

It would indeed be the Gospels if the divine model had already revealed itself. But, so long as Jesus had not shown forth in His person what the truth and goodness of God really are, the appeals which to us seem the purest, the richest of formulas, remain ambiguous. In a prayer such as the preceding, "For your kindness is before my eyes, and I walk in your truth," one may read a very high aspiration, the joy of a soul which has stripped itself of its own virtues and no longer can find repose except in the feeling of living immersed in the grandeur of God. But it is also possible to ask oneself legitimately whether this conviction of finding oneself on the right path is not the satisfaction of the Pharisee who takes as approbation from God the contentment he experiences in admiring himself. Because it is prophetic, because it is always speaking of realities which it does not yet see, the Old Testament remains full of equivoca-

82

tions and obscurities. The Christian revelation brings to light everything that the Old Testament already possessed in the way of riches, and the limitations which it could not overcome so long as Jesus had not come into the world.

As far as terms are concerned, in fact, the New Testament scarcely brings anything new to the themes of justice and fidelity, as they were consecrated by the tradition of Israel. But it shows them concretely lived and definitively accomplished in the person of Jesus.

Throughout the Gospels, one finds the original difference between the two themes. Justice is the object of expectation. Blessed are those who hunger and thirst after it,[176] those who suffer persecution to promote its coming.[177] The expectation of justice is what it has been since Isaias: the expectation of a regenerated world. This world is called by Jesus the Kingdom of God. "Kingdom" and "justice" are equivalent. Matthew's formula: "Seek first the kingdom of God and his justice"[178] is a good expression of this equivalence.

An eschatological grandeur, justice is nevertheless always a human grandeur, the coming in man of a state of innocence and fidelity to God's demands.[179]

The theme of goodness and fidelity also persists, quite recognizably, throughout the Synoptics. On two occasions, the Gospel of Matthew places in the mouth of Jesus the reproach addressed to the Jews who prided themselves on knowing their law:

But go, and learn what this means: "I desire mercy, and not sacrifice."[180]

This is a quotation from Osee,[181] but it is much more than that. In this word *hesed*, as we have seen, Osee summed up the Israelite ideal of brotherhood and human loyalty expressed in the traditional formula "goodness and truth." In canonizing this ideal, Jesus places in a definitive light one of the guiding lines of the Old Testament. He does so with deliberate solemnity. Setting Himself up as an infallible interpreter and supreme teacher of the Law, He proclaims this ideal as one of His basic points:

> Woe to you, Scribes and Pharisees, hypocrites! because you pay tithes on mint and anise and cummin, and have left undone the weightier matters of the Law, right judgment [χρίοις=*michpat*], and mercy [ἔλεος=*hesed*], and faith [πίστις='*emet*].[182]

These "three points," comments Father Lagrange, are "steeped in the tradition of the Bible, although all three are not found therein in any one place."

It is true that no one text brings all three together. At any rate, the last two are constantly associated.[183] The presence of justice, more exactly the practice of right, in this context, is considerably rarer, but still frequent.[184] In point of fact, these three words sum up the prophetic preaching, its constant fight against the injustice of those in high places, the hardness of everybody. It is worthy of note that each of them is characteristic of one of the three great pre-Exilic prophets: justice was the dream of Isaias, mercy, or goodness, that of Osee, faith that of Jeremias.

In the prophets also, these human virtues were already found to be the features of God Himself. Still, while the Old Testament, in its foreshadowings, placed the perfection of man in the imitation of God, only Jesus Christ, God and man, could set forth this still-implicit law, and proclaim: "Be ye perfect as your heavenly Father is perfect."[185] This precept, which remains general in St. Matthew, is made specific by St. Luke, who replaces τέλειοι with οἰχτίρμονες. The authentic perfection, of which God is the model, is this profound love of others, infinitely vaster than mercy, which makes us feel personally their sufferings and their joys, as if they were born in the same family. The Old Testament called this communion with others *hesed werahamim,* words which still presuppose the limited bonds of blood or of some individual commitment. The Synoptics remove all barriers in demonstrating that this fraternal

84

community embraces all men, sons of the same Father, but their vocabulary is still that of the Old Testament. The death of Jesus, who gave Himself completely out of love for His enemies, gives to the traditional words their ultimate meaning. In this fulfillment of all the promises, the unswerving truthfulness of God is revealed. In His generosity in sacrificing Himself for sinners, there bursts forth perfect goodness, which triumphs over evil through nobility. In the tenderness of a heart which deigned to know all the movements of our flesh, appears the indissoluble bond which joins God to our humanity.

To denote this perfection in the gift of self, Christianity consecrated a word which has almost completely replaced the Old Testament terms, namely, love. The love which has God for its object is not absent from the Old Testament. To formulate the great commandment, Jesus had only to quote Deuteronomy: "You shall love the LORD your God, with all your heart, and with all your soul, and with all your strength."[186] Nevertheless, the word is quite rare, and often has only an attenuated meaning. Generally, it serves to oppose those "who love the Lord" to those "who hate him,"[187] that is to say, those who observe the Law to those who violate it, and, in these juridical contexts, the word love often loses some of its force and depth.[188]

Love is rediscovered in the Gospel. Not that the formulas are very different. Jesus does not use the word love much more often than does the Old Testament. But He loves, He is loved. The love which He evokes and which He demands, the love which consumes Him and which He diffuses, His actions much more than His words, are the definitive revelation of love, the secret of the heart of God.

This revelation is at once purification and fulfillment. To translate "love," the Septuagint, anxious to avoid every suspect echo, chose the word ἀγαπᾶν. This dull word expressed in Greek a deliberate and considered preference, a love of the mind, far removed from the heart and from passion.[189] Still, inserted into so many burning texts, this word, which, from its very special use in the Bible, became a sort of sacred word, was charged with a new warmth. The life and death of Jesus, His power which regenerated hearts and transformed them, marked an unprecedented experience. In order to interpret it, St. John gave an absolute consecration to ἀγάπη. Thus, the most universal and most profound human sentiment comes to supplant the traditional phrases, which had more clearly-defined religious features, but which were too suffused with the Israelitic spirit to speak to all hearts. The purest Jewish hope awaited the revelation on earth of properly divine attributes:

> Near indeed is his salvation to those who fear him,
>   glory dwelling in our land.
> Kindness and truth shall meet;
>   justice and peace shall kiss.
> Truth shall spring out of the earth,
>   and justice shall look down from heaven.[190]

This hope, it knew, could not be fulfilled except in a renewed world. It had already stripped itself of the human perspectives of the sovereign and the kingdom in order to fix on the very traits of God, truth, goodness, justice. By means of a supreme purification, these features, still marked with the spirit of Israel, were disappearing, so that their substance might rise again in the Christian vocabulary.

The same phenomenon is found in the Christian and Pauline creation of grace. There too, a vague term, with a profane meaning, is substituted for words with a rich religious past. Mercy and kindness would have been more reminiscent, too reminiscent. Attention would have been concentrated on the wealth of their proper meanings. The word χάρις, without religious roots in tradition, does not interpose a screen before the reality which it denotes. Its whole wealth comes from the object it evokes: the gift of God in Jesus Christ.

This gift is without precedent, but the past does not, for all

86

that, disappear, never to return. When St. Paul reflects on the meaning of this gift, he formulates the Christian theology of grace in a vocabulary inherited from the Old Testament. The Epistle to the Romans, in particular, sees in the gift of grace the manifestation of the justice of God, "being attested by the Law and the Prophets."[191] This word justice, which is repeated thirty-two times in the Epistle, is indeed that of the Old Testament. With a perfectly clear vision, St. Paul defines very precisely the entire effort of Judaism, whose ideal is to find justice, to be found irreproachable before God's tribunal.[192] Such is the original meaning of the Hebrew word. But the fundamental deviation of Judaism is to seek this innocence in the observance of the Law. The Jews simply forgot all the prophets and their passionate expectation of God's justice. St. Paul puts himself squarely in the pure prophetic tradition, for which the justice of God denotes a new state of innocence and of perfection, transforming the hearts of men through an eschatological act of God, putting an end to the condemned world of sin.

The death of Jesus Christ has been this "revelation of the justice of God," destined to justify those who believe. The eschatological nature of this justice is clear, attested to by the quasi-technical epithets: revelation, manifestation, showing forth. Its interior nature is not less evident: it is a matter of the transformation of the believer, who passes from sin to life.[193] And, just as, in the Old Testament, the justice of Yahweh demanded the annihilation of evil before the reign of that justice could be established among the people, so too in St. Paul, the revelation of justice, without ever being identified with the revelation of wrath, presupposes it as a preliminary condition.[194] That is why the "revelation of the wrath of God" seems to be a part of the "revelation of His justice"; that is why the time of wrath is not that which preceded Christ, which is, on the contrary, the "time of his patience,"[195] but the very time of Christ. It is the coming of Jesus which manifests the true nature of sin; it is the attitude of man in the presence of the Gospel which determines his salvation or his condemnation. Such is the teaching of the Synoptics,[196] such is, even more explicitly, the thought of St. John. The hour of the Cross is also the hour in which the world is judged, in which those whom the light of Christ has shown to be incurably blind are found to be rejected, without excuse,[197] and the hour in which the Crucified "draws all things to himself."[198] The Epistle to the Romans, which presents those who are justified by faith—the saved—as opposed to the outcast, on whom falls the condemnation of the Law and of the religious conscience, has as its center the new propitiatory (Mercy Seat), the Cross.[199] This separation of the good and the wicked is indeed the aspiration of the entire Old Testament, but the fulfillment of this aspiration surpasses all human calculations. In this unique work of God His grace triumphs. The world transformed, consummated in a new innocence, this is the means by which His infinite generosity shines forth, so that "grace may reign by justice until life everlasting."[200] Such is, for St. Paul, the ultimate meaning of the world and its history.

St. John too, though he uses the Christian word "grace" only in his prologue, gives it the same fulness of meaning as St. Paul. For him too it is the word which sums up the work of God in the Incarnation. Reading, even in the history of Israel, the mysterious preparations of providence, he sees in the ancient law, because it had introduced a personal presence of God, a preparatory stage for grace. But this gift of God, transmitted by the hands of men, was still imperfect. Only Jesus Christ could bring the fulness of the gift: "For the Law was given through Moses; grace and truth came through Jesus Christ."[201]

John's expression, "grace and truth," recall the Hebraism commonly used to denote the good Israelite, "goodness and truth," *hesed we'emet*.[202] But, just as grace does in St. Paul, truth in St. John takes on a fulness of meaning unknown to

88

the Old Testament. In Jesus the ultimate truth is revealed. "I am the truth," He says.[203] Behind this affirmation, we must obviously place all the wealth of the Hebrew idea of truth, the unfailing solidity of a loyalty able to withstand any test. But the Gospels, and especially the Gospel of St. John, are the revelation among men of this unshakeable firmness. At the same time, the Greek idea of truth is also fully realized. The Hebrew word and the Greek word finally coincide. From the moment when the fidelity of God to His word becomes the revelation of His being, this decisive action is at once the testimony which brings with it a definitive confidence, and the total light on the true nature of God. Thus, the Johannine idea of truth is found to correspond, if not to a precise philosophical concept inherited from Hellenism, at least to the search for a substantial and supreme reality, of which Platonism is the most polished expression, inaccessible to the weaknesses and taints of the world. But at the same time, the Hebrew need for a concrete and active presence—"For the Jews ask for signs, and the Greeks look for 'wisdom' "[204]—is found to be fulfilled by this effort of God, who pushes generosity to the point of the total gift of Himself, and fidelity to men to the point of making Himself one of them.

NOTES

[1] In Amos 1: 9, the reference is to a political alliance with Tyre.
[2] Amos 5: 7, 24; 6: 12.
[3] Amos 8: 5.
[4] Amos 4: 1; 5: 11.
[5] Mich. 2: 9.
[6] Mich. 3: 1, 9.
[7] Mich. 3: 8.
[8] *Les douze petits prophètes*, Paris, 1908, p. 379.
[9] Many critics date these chapters from the Exile, seeing in them the destruction of Jerusalem. Van Hoonacker (*op. cit.*, pp. 347-353), while frankly acknowledging that they suggest different perspectives from those of the preceding chapters, underscores the points of contact, and thinks that these pages portray the fall of Samaria which had just come under the Assyrian sway.
[10] On the "justice of the Lord" of Mich. 6: 5, cf. *supra*, P. 28.
[11] Mich. 7: 8–9.

[12] Mich. 6: 8.

[13] Mich. 7: 18.

[14] A literary or perhaps liturgical tradition.

[15] Mich. 7: 20.

[16] Osee 12: 6.

[17] Osee 10: 12.

[18] Osee 6: 6.

[19] According to E. Sellin, *Das Zwölfprophetenbuch,* I, Leipzig, 1929, p. 72, *hesed,* for Osee, means piety toward God, but a piety which is proved by moral conduct. Osee chose this word because it most accurately expresses the bond which unites Israel to God, the union of marriage. It seems to us to be more in conformity with the usual meaning of the word *hesed* to see in it human relationships primarily, carefully considering, along with Sellin, that, for Osee, the love of God and the love of men are not separated.

[20] Osee 4: 1-2.

[21] Ex. 20: 2-17, except the Sabbath (20: 8-11).

[22] Cf. R. Bultmann in Kittel, *Theologisches Wörterbuch zum N.T.,* I, pp. 696-697.

[23] Osee 6: 4.

[24] Osee 1: 6, 8; 2: 3, 6, 25; 14: 4.

[25] Osee 3: 1; 9: 15; 11: 1; 14: 5.

[26] Osee 1-3.

[27] Osee 11.

[28] Osee 11: 8. Many authors propose to read *rahamy* instead of *nihumay,* by changing one letter in the parallel member, and thereby find that visceral emotion which characterizes *rahamim.*

[29] Osee 2:19-20.

[30] It is the *beth pretii:* cf. Joüon, *Grammaire de l'hébreu biblique,* Rome, 1933, par. 133c; and the dictionary by Brown, Driver and Briggs, III, 3.

[31] Cf. 2 Kings 3: 14. Custom prescribed that a portion of this "purchase price" be returned to the bride as a present. Lia and Rachel complained that Laban gave them none of the dowry paid him by Jacob (Gen. 31: 15). Cf. E. Sellin, *Das Zwölfprophetenbuch* I, Leipzig, 1929, p. 43.

[32] Is. 9: 6-7.

[33] Is. 16: 5.

[34] Compare Isaias 9: 6 and 16: 5 to 2 Kings 7: 13, 16.

[35] Is. 11: 3-5.

[36] Is. 1: 27; 9: 6; 11: 4; 16: 5; 28: 17; 32: 1, 16; 33: 5.

[37] Is. 5: 16.

[38] Is. 33: 5.

[39] Is. 5: 7.

[40] Is. 10: 2.

[41] Is. 1: 17.

[42] Is. 28:5-6.

[43] Is. 5: 23, according to the Septuagint text, and also that of the Targums and the Vulgate.

[44] Is. 9: 6; 32: 17.

[45] Is. 1: 26.

[46] Is. 1: 25-26.

[47] Amos, 1: 3—2: 16; 3: 14; 5: 18; Osee, 4: 1; 8: 13; 9:7, 9; 12:3, 15; Mich. 1: 2-4; 6: 1, 13; Soph. 3: 8; Jer. 1: 16; 25: 15, 31; Joel, 4: 2; Mal. 3: 2.

[48] Osee 2: 4; 4: 1; 12: 3; Jer. 2: 9, 29; 25: 31; Mich. 6: 1-2; Is. 1: 18; 3: 14; 5: 3.

[49] Is. 5:3, 6, 14-16. The objections of P. Condamin to the authenticity of verse 15 (cf. *Le Livre d'Isaïe,* Paris, 1905, p. 40), do not seem to be decisive.

[50] Is. 4: 3-5.

[51] Is. 1: 24.

[52] Is. 10: 22. In its present state, this verse is corrupted. Cf. H. Cazelles, *Revue Biblique*, 1951, pp. 176–182.

[53] Is. 1: 25–27, correcting verse 25 with Condamin.

[54] Is. 1: 21.

[55] Is. 11: 5.

[56] Is. 7: 9.

[57] Is. 28: 18.

[58] Is. 28, 16. The text clearly distinguishes between the stone and faith. Only the stone is the foundation, but only faith can attain it. From their coming together arises an unshakeable confidence.

[59] Is. 28: 17.

[60] The word *hesed*, in a rare usage, appears in Is. 40: 6. It is generally translated "All flesh is grass, and all the glory thereof as the flower of the field." This is the translation of the Septuagint ($\delta\acute{o}\xi\alpha$). But *hesed* never has the meaning of glory. Neither does it ever have the meaning of grace, beauty, charm, such as *hen* may have. Also, different modifications are proposed. If it is noted that this image of withering away has as its counterpart, a bit further on, the unfailing solidity of God (the grass dries up, the flower withers, but the word of our God remains forever), then it is possible that *hesed* means the consistency which is so cruelly lacking in the ephemeral creature: "All flesh is grass, and all the consistency thereof as the flower of the field." The Targum translates it "strength."

[61] Is. 55: 3.

[62] Is. 54: 10.

[63] Is. 54: 8.

[64] Is. 43: 19.

[65] Is. 45: 23–25.

[66] Is. 40: 23.

[67] Is. 54: 17.

[68] Is. 54: 12.

[69] Is. 54: 13–14.

[70] Is. 45: 13.

[71] Regarding the Servant of the Lord, the most recent study in French is the article by A. Feuillet, *Le Messianisme du Livre d'Isaïe*, in *Recherches de Science Religieuse*, 1949, pp. 203–228. Without neglecting the importance of certain recent collective interpretations, he insists on the personal nature of this mysterious figure. We do not need here to study these poems in themselves, but to locate them in the context in order to underline the common features between the Servant poems and their frame of reference.

[72] Is. 42: 6. It is true that here the word "alliance" appears in a context which is not that of fidelity, but we must note that the covenant is not placed in a direct relationship with justice.

[73] Is. 41: 2. The text is difficult. The translation adopted is that of Fr. Condamin (who, however, specifies "*my* justice"): Yahweh arises to combat His enemies, and has His chosen one follow "in his footsteps." Most of the commentators see in this chosen one Cyrus, named in 44: 28 and 45: 1, but mentioned without being named in 41: 2, 25; 45: 13; 46: 11; 48: 14–16. For C. C. Torrey (*The Second Isaiah*, New York, 1938, p. 312), it refers to Israel, represented by Abraham. H. Cazelles, *Revue Biblique*, 1951, p. 185, translates: "he whose justice meets his steps," he who goes from triumph to triumph.

[74] Is. 41: 8, 10.

[75] Cf. the common Hebraisms: the place of holiness—the sanctuary; a warrior of valiance —a valiant warrior; the scales of justice—accurate scales. P. Joüon, *Grammaire de l'hébreu biblique*, Rome, 1923, par. 129c, remarks on this subject that the adjective *saddiq* is not used of things. This is no doubt a sign that it keeps its original meaning of innocence, perforce personal.

[76] Is. 12: 1–39; 43: 9, 26; 44: 11; 50: 8; 54: 17.

[77] Is. 51: 17.

[78] Is. 51: 22.

[79] Cf. Is. 51: 23.

[80] Cf. Is. 41: 8, 10.

[81] Is. 54: 17.

[82] *Ibid.*

[83] 1 Kings 12: 7; Mich. 6: 2; Judg. 5: 11.

[84] Is. 40: 27.

[85] Is. 49: 4.

[86] In the sense of judgment in 41: 1; 50: 8; 54: 17; in the sense of right in 40: 27 and 49: 4; in the new sense of unique commandment, summing up the various commandments of the former texts, legislative texts, or formulas of Ezechiel, in 42: 1, 3, 4; 51: 4 (cf. Jer. 8: 7, and *infra* p. 73, n. 131).

[87] Is. 51: 5.

[88] Is. 46: 12.

[89] Is. 45: 8. Cf. the "just branch" of Jer. 23: 5; 33: 15.

[90] Is. 45: 21.

[91] Is. 45: 23. The translation of Fr. Condamin, who renders *sedaqah* as truth, is indeed the one which seems called for. It manifests the objective nature of the justice of God, which is a fact, not a quality.

[92] Compare Is. 46: 12 to Is. 51: 1, 7.

[93] Is. 51: 1.

[94] Is. 51: 7.

[95] Is. 51. 5.

[96] Is. 51: 4.

[97] Is. 51: 6; cf. 51: 8.

[98] In 57: 1, the just man, *saddiq*, is set alongside the men of *hesed*. Possibly the reference is to the *hasidim*, pious Israelites, opposed to the impious (cf. P. Volz, *Jesaia* II, Leipzig, 1932, pp. 209–211). In that event, we would be dealing with a new theme, one destined to a great future in the post-exilic community. The promise of 59: 21, whose relation to the context is not clear, envisages a new type of alliance, the gift of the spirit, on a level altogether different from that of the traditional covenant and its customary themes. Cf. pp. 262–263.

[99] Is. 56: 1; 58: 2; 59: 9, 14. In 50: 4, justice and fidelity are linked.

[100] Is. 58: 2, to be compared with 42: 1, 3, 4; 51: 4.

[101] Is. 61: 11.

[102] Is. 62: 2.

[103] Is. 32: 17.

[104] Is. 60: 17.

[105] Is. 61: 10.

[106] Is. 59: 17.

[107] Cf. Is. 62: 1.

[108] Is. 56: 1.

[109] Is. 59: 11.

[110] Is. 59: 1–2.

[111] Is. 59: 14.

[112] Is. 59: 9.

[113] Rom. 7: 28.

[114] Is. 64: 6.

[115] Compare Jer. 24: 7 with Osee 2: 25. Jer. 31: 31 with Osee 2: 21.

[116] Compare Jer. 2: 2 with Osee 2: 17.

[117] Compare Jer. 31: 20 with Osee 14: 4 and 11: 8 (especially if we adopt the correction suggested above, p. 48, footnote 28).

[118] Compare Jer. 5: 4; 9: 23; 24: 7; 31: 34, with Osee 2: 22 and 4: 1.

[119] Jer. 4: 2; 9: 23; 22: 3, 15; 23: 5.

[120] Jer. 7: 5.

[121] Jer. 5: 28; 22: 3.

[122] Jer. 21: 12.

[123] Jer. 22: 13, 15.

[124] Jer. 23: 5, repeated in 33: 15, whose authenticity is more in dispute.

[125] Jer. 23: 6.

[126] Jer. 5: 1.

[127] Jer. 5: 7.

[128] Jer. 5: 4; cf. 5: 5.

[129] Esd. 7: 10.

[130] Cf. *supra,* pp. 9, 10. Same parallelism in Is. 40: 27. In Amos 2: 7, the "way of the poor" is the equivalent of the "right of the poor."

[131] Jer. 8: 7. For "the will of the Lord," we might easily substitute "the ways of the Lord," which would be closer to the images evoked by the word. The unfortunate thing would be to lose the equally essential idea of God's commandment. However, it is an expression of His nature.

[132] Jer. 9: 1; 11: 19; 12: 6; 15: 10, 17; 20: 7.

[133] Jer. 6: 27.

[134] Jer. 11: 20; 17: 10; 20: 12. Jeremias seems to be the originator of this formula, unknown before him. Cf. also Jer. 9: 6; 12: 3.

[135] Jer. 11: 20. The text of 20: 12 is very similar, almost identical, in the Septuagint and the Targums. At any rate, it attests to the fact that *chaphat* in 11: 20 has its corresponding expression in 20: 12, *bahan.*

[136] Jer. 14: 13; 23: 28; 26: 15; 28: 9; 32: 41.

[137] Cf. J. Pedersen, *Israel, its Life and Culture,* London–Copenhagen, 1926, pp. 336–339.

[138] Is. 1: 26.

[139] Is. 28: 16.

[140] Jer. 7: 28.

[141] Jer. 9: 3.

[142] Jer. 5: 3.

[143] Jer. 2: 21.

[144] John 15: 1. See *infra,* Ch. VI, Sec. 4.

[145] The only instance where God is called "the God of truth" (Jer. 10: 10) is considered doubtful by so competent an exegete as F. Notscher (*Das Buch Jeremias,* Bonn, 1934, p. 101).

[146] Jer. 2: 1: "I have remembered thee, pitying thy youth and the love of thy espousals." The parallelism with *'ahabah* gives *hesed* a very marked accent of love. The word expresses, in this love, loyalty, fidelity to promises made.

[147] Jer. 31: 3.

[148] Jer. 16: 5.

[149] The last line of the verse: "for these things please me," recalls both Mich. 7: 18: "He delighteth in mercy," and Osee 6: 6: "I desired mercy and not sacrifice." Once more, the attitude that God demands of man is that which He affirms as being His personal characteristic.

[150] Osee 6: 4.

[151] Jer. 33: 11.

[152] Jer. 32: 18.

[153] Ex. 34: 6. The Septuagint version adds: "keeping *justice* and goodness." This is no doubt an addition from an age when the words were quasi-synonomous and continually associated. The Hebrew text does not have this intervention of justice. The perspectives are solely those of God's loyalty to His covenant, to His true nature.

[154] Ps. 102: 8; 2 Esd 9: 17; Joel 2: 13, applied to Israel; Ps. 144: 8; Jonas 4: 2, extended to humanity.

[155] Though the psalms are treated here after the prophets, it is not because all, or even a majority of them, date from after the Exile. This method was necessary to show a de-

velopment, since there was no question of dating each of the psalms, but it does not indicate any intent to determine the date of their composition. We have taken the Psalter, the liturgical collection of the second Temple, as a whole.

[156] *tehinnah* in Ps. 6: 10; 118: 170; *tahanun* in Ps. 27: 2, 6; 30: 23; 85: 6; 115: 1; 129: 2; 139: 7; 142: 1; almost always in the expression "hear the voice of my supplication" or some similar formula.

[157] In the two examples, Ps. 44: 3, and 83: 12, it is not a question of God's favor, but of a quality of man.

[158] Gen. 6: 8; 18: 3; 19: 19; Ex. 33: 12, 13, 16; 34: 9; Num. 11: 11, 15; Judg. 6: 17; 2 Kings 15: 25; Jer. 31: 2; Zach. 4: 7; Prov. 3: 4, 34. Cf. the Yahwist theophoric name, Hananias.

[159] Cf. in Carthage, names like Hannibal (Grace of Baal), Hamilcar (=Hanmilcar, the Grace of Melqart).

[160] Ps. 35: 6-8, 11; the same juxtaposition of themes is found in Ps. 5: 8-9; 11: 11, 12; 84: 11-12; 87: 12-13; 88: 15.

[161] Ps. 102: 17-18.

[162] Ps. 102: 6-7.

[163] Ps. 102: 8, 11-13.

[164] Ps. 34: 23-24; cf. 7: 10, 12; 9: 5, 9; 30: 2; 64: 6; 70: 2.

[165] Ps. 23: 4-5.

[166] Ps. 47: 11.

[167] Ps. 102: 3-4. This is generally translated: who "crowns" you with kindness. The root TR, indeed, often has the sense of crowning, but its original meaning is "to surround" (cf. 1 Kings 23: 26); it is found again, in an analogous passage, in Ps. 5: 13: "For you, O LORD, bless the just man; you surround him with the shield of your good will."

[168] Ps. 24: 10; 39: 12; 56: 4; 60: 8.

[169] Ps. 51: 3; 88: 3; 99: 5.

[170] Ps. 24: 6; 97: 3.

[171] Ps. 49: 1, 3, 6.

[172] Ps. 68: 25, 28-29.

[173] 1 Mac. 2: 29.

[174] Ps. 62: 3-4.

[175] Ps. 25: 3.

[176] Matt. 5: 6.

[177] Matt. 5: 10.

[178] Matt. 6: 33. The parallel passage in Luke 12: 31, does not mention justice. Justice is one of the fundamental concepts of the first Gospel, one of whose aims is to show the fulfilment of Judaism in Christianity, the establishment of an authentic justice. Cf. A. Descamps, "Le Christianisme comme justice dans le premier évangile," in *Ephemerides Theologicae Lovanienses*, 1946, pp. 5-33.

[179] Cf. Matt. 3: 15; 5: 20; 21: 32.

[180] Matt. 9: 13; 12: 7.

[181] Osee, 6: 6.

[182] Matt. 23: 23=Luke 11: 42.

[183] Fr. Lagrange quotes Prov. 14: 22. But the examples, as we have seen, are without number.

[184] Fr. Lagrange quotes Mich. 6: 8 and Zach. 7: 9. If we were to collect all the texts which combine, along with χρίσις and πίστις, their synonyms, χρίμα and ἀλήθεια, we would multiply quotations rapidly.

[185] Matt. 5: 48=Luke 6: 36.

[186] Deut. 6: 5.

[187] Ps. 21: 9; cf. 82: 3; 144: 20.

[188] Ps. 10: 7; 44: 8; 49: 17; 96: 10; 118: 47, 48, 97, 113, 119, etc.

[189] Cf. E. Stauffer, in Kittel, *Theologisches Wörterbuch*, I, 21, 39.

94

[190] Ps. 84: 10–12.

[191] Rom. 3: 21.

[192] ". . . . secured justice," Rom. 9: 30.

[193] Rom. 3: 24; 5: 18.

[194] A. Feuillet very precisely defines judgment in the biblical tradition as "the divine intermediary act which assures the passing of the present time and the present world, which is evil, into the age of salvation." *Revue Biblique*, 1949, pp. 81–82. Fr. Lyonnet, in a series of articles appearing in *Verbum Domini*, 1947, "De justitia Dei in Epistola ad Romanos," pp. 23–24, 118–121, 129–144, 193–203, 257–263, has shown quite clearly that, even in the text which seems best to demonstrate this, the justice of God, as far as St. Paul is concerned, is not distributive, vindictive justice. Still, in simply identifying the justice of God with fidelity to His promises of salvation, he seems greatly to weaken its eschatological nature. The revelation of justice presupposes God's fidelity to His promises, but it is also something quite different, the triumph of God through the regeneration of the world. That is why, though it may be opposed to wrath, as Fr. Lyonnet justly notes (p. 143), it does presuppose the prior extermination of sin.

[195] Rom. 1: 17–18; 3: 25.

[196] Matt. 12: 38–42; 16: 1–4; 21: 33–46.

[197] John 15: 22.

[198] John 12: 31.

[199] Rom. 3: 25; cf. T. W. Manson, ἹΛΑΣΤΗΡΙΟΝ, *Journal of Theological Studies*, 46, 1945, pp. 4–6.

[200] Rom. 5: 21.

[201] John 1: 17. In verse 16, the Greek Fathers see in χάριν ἀντὶ χάριτος, the substitution of the new grace for the ancient grace, and read: "grace for grace." Cf. D. Frangipane, "Et gratiam pro gratia," in *Verbum Domini*, 1948, pp. 3–17. To which we raise the objection that John cannot consider the Law as a grace, since he is about to specifically oppose the grace of Jesus to the Law of Moses. Also, a number of modern authors translate: "grace upon grace," despite the rare use of ἀντὶ which this formula involves.

[202] It is even quite likely that John is alluding not only to the gift of the Law and the presence of Yahweh in the Old Testament, but, specifically, to the revelation made to Moses on the top of Sinai (Ex. 34: 6). Cf. M. E. Boismard, *Le prologue de Saint Jean*, Paris, 1953, pp. 74–79; 165–175.

[203] John 14: 6.

[204] 1 Cor. 1: 22.

Chapter IV

THEMES OF SIN

1. SOME NAMES FOR SIN

The Hebrew vocabulary on sin is extraordinarily rich.[1] More-over, none of the words capable of denoting sin has this mean-ing exclusively. All can preserve a more or less profane usage. The original images are still near-to-hand. The offense done to God remains a concrete act, instead of being obscured in some abstract category, without any reference to life. It is a lie, (*cheqer*), a denial, (*kahach*), an aberration (*chegagah*), an act of violence (*hamas*), an offense (*'acham*), a nothingness (*chaweh*), a perjury (*ma'al*), a horror (*to'ebah*), etc. This wealth indicates an awakened conscience, attentive to the di-verse aspects of sin, while at the same time, the persistence of the concrete meaning of the words attests to the fact that God is always treated as a living person.

However, it is not always these words, which are the most expressive in themselves, that bear witness to the most acute sense of sin. The most poignant cries of the prophet who is the most sensitive to sin's horror, Jeremias, give it only the most ordinary of names: evil, or wickedness:

96

Wash thy heart from wickedness, O Jerusalem, that thou mayest be saved.

. . . .

Thy ways and thy devices have brought these things upon thee: this is thy wickedness, because it is bitter, because it hath touched my heart.[2]

Be astonished, O ye heavens, at this: and, ye gates thereof, be very desolate, saith the Lord. For my people have done two evils: they have forsaken me, the fountain of living water, and have digged to themselves cisterns, broken cisterns, that can hold no water.[3]

This identification of sin with evil is more expressive than many reproaches. Evil is always that which horrifies man. Sin is evil. pure and simple, and the evils that mankind suffers are but the diverse symptoms of this essential evil.

Of itself, this acute consciousness of the affront to God that sin is would be enough to provide the unifying strand for such a rich vocabulary. Indeed, the vocabulary itself manifests a very clear movement toward unification. Up to the final pages of the Old Testament, the most varied words continue to denote sin. But, more and more, they gravitate around a central series which will ultimately provide, if not the exclusive terms, at least the proper words for denoting sin.

This array has as its central point the root HT'. It is the derivatives of this series which appear first. In the oldest pages of Genesis, in the accounts concerning Cain, the Deluge, or Sodom, these words have their full sense.[4] They denote more than a wicked action; rather, they denote an act hostile to God Himself which God cannot tolerate. If they simply want to refer to the action according to the norms of human morality, these same groups of accounts speak rather of doing evil.[5] HT' therefore seems to underscore the religious aspect of sin, the affront to God. Later, as the vocabulary of sin becomes richer, the root HT' remains the focal point of all the new associations. And it remains the most frequent right up to the end of the Old Testament. It represents most accurately of all, the general notion of sin.

The Septuagint translation, in generalizing the series ἁμαρτία ἀμαρτάνω, to denote sin, even where the Hebrew used different words, only serves to prolong to its conclusion an evolution already evident in Hebrew.[6]

In choosing the ἀμαρτία series as a generic term for sin, the Septuagint evidently sought to translate the root HT'. That was indeed the Greek equivalent of the Hebrew root. The latter, like the root "to miss" in English, means to fall short of the goal. The material sense, without being very frequent in the Bible, is nonetheless common enough to insure the persistence of the metaphor in the background of the ordinary meaning of sin. Among the Israelites mobilized by the tribes to seek revenge for the affront of the Benjaminites to the Levite enroute to Gabaa, there were "seven hundred picked men who were left-handed, every one of them able to sling a stone at a hair *without missing*."[7] On the earth renewed by God at the time of the new creation, human life will re-discover the longevity of the patriarchs:

> If a man dies at one hundred years, that will be to die young; to *miss* one hundred years, will be to be accursed.[8]

Morally, to miss one's target is to be deceived. The root HT' also has this sense. Eliphaz, preaching to Job the avowal of his faults, promises him God's favor:

> and you shall know that your tent is secure;
>   taking stock of your household, you shall miss nothing.[9]

Among the imprecations which Psalm 108 heaps upon the wicked man, the poet demands:

> May his plea be in vain,[10]

that is, not exactly like an action culpable before God, but rather like an action which falls short of its goal. And the "delinquentibus in via" of Psalm 24 are not those who are stopped along the way by some fault, but rather those who lose their way.[11]

In the case of sin properly so-called, the goal that is missed

98

is a person. Sin is conceived as a *failing* toward someone, a violation of the bond which unites persons to each other, an act which, because it does not respect this organic bond, only affects the person concerned by injuring him. The first person of the perfect tense, *hata'ti* is the common formula of avowal: "I have failed you." Abimelech refuses to say it to Abraham,[12] Jephte to the King of Ammon,[13] Saul is forced to it by David's generosity,[14] and Ezechias tries by means of this act of submission to appease the ambitions of the King of Assyria.[15] Usual among men, this formula also expresses the contrition of the one who has offended God, of Pharaoh struck by the plagues of Yahweh,[16] of Achan,[17] of Saul convicted of disobedience by Samuel,[18] of David made to own up to his adultery by Nathan,[19] or convicted by Gad of having usurped the rights of Yahweh in ordering a census of the people.[20] It is, in its simplicity, the word by which the author of the Miserere expresses, in definitive terms, the essence of his crime:

> Against you only have I sinned.[21]

This is to be the avowal of the Prodigal Son: "I have sinned against heaven and before thee."[22] The most common idea of sin is, therefore, that of a personal failing in regard to God.

However, this failing reflects on the sinner. To fail God is to fall short of the mark that God has set for us, it is to miss our destiny; it is, therefore, to fail ourselves. A text from Proverbs shows that there was awareness of this. It dwells on the persistence, in the verb "to sin," of the primitive meaning of falling short. It has Wisdom saying:

> For he who finds me finds life,
> and wins favor from the LORD;
> But he who misses me harms himself;
> all who hate me love death.[23]

The opposition between "to attain" and "to fall short," the connection between failing wisdom and failing oneself, attests to a profound religious intuition. In other languages there is evidence of similar efforts, a sign that man, in sinning, is not unaware of the scope of his action. Our word "fault," for example, from the root "to fail," also evokes the image of a mark undershot. To be at fault is both to fail God and simply to fail, to fall short of the mark. However, the etymological relationship remains an unconscious one in everyday English. In Hebrew, the persistence of the root in its derivatives assures the continuance of the primal image. To sin is to become lost. The Christian vocabulary, arising out of the Gospels, will see in perdition the simple manifestation of sin.[24]

Among the words grouped around HT', two are especially frequent, *pecha'* and *'awon,* translated as revolt[25] and iniquity. These words are by far the ones most frequently used to denote sin. They evoke one another in a quasi-automatic way, and are easily interchanged. After the apostasy of Israel, Yahweh is revealed as he who "forgives wickedness and crime and sin."[26] Psalm 31 sings of the happiness of the man who sees "[his] fault . . . taken away, whose sin is covered . . . to whom the LORD imputes not guilt."[27] The Miserere begs God:

> . . . in the greatness of your compassion wipe out my offense.
> Thoroughly wash me from my guilt
> and of my sin cleanse me.

In all these texts,[28] the three words cover but one single concept, that of sin. Each of them loses its own shades of meaning, but the total group is enriched by each component. *Pecha'* denotes transgression, the violation of the rights of others. The word easily takes on a juridical sense and "underscores the damage done to the victim: his rights have been trampled on, the sinner has gone beyond the limits that have been reserved to him."[29] But its original meaning seems to be more general and to denote the hostility which sets the rebellious sinner against God, as it sets individuals and peoples one against the other. Jacob defends his yielding to it against Laban,[30] and David against Saul.[31] It is this which set his brothers against

100

Joseph,[32] Israel against the dynasty of David,[33] and Edom against Juda.[34] This word, however, in its religious meaning of sin, is missing from Genesis. It only appears in Exodus,[35] and denotes a new quality of sin in God's people. It is a revolt declared against manifest intentions, a direct blow struck against a God who, by His Covenant, has involved Himself in the world and made Himself vulnerable. The word *pecha'* will be constantly reserved for Israel. Especially frequent in the prophets, it stigmatizes the special malice of those whom Yahweh has chosen to be His own.[36] If Amos uses it to condemn the crimes of the pagans of Damascus, Gaza, Tyre, Ammon, Moab, it is because, in their footsteps and more guilty than they, he sees Juda and Israel sinning.[37]

While *pecha'* denotes, in sin, failing God, turning away from Him, *'awon* in its turn, denotes the interior state of the guilty man. The word seems exclusively religious.[38] To the extent that we can gather from several rare usages of the root 'WH in the physical sense, the original images seems to have been that of a twisted body.[39] In fact, *'awon* would seem to denote all the disorder, the deviation, the falseness which sin involves. The traditional translation, "iniquity," has the advantage of being quite vigorous, provided we do not consider the etymology of the word, which would connect it to injustice and to *pecha'*. Iniquity has a note of monstrousness, of something intolerable. The most constant aspect of *'awon,* as a matter of fact, is precisely the burden whose weight bears down on the sinner. The verb most frequently associated with *'awon* is "to bear," *nasa'*. Common in Leviticus, the expression has primarily a legal value.[40] "To bear one's iniquity" is the equivalent of "to be guilty."[41] In fact, *'awon* always designates guilt. The guilty one can be absolved from this culpability. The Levitical priesthood,[42] the scapegoat,[43] are thus, through a juridical fiction, charged with the sins of the people. This substitution does not always remain fictitious. Ezechiel feels his responsibility profoundly.[44] The Servant of Yahweh dies, the victim of the crimes with which he has been charged.[45]

The verb "to bear" in Hebrew can, as can the Latin *tollere*, mean to support, and also to take away. From this, no doubt, the formula "to bear iniquity" may also come to mean the forgiveness of sins, their suppression. In this usage, it is reserved to God. It does not seem possible that this expression should arise out of those cases where someone is substituted for the guilty party, in order to take on his sins. It is clear that God does not take the sins upon Himself. And the cases of substitution are more recent than the first texts which use *nasa'* in the sense of taking away.[46] As difficult as it may be to clarify the relationship between these two meanings, it must be noted that they come together as early as the Old Testament itself. The Servant of Yahweh, in bearing our woes and taking upon himself our iniquities, assures us healing and peace.[47] The two meanings brought together in the Johannine formula "the lamb of God, who takes away the sin of the world"[48] are already united.

The image of this burden to be lifted never ceases to accompany the word *'awon*. It causes Cain, brought face to face with his crime by the Lord, to tremble:

My punishment is too great to bear.[49]

Even where the verb "to bear" does not appear, the words which *'awon* evokes are those of burdening:

Woe to the sinful [*hote'*] nation, a people laden [*kebed*] with iniquity [*'awon*].[50]
For my iniquities [*'awon*] have overwhelmed me;
    they are like a heavy [*kabed*] burden [*masse*], beyond my strength [*yikbedu*].[51]

2. ALL ENCOMPASSED IN SIN

The Epistle to the Romans evokes both the revelation of the wrath of God because of sin,[52] and the revelation of His justice which comes, through faith, to free guilty man.[53] All of mankind, Jewish and pagan, appears to undergo God's judgment before receiving His pardon. This grandiose tableau is the denouement of a drama which extends throughout the entire Old Testament. In order that the true nature of sin might become apparent, it was necessary first that the Scriptures should come, in order to "shut up all things under sin, that by the faith of Jesus Christ the promise might be given to those who believe." [54] Surely, St. Paul is thinking primarily of the Law, which, by requiring of man a justice greater than he is capable of, obliged him to expect his salvation as the free gift of God. But for Paul, the Law is inseparable from the Scriptures. [55]

How then does the Old Testament go about "shutting everything up in sin"? In St. Paul, this concise formula involves a twofold aspect. On the one hand it signifies that all of mankind is delivered up to sin, that all, Jew and Greek alike, "are under sin," [56] that "the result was unto condemnation to all men" [57] so that "every mouth may be shut, and the whole world may be made subject to God." [58] It also signifies that corruption is without remedy, slavery without solution, that man cannot snatch himself from sin, [59] and can expect from the tyrant to whom he is delivered up, the only kind of wages at his disposal: death. [60] This is the universal power of sin, the definitive slavery of sin. It affects all men and entirely corrupts man.

Paul sees proof of the universality of sin in the Old Testament, in the story of Adam. Adam, the chief of mankind, is at the source of the sin which affects all mankind. Without, to be sure, having invented the formula which St. Augustine, led astray by the Latin version, read in him: "All men have sinned in Adam" ("as through one man sin entered into the world"), [61] without, perhaps, having explicitly taught that all men are born sinners, St. Paul, at any rate, inculcates with irresistible vigor a twofold truth in this famous passage: all men without exception, and regardless of their situation with regard to the positive law of God, are subject to the slavery of sin—and all are in this condition because of the fact that they are all sons of Adam and all partners in his sin.

There is here, obviously, a new teaching. No text of the Old Testament formally teaches a participation by his descendants in the sin of Adam. No doubt Genesis, in exiling all of mankind from Eden and from the divine familiarity, already gave some glimpse of the interior effects of the first sin upon the entire race. But these lessons seem to have remained implicit. The sages, for instance, had drawn only obvious lessons from the account, and had attributed to the sin of Eden all the sufferings of humanity, and above all, death. The trenchant remark of Ecclesiasticus regarding Eve:

> In woman was sin's beginning,
> and because of her we all die,[62]

assumes in fact, that all men are victims of the sentence pronounced against Adam: "You must die."[63] The Book of Wisdom refers to an identical interpretation when it underlines another aspect of the account: the role of the devil.

"By the envy of the devil, death entered the world."[64] The Wisdom account is concerned with the serpent, Ecclesiasticus with Eve, but both assume one point made without contest; that death comes from this sin. This is, moreover, the teaching which Chapter 3 of Genesis probably intends to convey. Here it is a question of explaining the most scandalous facts of the world in which we live: man's troubles, woman's suffering, and, to top it all, death. There is no doubt that death is, for the Hebrews, the sign of a curse. Still, St. Paul gives a new bearing to the text.[65] Is this purely arbitrary on his part? Is he using at random an example which seems meaningful to him? It is quite true that St. Paul often takes liberties with Scripture. To the liberties of the rabbis, influenced by the words but scarcely attentive to the contexts, he adds the sovereign liberty of the heir who knows he is in his own house.[66] But these liberties, and this freedom, are joined to a profound understanding of Scripture

104

and of its overall meaning. Whatever the ways of his thought, Paul has an authentically biblical vision of history. When he finds in Scripture the spectacle of mankind all joined together in sin, of an unique army of God's enemies, he is being quite faithful to the entire Old Testament.

In his view, the account of the fall of Adam shuts all mankind up under sin. For it begins a history in which sin will spread over all men. To understand Genesis, it is necessary to pay as much attention to the aim which the overall arrangement reveals, as to the details of the story themselves. Now the history of salvation, which begins in Chapter 12 with the election of Abraham, is the counterpart of the history of sin, which opens in Chapter 3. The blessing of Abraham, the type of all the blessings destined for man,[67] corresponds to the curses which the sin of Adam has merited for the world.[68] While the blessing of God never ceases to accompany the patriarchs and to protect their steps, the first chapters, on the other hand, show the inexorable proliferation of sin. The murder of Abel is but the first crime in an unending series. Hatred grows without let-up, dictating its laws, ever more pitiless:

> If Cain shall be avenged sevenfold,
> Lamech seventy times sevenfold.[69]

So much so that finally, the earth is "full of violence,"[70] and man is completely dominated by the evil which possesses his heart.[71] Only Noe and his kin escape this universal corruption. God then takes the initiative, the first move in a series which will come after. He makes a covenant with Noe. He draws His chosen one from the mass of humanity which is vowed to destruction, and, miraculously, saves him and makes him the father of a renewed mankind.[72]

This humanity in its turn succumbs again to sin. The episode of the Tower of Babel,[73] shows that man has not given up making himself God's equal. It also shows that, while God has forbidden Himself ever to annihilate mankind, sin nevertheless continues to provoke catastrophes. Present-day humanity, with its barriers and its divisions, bears constantly the sign of Babel, just as it is at all times the victim of the sin of Adam. Of this punishment, the nation of Babylon, so proud of its power and its accomplishments, bears the indelible trace: the boldest of its monuments is only a ruin.

From the midst of this land struck by God, from this world delivered up to sin, Yahweh draws forth Abraham. In place of the cursed structure, symbol of a humanity torn asunder, God gives to all the peoples the figure of His chosen one as a rallying point and type of the blessings He has destined for them.[74] Abraham, indeed, inaugurates a new world. His adventures, his very trials, take place in an almost paradise-like atmosphere. But this situation is not a natural one. It comes as a result of God's exceptional favor. Around this luminous existence, there are only wars, deceits, violence, crimes and catastrophes. In varying degrees, Ismael and Abimelech, Sodom and Gomorrha, constitute the real mankind, sunk in evil.

From the time of Jacob, the aura of innocence and of happiness which surrounded the patriarch becomes obscured. Without being directly condemned, his craftiness is presented by the author of Genesis as the source of his troubles, in particular, of his long exile. Still, God does not abandon him, and his trials all have happy endings.[75]

The opening chapters of Exodus have an altogether different tone from that of Genesis. The era of favor seems at an end. The Hebrew people is living in the midst of the Egyptians, subject to the most arduous labors. Undoubtedly, it is still aware that its fathers have received from God some magnificent promises,[76] but "their dejection and hard slavery"[77] have crushed all resilience in the people and have left them deaf to the message of Moses. Their souls have become those of slaves, dominated by the fear of death. The generous reaction of Moses, indignant at the treatment of his people, only arouses jealousy and fear.[78]

106

And his intervention with Pharaoh, far from awakening the people's courage, unleashes a rash of servile cowardice:

The Lord look upon you and judge! You have brought us into bad odor with Pharaoh and his servants and have put a sword in their hands to slay us.[79]

That is the point to which the descendants of Abraham have come—reduced to slavery.

What is this slavery? In the first place, certainly, that of a hostile tyranny. Still, behind it, one can feel a power other than the political power, a force hostile to God. No text mentions it by name, no text even allows us to suppose that the author of these chapters sees in the servitude of the Hebrews the penalty for some failing. But the atmosphere is that of sin. Not of any specified sin: it seems merely that the chosen people themselves have lost their familiarity with the God of Abraham, as if this were more or less tied up with the holy places of Palestine. The Hebrews have fallen back into the normal condition of mankind: sin.

The Israelitic tradition will spell out this confused impression which is brought to light in the pages of Exodus. It will retain the name of "that place of slavery"[80] to refer to Egypt, but, rather quickly, it will also see in the sojourn on the banks of the Nile a period of sin, a return to the paganism from which God had drawn Abraham.[81] When Osee threatens the people with a return to Egypt,[82] he is not simply calling to mind the land of forced labor, but the impure land from which Yahweh is missing. And Ezechiel accuses Israel of having, from the Egyptian period on, multiplied its prostitutions,[83] to the point where Yahweh was then tempted to "pour out . . . indignation upon them, and accomplish my wrath against them."[84] For him, the sin of Israel, to which he was always returning, was the sin of its youth, the sin of Egypt.[85]

There is here, a special interpretation of history. In making the sojourn in Egypt a time of sin, Ezechiel does not get away from the explicit statements of Exodus, but rather, extends them. He gives a fuller meaning to indications whose full scope the author of Exodus did not grasp. As far as the latter is concerned, it is impossible to celebrate Yahweh in Egypt;[86] Yahweh wants to be served on His mountain.[87] For Osee, Yahweh exiles His unfaithful people[88] in Egypt, far from their own land, that is to say, far from His presence. This transposition reveals, in the light of subsequent experience, the somber atmosphere which presses down on these accounts, and which is, in the last analysis, that of sin.

Thus clarified, the initial chapters of Exodus are to be placed naturally after the beginning of Genesis, and correspond thereto. They manifest the same law of the proliferation of sin. From Adam was born the generation of the Deluge; from Noe were born the builders of Babel; from Abraham were born the slaves who, for a piece of bread, prefer their servitude to the service of the God of their father.[89] Sin pervades all.

Only those privileged with a miracle escape the contagion. An exceptional intervention by God saves Noe and his kin from the waters of the Flood, snatches Abraham and his heirs from Babylonian heathenism, saves Moses, abandoned to the waters of the Nile,[90] and, finally, draws Israel out of Egypt. We could multiply, with regard to the passage through the Red Sea, the most documented studies, the most ingenious hypotheses, yet we would not be giving the account of Exodus its proper meaning if we did not recognize that it is founded entirely upon a miracle, and on a miracle of the first order, analogous to Noe's Ark. An authentic miracle, because the marvelous fact is the sign of a divine event. Only an act of God can rescue the Hebrew people from their slackness and make them the people of Yahweh. The ultimate reality of the Exodus, a properly historic reality, is this literally miraculous birth.

The greatness of this miracle is only insofar as it is a triumph over sin. In the origins of Israel there is, therefore, sin, sin in which the people itself was mired. Noe had kept himself just;[91]

Abraham, in order to obey Yahweh, had had to leave his homeland,[92] tear himself away from the paganism of his fathers.[93] In Egypt, the breakdown was complete. The Exodus is literally a new birth.

This birth opens an era. The Covenant with Israel[94] marks it forevermore. It gives to the sin of the chosen people a new scope and gravity. Its sin is a return to Egypt. No more than Baptism erases concupiscence, was the passage through the Red Sea capable of abolishing, among the Hebrews, the remembrance of this rich and verdant land, this brilliant civilization, these seductive gods. This "place of slavery" seems to them now to be the land of "fleshpots [where we] ate our fill of bread."[95] The savagery of the desert, the uncertainty of an adventure without conclusion, revives their nostalgia. But it is no longer possible for them simply to turn back. The passage through the Red Sea definitively marked the end of an era. To return to Egypt now would be to take sides against God; to render homage to an image is to apostasize.

The vocabulary of these episodes reveals these changes. Now there appear the words reserved for the sin of Israel, the temptation,[96] the quarrel between God and His people.[97] Now especially, there appears the new name for sin, *pecha'*, offense.[98] This revolt, however, is the doing of the entire people. The idolatry scene at the foot of Sinai is obviously told with intention of showing that, from its beginnings, Israel is guilty in each of its children. The biblical tradition was not afraid to show the first generation of the chosen people entirely unfaithful and condemned.[99] The lesson was not lost. The Canticle of Moses, at the end of Deuteronomy, stigmatizes this "perverse and crooked race,"[100] a "fickle race . . . sons with no loyalty in them."[101] Just as all mankind had come from Adam, the sinner, Israel is forever marked by the failure at its birth.[102]

In their struggle against sin, the prophets feel profoundly the collective, universal aspect of their people's crime. No doubt the national cohesiveness, supported by the monarchical idea, helps them persuade their compatriots that the sin of the king is the sin of Israel, according to the refrain which runs through so many scandalous reigns, in the Book of Kings.[103] But their religious sagacity soon makes them go beyond the still too external area of collective responsibilities. In the face of impurity:

Woe is me, because I have held my peace; because I am a man of unclean lips.[104]

But in the same instant, he perceives that he shares this impurity with the people of his birth:

And I dwell in the midst of a people that hath unclean lips.[105]

Jeremias is so obsessed by the "breach of the daughter of my people"[106] that this breach or wound becomes his own:

Why is my sorrow become perpetual, and my wound desperate so as to refuse to be healed?
For the affliction of the daughter of my people, I am afflicted and made sorrowful.[107]

This wound, this "wickedness . . . [which] hath touched my heart,"[108] is the sin of Israel.[109] All are guilty of this sin. Like Sodom of yore, Yahweh looks at Jerusalem in vain; in vain does His eye search the streets and by-ways to find a man, "a man that executeth judgment, and seeketh faith,"[110] on behalf of the city. But He can find no one. Not only the little ones, "those who do not know the ways of the Lord," but the great ones also, those who have "known the way of the Lord, the judgment of their God. And behold these have altogether broken the yoke more and have burst the bonds."[111]

All these princes go out of the way: they walk deceitfully, they are brass and iron, they are all corrupted.
The bellows have failed, the lead is consumed in the fire, the founder hath melted in vain: for their wicked deeds are not consumed.[112]

As before in the desert, God's efforts to keep His people are in

110

vain; just as He had to abandon the generation of the Exodus, so He must abandon that of Jeremias:

Cut off thy hair, and cast it away: and take up a lamentation on high; for the Lord hath rejected and forsaken the generation of his wrath.[113]

The sin of this generation is similar to that of its fathers, but worse:

And when thou shalt tell this people all these words and they shall say to thee: Wherefore hath the Lord pronounced against us all this great evil? What is our iniquity, and what is our sin, that we have sinned against the Lord our God?

Thou shalt say to them: Because your fathers forsook me, saith the Lord, . . . and kept not my law.

And you also have done worse than your fathers; for, behold, every one of you walketh after the perverseness of his evil heart.[114]

Could this "evil heart" be the source of the expression by which the Fourth Book of Esdras and the Apocalypse of Baruch explain the fact that men have sinned following Adam? It is because they always bear this "evil heart" which led Adam to sin.[115] Is there, in the writings of St. Paul, a harking back to Jeremias? In any event, this text offered for consideration more than just the expression "evil heart"; it clearly suggested the idea of a sin passed on from generation to generation. The apostasy of the ancestors has its effects even on the present generation.[116] Jeremias is closer to the Christian formulations of original sin than the Jewish writings which think only of the repetition of analogous effects produced by the same cause. Ezechiel, following Jeremias, develops this theme at great length, showing throughout the history of the people the permanence of this sin which goes back to its impure origins, to its birth in Egypt.[117]

Another theme of the prophets shows even more clearly how deeply sin has become ingrained in the people: the theme of the uncircumcised heart. Indeed, it implies a congenital impurity:

Be circumcised to the Lord, and take away the foreskins of your hearts.[118]

111

But how to act upon one's own nature? That is not man's work. This purification, also, is reckoned by Deuteronomy among Yahweh's promises:

> The LORD, your God, will then bring you into the land which your fathers once occupied, . . . [he] will circumcise your hearts and the hearts of your descendants, that you may love the LORD, your God, with all your heart and all your soul, and so may live.[119]

Uncircumcised of heart, Israel falls back to the level of the heathen. Long before St. Paul, the "prophet of the Gentiles" had drawn this conclusion from the irremediable corruption which was defiling his people:

> Behold the days come, saith the Lord, and I will visit upon every one that hath the foreskin circumcised.
> Upon Egypt, and upon Juda, and upon Edom, and upon the children of Ammon, and upon Moab, and upon all that have their hair polled round, that dwell in the desert: for all the nations are uncircumcised in the flesh, but all the house of Israel are uncircumcised in the heart.[120]

Israel's privilege is abolished: as guilty as the heathen, guilty of the same faults as they, it falls under the common judgment of God.

This universal judgment is prophesied in Isaias. At Tophet, the infamous place where the "wicked kindred," the "generation of his wrath,"[121] must pay for its crimes, the "carcasses of the men that have transgressed against me"[122] are gathered together, spread out on the ground like manure,[123] to be delivered up to torments without end. The word which denotes the transgression here is *pecha'*, the term heretofore reserved for the sin of Israel against its God, apostasy. Now all the nations have had access to Jerusalem, God's people extends to all mankind. "Tribulation and anguish shall be visited upon every man who works evil; of Jew first and then of Greek."[124] The latter is equally guilty. Thus, the experience of the prophets concludes by bringing together in a common condemnation both Israel and the Gentiles. After having constantly reproached their people for denying their God in order to give themselves up to

112

the sin of the pagans, they discover that the sin of the pagans is identical with that of their own people. No one has any right to glorify himself.

From these unburied corpses, from these rotted bones, God can, however, bring forth living souls.[125] Israel, annihilated by the Exile, will find renewed existence. As mediocre as this renaissance might at this time have seemed to be, at least the great temptation of idolatry was finally put aside. Was the promise of God fulfilled? Was the heart of the people truly renewed, circumcised? Was gehenna, "valley of the dead bodies and of ashes," finally purified, its fields now "the Holy of the Lord"?[126] Those who had hoped so were to be mistaken. The community after the Exile shows, on the whole, a greater fidelity to the Law. But many signs indicate the presence of serious shortcomings. Two factions are indicated: that of the just and that of the wicked. The sapiential literature and the psalms are continually opposing one to the other. Until the Exile, the world was divided up between the people of God and the pagan peoples. Yahweh's enemies, so recently the heathen nations, are still the adversaries, the oppressors, but their victims are now "the poor of Israel."[127]

How many psalms were written to ask God for deliverance from the pursuit of an ambitious calumniator, the rapacity of some intriguer! Often, these appeals seem terribly self-interested, these invectives quite impermeable to Christian charity. To understand them, it is necessary to put them into their proper place, to recognize that the unfortunate one who cries out his distress is putting his faith into play. It is not simply a question of asking God for an end to one's troubles, but to escape from scandal, from the temptation of rejoining the party of the wicked, of those for whom everything succeeds. Such a psalm expresses with emotion the confusion which seizes the man who is burdened by misfortune, tempted to be "false to the fellowship of your children."[128]

113

The danger in this situation was Pharisaism. The party of the just becomes the party of those who have nothing with which to reproach themselves. The Gospels bear witness that Judaism had largely succumbed to this danger, and Jesus was often to scandalize the well-intentioned by the sympathy He would show for sinners.[129] But Pharisaism was not faithful to the spirit of the Old Testament. A psalm such as the Miserere is proof of the kind of awareness of sin Israelitic piety could come to.[130] Its testimony is all the more significant because this avowal, completely permeated with the feeling of the fundamental impurity of the creature in the presence of the divine holiness, was attributed by tradition to David.[131] David had sinned, and Scripture had not feared to bring out the particularly odious nature of his crimes. David, nonetheless, remained at all times the ideal type of the monarch chosen by the Lord, the type of the Messias. Still, there was no timidity about placing on the lips of this venerated personage these pitiless words regarding his guilt and his lack of power to raise himself up again. There was a firm conviction that "before you [God] no man living is just":[132]

> If you, O Lord, mark iniquities,
> Lord, who can stand?[133]

While there is not, in the Old Testament, any formula which corresponds to the Christian dogma of original sin, and which attributes explicitly the state of condemnation in which all men are born to their solidarity with the sin of Adam, there is the profound feeling of belonging to a race of sinners born of sinners:

> In guilt was I born,
> and in sin my mother conceived me.[134]

National pride in no way weakened this conviction; on the contrary, the authentic Israelitic tradition reinforced it. It showed the chosen people itself, born of a condemned genera-

114

tion, dragging the heritage of this sin throughout its history, without ever being able to detach itself from it.

Man does not come forth out of this sin. On this point, too, the biblical vision announces the Christian vision. Since the first man, God's action has consisted in snatching His chosen ones from a mankind of sinners. This intervention has always been miraculous. The building of the Ark, the supernatural blessing which protects Abraham, the passage through the Red Sea, are actions which raise their beneficiaries above the human condition.

Yet they do not succeed in changing hearts. This supreme miracle can only be awaited by the prophets. Only Jesus can perform it.

Jesus, however, faced with His contemporaries, is in exactly the same position as Yahweh had been since the birth of Israel. After having tried for centuries to make Himself heard through the mouth of His prophets, Yahweh's Word comes in person to address Himself to His people. This supreme effort encounters a total hardening. Bringing to full fruition the crimes of their fathers, the Jews refuse to listen to Jesus. They therefore call down upon their heads the judgment of God. To express the sin and the fate of these last heirs of the people born at the Exodus, Jesus repeats the phrase which Scripture had used in describing the forefathers: "perverse and crooked race!"[135] He often adds to the Deuteronomic formula a second qualification that is missing in Deuteronomy, but in which a whole prophetic tradition lives again: the complete expression in the Gospel is: "an evil and adulterous generation."[136] Thus He affirms the solidarity of His contemporaries with the sins of their fathers, but above all, with the generation of the beginnings. But that is not for the purpose of lessening their responsibility. They have filled up the measure of their fathers. On them

115

. . . may come all the just blood that has been shed on the earth, from the blood of Abel the just unto the blood of Zacharias the son of Barachias, whom you killed between the temple and the altar. Amen I say to you, all these things will come upon this generation.[137]

The judgment will also sound forth. It still remains for this generation to reject the Son of Man.[138] Then will the signs which it seeks, as did in former times the generation of the desert,[139] appear, and it will be unable to recognize them. The sign of Jonas, the supreme sign of the Resurrection, will remain hidden to it.[140] God will have rejected this generation. "Amen I say to you, this generation will not pass away till all these things have been accomplished."[141] The threat of Jeremias is fulfilled:

The Lord hath rejected and forsaken the generation of his wrath.[142]

Behind the generation which rejected Jesus, the Gospels give a glimpse of another, vaster grouping, to which St. John gives a lasting name, "the world."

In the Synoptics, certain features of "this generation" already seem to go beyond the limited framework of the original expression. Mark's formula: "For whoever is ashamed of me and of my words in this adulterous and sinful generation, of him will the Son of Man also be ashamed when he comes with the holy angels in the glory of his father,"[143] evokes such a vast field of action that Luke and Matthew substituted in the parallel passages the general formula: "Whoever disowns me before men."[144] Jesus' comment at the conclusion of the parable of the unfaithful steward: "For the children of this world, in relation to their own generation, are more prudent than the children of the light,"[145] is obviously a phrase of universal scope. It divides men into two categories. But what are the words "their generation" doing here?[146] Are they not witness to the perspective in which Jesus lived, that of a condemned generation? Of course, they could be accurately translated "in their sinful environment." The interesting point here is that the men

116

of his generation have become the children of this world. For, the present world, or, according to the usual formula, *this* world (as also *this* generation), is likewise the world itself. It seems that it is St. Paul who made the transfer from one word to the other. These expressions, "this generation" and "this world" are completely interchangeable in his writings.[147] St. John, who gave to the world rejected by God its definitive features, also takes up quite frequently the demonstrative "this world."[148]

The world, as St. John sees it, is committing the very sin of the Hebrews in the desert, then of the Jews who rebuffed Jesus. Like them, it is refusing to receive the Word of God who comes unto His own.[149] Like them, it is remaining insensitive to all the signs, blind to the light.[150] Like them, it is condemned without appeal.[151]

The idea of "this world," whether limited to Israel or expanded to all of mankind, implies the same reality: a collectivity which acts as one in its hostility to God. This is a condition imposed upon each individual like his environment, a natural habitat no one can escape.

The miracle of Christianity, one that has no common ground with those miracles of the Deluge and the Red Sea, is to break the limitations of this environment. The first Christian preaching, on the morning of Pentecost, affirms that the Spirit makes a second birth possible: "Save yourselves from this perverse generation."[152] It is in this vocabulary that the Christians of Phillipi considered their conversion. No doubt, they have practically nothing in common with the Jews to whom Jesus spoke. St. Paul, nevertheless, writes to them to keep themselves "blameless and guileless . . . in the midst of a depraved and perverse generation."[153] Thus, in St. John, the disciples may indeed have been born into the world. But they have been taken "out of the world";[154] since they were chosen, they have been "chosen out of the world,"[155] and henceforth are "not of this world."[156]

For John as for Paul, God draws forth His own out of a sin which has spared no one.

3. HORROR OF SIN

As far back as we can determine, the religion of Yahweh developed an acute sense of sin. The fall of Adam and Eve is told with sober and serious depth. The ancient author of these pages knew souls and was a man of God. Not all in Israel reached these heights. The accounts in Genesis are incomparable but still isolated testimonies. The Books of Kings, at the beginning of the monarchical period, give us the average reactions of the people during the years in which they were implanting their religion in the country. These are at a much more common level.[157] Sin often seems to consist of an external act. Some combatants are guilty because, exhausted, they sought to refresh themselves by striking down beasts without respecting consecrated formalities.[158] Jonathan, unaware of Saul's oath, is at fault for having eaten a bit of honey.[159] The intention counts for nothing. In the offended one Himself, God, the reaction seems automatic. He takes at face value Saul's oath, and refuses, because of Jonathan's action, to respond to the ritual consultations.[160] He strikes down Oza, who was guilty of having, in his piety, touched the Ark to keep it from falling.[161]

This mechanical aspect of sin and sanction surely reveals some rudimentary concepts; these interdicts, moreover, protect impure objects equally as much as they do sacred areas. Might not, in its origins, the horror of sin have been but a panicky fear in the presence of forces whose power made one tremble? This idea has often been maintained, but at the price of confusion—a confusion well justified by appearances. "Holy things are those whose use is withdrawn, in whole or in part, from man, so that they may be set aside for divinity. Impure things are those of which divinity has a horror, and which, for

118

this reason, cannot be tolerated in its service."[162] Both forbidden for reasons which are different but still religious in nature,[163] impure objects and sacred objects, brought together in this way by many common features, easily come to exchange even the characteristics which make them opposites. The impure is to be avoided in all circumstances, because it is in itself repulsive; the sacred, on the other hand, is in itself attractive, but is to be avoided as dangerous in certain cases, owing to a lack of preliminary precautions. Supernatural fear provoked identical attitudes of repulsion, although situations were altogether different.[164]

Israel could not escape this confusion entirely. "Unceasingly, under the lash of these impurities which extended to every moment of life . . . the believer was led accordingly to conceive his sins against Yahweh in their image, to see in them the external action more than the intention, to look upon his God as a force more than as a person. . . . That was the path of least resistance and we have not forgotten it."[165] Still, this confusion did not obliterate in practice the essential difference between the sacred and the impure. In Samuel's time, in the popular religion which is presented to us by the accounts of this period, the distinction between sin and impurity is perfectly clear. Sin is "a personal offense against Yahweh; in the outraged Ark, it is He who is annoyed and who is appeased. But the one who incurs some impurity does not, in any text of the Bible, refer it to a supernatural person. He manifests neither repentance nor prayer; he sees only the stain which has sullied him, and he purifies himself of it by an infallibly efficacious procedure."[166] The representation of sin, still very materialistic, co-exists, among the believers of this period, with a profound sense of the grandeur of God, but also with a profound confidence in His goodness, a personal intimacy with Yahweh.[167] From the moment of Israel's birth, its God is the true God. All subsequent progress depends on that faith.

The master artisans of this progress are the prophets. One of the first, Isaias, goes immediately to the heart of the matter. The vision which determines his vocation marks a major experience.[168] Isaias finds himself in the Temple, and the vision which appears to him is that of Yahweh in His glory.[169] Before this vision, Isaias is seized with terror, his fundamental impurity appears to him:

> Woe is me, because I have held my peace; because I am a man of unclean lips, and I dwell in the midst of a people that hath unclean lips, and I have seen with my eyes the King the Lord of hosts.[170]

The impurity with which the prophet feels himself permeated is this blemish which sets off the beings with whom divinity refuses to deal, and which it proscribes from its presence and its service.[171] It is a ritual impurity. But it is much more: it is the basic impurity of the creature in the presence of God. Only some act from on high can efface the impurity of Isaias and consecrate him for his mission.[172]

This mission is a fight against sin, and the impurity which excludes Isaias from it is the presence, in himself, of sin. The purifying action of the seraphim destroys this sin:

> Behold this hath touched thy lips, and thy iniquities shall be taken away, and thy sin shall be cleansed.[173]

One of the essential features of this vision is the fusion that takes place in it between the liturgical expressions and the interior sentiment. Impurity and sin coincide. But, far from sin deteriorating into a material impurity, as was the ordinary tendency, in this case it is the ritual impurity which becomes interior. The quasi-automatic reflex by which Yahweh, without considering the pious intention, had struck down Oza when he touched the Ark, herein finds its justification. The trembling that shook the Israelite in the presence of God: "We will certainly die, for we have seen God,"[174] is no longer the irrational fear in the presence of some redoubtable greatness, but the clear vision of the essential impurity of man in the presence of God's

120

holiness. Sin and impurity continue to exchange features, but, at this level, only the purely religious features persist. The only real impurity is sin, and sin, for its part, is no longer some fleeting gesture, but a blemish that penetrates man and marks him with a curse. The vision of Isaias transforms both the liturgy, whose symbolic scope it reveals—its truly spiritual meaning— and also the awareness of sin, by putting this completely within God's presence.

The images which describe sin as a stain are multiplied in the prophets. But it is a question of living impressions, and the ritual words themselves, in this context, regain all their vigor.

Isaias describes the "blood" which covers Jerusalem,[175] or the "filth of the daughters of Sion," using the vulgar word he uses elsewhere to denote human excrement or the vomiting of drinkers.[176] The vocabulary of Jeremias generally lacks this vigorousness. His words are those of the common vocabulary. The prophet appeals less to images than to emotion. True, he uses the comparison of washing:

Though thou wash thyself with nitre and multiply to thyself the herb borith, thou art stained in thy iniquity before me, saith the Lord God.[177]

In this context, the following verse:

How canst thou say: I am not polluted?[178]

in which the verb "to pollute," from the root TM', is the consecrated word for denoting ritual impurity, the word that Isaias applied to himself when in Yahweh's presence, takes on its full force. But Jeremias tries above all to awaken the reflexes of the heart:

If a man put away his wife, and she go from him and marry another man . . . shall not that woman be polluted? (HNP). . . . Lift up thy eyes on high, and see where thou hast not prostituted thyself . . . thou hast polluted (HNP) the land with thy fornications and with thy wickedness.[179]

The words are the ritual terms,[180] but emotion robs them of all formalism.

The prophets, in order to express the horror of sin, consecrated the word for horror (*to'ebah*). It appears already in some ancient texts, but initially it only denotes instinctive and quasi-physical revulsion in the presence of the usages and customs of a strange race, such as the Egyptians' revulsion for the nomadic life of the Hebrews,[181] their way of eating,[182] their religious rites.[183] Isaias uses it to depict the wave of disgust which comes over Yahweh at the sacrifices offered to Him by criminals.[184] It becomes frequent in Jeremias to denote the great sin of Israel, idolatry, and points up the almost physical horror that God has for this sin. The corruption of the people was such that it even lost this reflex action; they committed these horrors, yet:

they were not confounded with confusion and they knew not how to blush.[185]

It is these horrors which have made the Temple of Jerusalem a "den of robbers."[186] The word is one of the refrains of Deuteronomy, and even more, of Ezechiel. As trite as it may seem in the latter, it still preserves its power of evocation in describing Jerusalem, the prostitute who goes on sinking ever deeper into her crime, and "has made [her] beauty abominable [*ta'ab*],"[187] becoming more and more hideous.

This horror of sin finally reveals itself in the ruins which it brings on. The catastrophes of which the prophets are witnesses and announcers, are, for them, much more than frightening symbols of the crimes of Israel. They are the very revelation of its sin. It is often difficult to decide if their expressions are aimed at the sins committed or the punishments these have unleashed. Yahweh announces by the mouth of Osee that He will be, with regard to the Kingdom of the North "like a moth," and with regard to the Kingdom of the South, "like rottenness."[188] Reduced to the status of old clothing ready for the junk heap, Israel and Juda will run in vain to seek a remedy from King Assuerus, in condemned alliances. Their lot is set.

There is no doubt that we are to see in these images of decomposition the announcement of the internal dissolution which will undermine the two states.[189] But this incurable wound, this sickness without remedy,[190] is of an order outside the political arena. Moral rottenness, religious deterioration, are implacably at work.

There is, of course, in this strict relationship between sin and its horrible consequences, a permanent feature of the Hebrew mentality, the tendency to fuse into a synthesized whole aspects which we try to isolate through analysis. Thus, among the common words of the vocabulary of worship, which is not very sensitive to prophetic influences, one of the terms in use for sin, 'acham, denotes both the sin and its consequence, the sanction, in a twofold aspect: that of the sin reflecting back upon the delinquent one, leaving him with a responsibility, and that of the sacrifice which must accompany the material reparation.[191] In this way, also, the most frequently used word for sin, hattat, is the name of the ritual sacrifice of expiation "for sin."[192] There are some examples of the tendency to synthesize which is characteristic of the Hebrew mentality, and, along with it, a state of culture and a type of thought.[193] We too, however, with the same word, "fault," denote at once the guilty act and the guilt itself which it involves. This is a basic fact of the human conscience.

The prophets experienced this fact with exceptional lucidity and sensitiveness. In the ruin of their country, they saw its sin as a damning force ravaging Israel. In picturesque imagery, an old text of the Book of Numbers already was threatening Hebrews who were unfaithful to their compatriots:

You will sin against the Lord, and you can be sure that you will not escape the consequences of your sin.[194]

This visiting of sin upon its victims is the entire history of the Hebrew people. Isaias sees it,

As a breach that falleth and is found wanting in a high wall. For the destruction thereof shall come on a sudden.[195]

The wall which falls, crumbled to dust so that

there shall not a shard be found of the pieces thereof, wherein a little fire may be carried from the hearth, or a little water be drawn out of the pit,[196]

is both Israel, condemned to total destruction, and its sin, established in the midst of the nation like a rotted structure. It is impossible to distinguish sin from its consequences.

There is the same coincidence between material ruin and interior devastation in Jeremias:

Guards are coming from a far country and give out their voice against the cities of Juda. . . .
Thy ways and thy devices have brought these things upon thee: this is thy wickedness . . . it hath touched thy heart.[197]

What is this evil which penetrates to the heart? Sin or its punishment? Misfortune or wickedness? Both, because the prophet, at the sight of his country's ruins, perceives the fathomless distress of his people, the incurable wound;[198] here is another image in which the suffering and the stain are identified.

In their lucidity, the prophets give new depth to the ordinary patterns of everyday experience, which is content to invoke the laws of immanent justice. The proverb "He who sows iniquity reaps calamity,"[199] was quoted. Job saw "those who plow for mischief and sow trouble, reap the same."[200] In the face of catastrophes without parallel, Osee reveals an otherwise terrible fatality and his words take on a different tone: "You have ploughed wickedness, you have reaped iniquity."[201] It was well known that "By his own iniquities the wicked man will be caught, in the meshes of his own sin he will be held fast."[202]

For Osee, this is not a natural law, the normal consequence of a life of disorder. There is a mysterious force at work: "The iniquity of Ephraim is bound up: his sin is hidden,"[203] so as to return again as a divine punishment. It was a common experience that "what the wicked man fears will befall him,"[204]

124

but the disaster is infinitely more terrifying when the punishment comes down from heaven above: "I . . . will bring upon them the things they feared."[205] "And I will visit their ways upon them: and I will repay them their devices."[206]

When Jeremias reveals to Israel the meaning of the catastrophes which beset it—"Thy own wickedness shall reprove thee, and thy apostasy shall rebuke thee"[207]—he is evoking a divine judgment, the sanction for an offense against God. Rephrasing the traditional formula which announced the pouring forth of Yahweh's spirit, the prophet threatens: "And I will pour out their own wickedness upon them."[208] The rain from on high, the promised divine blessing,[209] becomes a cursed rain. The image expresses both the fatal logic of sin and its supernatural dimensions.[210]

Throughout the entire Bible, one refrain comes back at each of Israel's new sins, indicating God's reproof: "Then the Lord delivered them into the hands of their enemies."[211] This is the outline of the nation's history. Originally, this outline sees in oppression a trial destined to bring the people back to their God. The struggle of the prophets against the seductions of sin reveals other depths to them. Israel has desired idolatry: it shall have it. It has wanted to sample heathenism: it shall know this world of hatred and despair:

Therefore have I delivered her into the hands of her lovers, into the hands of the sons of the Assyrians, upon whose lust she doted.
They discovered her disgrace, took away her sons and daughters, and slew her with the sword.[212]

After the Madianites and the Philistines, after the kings of Assyria and Babylon, the last tyrant of Israel, the most terrible of all, its own sin, is then revealed:

Thou hast . . . delivered us into the hand of our iniquity.[213]

This discovering, through the events of history, of a power proper to evil—this, precisely, is the spiritual interpretation.

This spiritual vision of history, while animating the entire

Old Testament, manifests itself only in flashes—lightning intuitions that the prophet himself cannot grasp, but which, nonetheless, make him a prophet, and bring him to the threshold of the revelation of Christ. Was St. Paul thinking of the above phrase from the Book of Isaias when, in his Epistle to the Romans, he repeated, on three occasions, the formula "delivered them up"?

God has delivered them up in the lustful desires of their heart to uncleanness . . . delivered them up to shameful lusts . . . delivered them up to a reprobate sense.[214]

If the coincidence was not deliberate, it is even more remarkable.

Moreover, the biblical recollections and, what is much more important, the biblical dialectic, seem close to this first chapter of the Epistle to the Romans. The abandonment of the sinner to the power of sin is, for St. Paul, the punishment of idolatry. He denotes this in a typical expression:

they have changed the glory of the incorruptible God for an image.[215]

The word seems to have been coined by Jeremias:

If a nation hath changed their gods, and indeed they are not gods: but my people have changed their glory into an idol.[216]

Psalm 105 repeats the expression, referring to the idolatry at the foot of Sinai:

> They exchanged their glory
> for the image of a grass-eating bullock.[217]

After a lengthy review of the sins of the people throughout history, the psalm lets the punishment burst forth:

> And the LORD grew angry with his people,
> and abhorred [ta'ab] his inheritance;
> He gave them over into the hands of the nations
> . . . .
> and [they] were brought low by their guilt.[218]

In the perspectives of the Old Testament, of a temporal history

126

with temporal sanctions, this movement of thought is absolutely parallel to that of St. Paul. Here again, it is impossible to state that St. Paul was aware of his parallelism. Without such awareness, it would be all the more striking, like the resemblance between two relatives who had never met.

Perhaps this theme of sin being its own punishment furnished St. Paul with another image. Death for him is the "wages of sin."[219] Sin, after having reigned tyranically over its own, reserves for them, to reward them for their pains, this manner of settling the debt which it owes them. Ezechiel, recalling the wages which prostitutes asked for their bodies, was astonished to see Israel, against all custom, offering to pay to be dishonored:

> It hath happened in thee contrary to the custom of women in thy fornications, and after thee there shall be no such fornication: for in that thou gavest rewards and didst not take rewards, the contrary hath been done in thee.[220]

The situation is not exactly the same, but it is the same biting irony, in reference to the same theme.

It is the same theme, they are the same expressions, but this identity of expressions must not deceive us. In the prophets, these expressions are, in the real sense of the word, prophetic. In one sense, they are definitive. The Epistle to the Romans does not describe the nature of sin any more accurately than does Jeremias when he announces "I will pour forth their wickedness upon them." Still, the most spiritual texts of the Old Testament are full of ambiguity. Jeremias reveals the sin of his people through the "wound" which ravages them, and, while he is able to see the essential evil therein, his human compassion as yet prevents him, in his purity, from experiencing the horror of sin. But the major difference between St. Paul and Jeremias seems to bear on the nature of their certitude. That of the prophet, to be sure, is not groping, but it is strained, threatening more than convincing. In St. Paul, however, the light has arisen. Despite all the terror of God's wrath being let loose upon sin, the atmosphere is serene. This is because a revelation has been made, the mystery of sin is unveiled, an unshakeable ground has been attained, a definitive truth.

This serenity is not that of St. Paul and his temperament. It is that of the Christian faith, which is possession. It is born of the encounter with Jesus. For Jesus reveals the true nature of sin—less by descriptions, by teachings or by threats, than by His very presence, by His spontaneous reactions.

The Old Testament, as we have seen, knew that every man is a sinner, that all his justices are but "a filthy rag."[221] In its most exalted figures, a David, an Isaias, it revealed the most acute awareness of the basic impurity of the human heart. In the presence of Jesus, this still-abstract conviction becomes proof. The believer who reads the Gospels no longer needs any prophet to tell him that all human justice is tainted. He has but to see the unique holiness of Jesus. In this presence, the figure of the Baptist is troubled. This is the Christian experience, which gives the New Testament its characteristic tone. St. Paul's words: "all have sinned and have need of the glory of God,"[222] could be in the Old Testament. The expression has its equivalents there. His sovereign certitude comes from the fact that his meeting with Christ, from the very first moment, placed Paul beyond all individual experience, into the heart of the world, in the mystery of Jesus.

The Incarnation was necessary for man to discover the mystery of sin, so that he might see revealed toward sin the wrath of God—no longer in its signs or its effects, but in its inmost self, at its source. The Gospels give us God's reaction in the face of sin, His reaction of horror. The word echoed throughout the Old Testament, but the action is in the Gospels. It appears, for instance, in the condemnation of the "unfaithful and blind generation." To the Jews who ask Him for a sign from heaven, Jesus replies with a deep sigh and a refusal: "Amen I say to you, a sign shall not be given to this generation."[223] Jesus' reply, as

Mark relates it, refers explicitly to a verse of Psalm 94, whose Hebrew nature He preserves:

> Forty years I loathed that generation,
>> and I said: They are a people of erring heart,
>> and they know not my ways.
> Therefore I swore in my anger:
>> They shall not enter into my rest.[224]

But there definitely seems to be in Jesus' answer more than a literary allusion. Christ seems to put Himself in the very place of Yahweh. Just as Yahweh was tempted during forty years by the Hebrews, so too Jesus is tempted by the Jews. Yahweh is filled with disgust for this generation, and Jesus gives a sigh of sorrow; and perhaps Yahweh's oath condemning this generation to die without seeing the promised land, finds its echo in Jesus' solemn Amen, which, for the Jews, had the value of an oath.

Elsewhere there are similar coincidences: Jesus' sigh in the presence of this generation is repeated, after the Transfiguration, in the cry which escapes Him before the crowd which is disturbed by the failure of the disciples: "O unbelieving and perverse generation, how long shall I be with you? How long shall I put up with you?[225] No doubt this is sadness only at finding such weak faith. Still, these are people of good will, and His complaint would be more natural in the face of ruthless adversaries. Perhaps we have to put the words back into their frame of reference. Jesus is coming down from the mount of God. There He has found Moses and Elias, the two privileged ones permitted of old to enter the sacred places and speak with God. Now He must plunge once again into this world of sin. His repugnance reveals the horror for sin of the holy God, the God who refused, after the apostasy of His people, to "go up in your company,"[226] to grant it the gift of His presence.

It is difficult to distinguish, among all these relationships, those which are deliberate and are consciously suggested by the Gospels, and those which arise from the sameness of situations. This very difficulty is a sign of profound continuity; throughout the entire Bible, both the features of God and the features of sin are found unchanged. But it takes the horror of Jesus, in agony before the chalice which awaits Him, to reveal what the Old Testament used to call, in an expression which had become hackneyed, that "which the Lord detests."[227]

This revelation is not an emotion brought forth by a moving scene. It is the manifestation, through the Holy Spirit, of the profound meaning of the evangelical actions. The agony of Jesus remains an enigma until the Christian experiences the literally mortal nature of sin. But, once admitted to the intimacy of God, once introduced by the Spirit into the ecstasy of love which unites the Father and the Son, the Christian discovers the true name of the sin which tears him away from this home: death.[228]

NOTES

[1] Cf. the statistics on these words and their translations in the Septuagint, arranged by G. Quell, in Kittel, *Theologisches Wörterbuch*, I, pp. 268–269. On the opposition between *racha* and *saddiq*, see *supra*, Ch. II, n. 32.

[2] Jer. 4: 14, 18.

[3] Jer. 2: 12–13.

[4] Gen. 4: 7; 13: 13; 18: 20.

[5] Gen. 6: 5; 8: 21; 19: 7.

[6] Cf. G. Kittel, *Theologisches Wörterbuch*, I, p. 279 (G. Quell); p. 290 (G. Bertram).

[7] Judg. 20: 16 (according to Lagrange).

[8] Is. 65: 20.

[9] Job 5: 24; cf. G. Quell, *art. cit.*, p. 271.

[10] Ps. 108: 7.

[11] Ps. 24: 8; cf. G. Quell, *art. cit.*, pp. 271–272.

[12] Gen. 20: 9.

[13] Judg. 11: 27.

[14] 1 Kings 26: 21.

[15] 4 Kings 18: 14.

[16] Ex. 9: 27; 10: 16.

[17] Jos. 7: 20.

[18] 1 Kings 15: 24, 30.

[19] 2 Kings 12: 13.

[20] 2 Kings 24: 10, 17; regarding this sin, see A. George, "Fautes contre Yahweh dans les Livres de Samuel," in *Revue Biblique*, 1946, p. 178.

[21] Ps. 50: 6.

[22] Luke 15: 18.

[23] Prov. 8: 35–36.

[24] Matt. 7: 13; Mark 8: 35; John 12: 25; 17: 12.

[25] "Offense" would be more accurate than the common word "revolt." We will use it from this point on.

[26] Ex. 34: 7.

[27] Ps. 31: 1-2.

[28] And a number of others: cf. Ezech. 21: 29; Is. 43: 24-25; Job 13: 23; 14: 16-17; Dan. 9: 24.

[29] H. Cazelles, *Études sur le Code de l'Alliance*, Paris, 1946, p. 68.

[30] Gen. 31: 36.

[31] 1 Kings 24: 12.

[32] Gen. 50: 17.

[33] 3 Kings 12: 19.

[34] 4 Kings 8: 20. Even the juridical text of Ex. 22: 8, generally translated as "fraud" or "crime," envisions the case of a protest against a given situation, and keeps the original meaning of relief. Cf. L. Kohler, *Zeitschrift für die alttestamentliche Wissenschaft*, 1928, pp. 215-218.

[35] Ex. 23: 21.

[36] Osee 7: 13; 8: 1; 14: 10; Mich. 1: 5; 3: 8; 7: 18; Is. 43: 27; 46: 8; 48: 8; 53: 12; 59: 13; Jer. 2: 8; 2: 29; 3: 13; 5: 6; 33: 8; Ezech. 2: 3; 18: 31; 20: 38.

[37] Amos 1: 3, 6, 9, 11, 13; 2: 1, 4, 6.

[38] Even in 1 Kings 20: 8, where David does not acknowledge his guilt as regards Saul, he understands that his conscience does not charge him with any sin, and his viewpoint is religious.

[39] Cf. Is. 21: 3; Ps. 37: 7.

[40] Lev. 5: 1; 7: 18; 20: 17; Num. 5: 31; 14: 34; Ezech. 14: 10; 44: 10, 12.

[41] But nowhere directly, despite appearances (Lev. 17: 16; 20: 17), "to suffer the punishment."

[42] Ex. 28: 38; Lev. 10: 17; Num. 18: 1.

[43] Lev. 16: 22.

[44] Ezech. 4: 4-6.

[45] Is. 53: 11; the verb "to bear" here is not the usual *nasa'*, but the more expressive *sabal* (cf. Is. 53: 4).

[46] Ex. 34: 7; Num. 14: 18; Osee 14:3; cf. Ps. 84: 3.

[47] Is. 53: 5.

[48] John 1: 29.

[49] Gen. 4: 13.

[50] Is. 1: 4.

[51] Ps. 37: 5.

[52] Rom. 1: 18.

[53] Rom. 3: 21.

[54] Gal. 3: 22; cf. Rom. 3: 20.

[55] Compare for example, Gal. 3: 21 with 3: 22; or Rom. 3: 10 with Rom. 3: 9-18, where the quotations of the "Law" are all taken from the psalms and the prophets.

[56] Rom. 3: 9.

[57] Rom. 5: 18.

[58] Rom. 3: 19.

[59] Rom. 6: 16, 22.

[60] Rom. 6: 23.

[61] Rom. 5:12. For an explanation of the text, refer, for example, to *L'Épître aux Romains*, translation and commentary by P. J. Huby (*Verbum Salutis*), Paris, 1949, pp. 189-194. For its place in the work of St. Paul, see J. Bonsirven, *L'Évangile de Paul*, Paris, 1948, pp. 107-115.

[62] Ecclus. 25: 23.

[63] Gen. 2: 17.

[64] Wis. 2: 24.

[65] A new bearing even with reference to the ideas of his time. Two apocryphal Jewish apocalypses, the Fourth Book of Esdras and the Second Book of Baruch, both from a time shortly after St. Paul, see in the sin of Adam a moral catastrophe whose consequences humanity must suffer. But the viewpoints are quite different from those of St. Paul. They remain moral. That which mankind inherits from Adam is a weakness which makes it incapable of resisting evil. Also, it sins like Adam, and the few beings which have remained faithful to the Law escape death. Man sins freely. He can imitate Moses as well as Adam. Each of us is his own Adam. If Adam himself sinned, it is because he had in himself an inclination to evil, this "wicked heart" buried in each man. In these moral perspectives, there is no question, as in St. Paul, of a unity of sinful mankind gathered together in Adam. See the translated texts with commentaries by J. Bonsirven, *Le Judaïsme palestinien au temps de Jésus-Christ*, Paris, 1935, II, pp. 15–16.

[66] Cf. J. Bonsirven, *Exégèse rabbinique et exégèse paulinienne*, Paris, 1938, p. 350.

[67] Gen. 12: 3.

[68] Gen. 3: 17.

[69] Gen. 4: 24.

[70] Gen. 6: 12.

[71] Gen. 6: 5.

[72] Gen. 6: 18; 9: 8–17. These texts are generally assigned to a relatively recent date, that of the sacerdotally-inspired account, source P. One of the characteristics of its theology is the extension throughout history and even throughout the creative work of God, of the pattern of the covenant, originally reserved to the privileged relationship between Yahweh and His people. (Cf. J. Chaine, *Le Livre de la Genèse*, Paris, 1948, pp. 124–125.) It is, as a matter of fact, possible. But this outline simply brings out all the more clearly an undeniable parallelism, born of the very structure of Genesis, between the situation of Noe and Abraham, and that of the people of the Book of Exodus.

[73] Gen. 11: 1–9.

[74] Gen. 12: 3; 18: 18; 22: 18; 26: 4; 28: 14. The generally accepted meaning: "All the nations of the earth will be blessed in thee," is the one which most naturally corresponds to the context, where it is obviously a question of a positive promise by God bearing on all mankind. It was interpreted in this way by the tradition of Israel. Even if we feel we must strictly respect the reflexive sense of the *nifal* and *hithpael*, the translation we obtain: "All the peoples will take your lot as the object of their wish," gives Abraham a central place in mankind. See J. Chaine, *op. cit.*, p. 181.

[75] On the judgment made by the author of Genesis about Jacob, see J. Chaine, *op. cit.*, p. 312. It is quite possible that the reference by Osee to Jacob does not recall his zeal but, on the contrary, his resistance to God.

[76] Ex. 3: 15.

[77] Ex. 6: 9.

[78] Ex. 2: 11–15.

[79] Ex. 5: 21.

[80] Ex. 20: 2; Deut. 5: 6; 8: 14; 13: 6, 11.

[81] Jos. 24: 14.

[82] Osee 8: 13; 9: 3.

[83] Ezech. 16: 26.

[84] Ezech. 20: 8.

[85] Ezech. 21: 29; 23: 3, 8.

[86] Ex. 5: 1.

[87] Ex. 3: 12.

[88] Osee 9: 3.

[89] Ex. 5: 21.

[90] Moses is enveloped in a box whose name *tebah* (Ex. 2: 3, 5) is exactly the same as that of Noe's Ark (Gen. 7: 1, etc.).

[91] Gen. 6: 9.

[92] Gen. 12: 1.

[93] Jos. 24: 14.

[94] Ex. 19: 5.

[95] Ex. 16: 3

[96] Ex. 15:25; 16:4; 17:2, 7; 20: 20; Deut. 6: 16; 8: 2; 8: 16; 13: 4; 33: 8; Num. 14: 22.

[97] Ex. 17: 2, 7; Num. 20: 3, 13.

[98] Ex. 23: 21.

[99] Num. 32: 13; Deut. 2: 14.

[100] Deut. 32: 5.

[101] Deut. 32: 20.

[102] Regarding the consciousness in Israel of an hereditary fault, see W. Eichrodt, *Theologie des A. T.*, 3rd ed., Berlin, 1948, pp. 188–189, 193.

[103] 3 Kings 14: 16; 15: 26, 30, 34; 16: 2, 19, 26; 21: 22; 22: 53, etc.

[104] Is. 6: 5.

[105] *Ibid.*

[106] Jer. 6: 14.

[107] Jer. 15: 18; 8: 21.

[108] Jer. 4: 18.

[109] Jer. 10: 19.

[110] Jer. 5: 1; cf. 23: 14.

[111] Jer. 5: 4, 5.

[112] Jer. 6: 28–29. The image is that of lead melted down to extract the silver. Cf. article on "Plomb" (lead) in the *Dictionnaire de la Bible*, V., p. 469.

[113] Jer. 7: 29.

[114] Jer. 16: 10–12.

[115] Cf. J. Bonsirven, *Le Judaïsme palestinien au temps de Jésus-Christ*, Paris, 1935, II, pp. 15–16.

[116] Perhaps we must interpret in the same sense the prototype role given to the sin of Jacob, "thy first father," in Is. 43: 27. Cf. also Osee 12: 4.

[117] Ezech. 20: 8; 23: 3, 8.

[118] Jer. 4: 4; cf. Deut. 10: 16. See W. Eichrodt, *Theologie des A.T.*, 3rd ed., Berlin, 1948, III, p. 87.

[119] Deut. 30: 5–6.

[120] Jer. 9: 25–26.

[121] Jer. 8: 3; 7: 29.

[122] Is. 66: 24.

[123] Jer. 8: 1–2.

[124] Rom. 2: 9.

[125] Ezech. 37: 1–14.

[126] Jer. 31: 40.

[127] Many psalms identify the "oppressors" of Israel with the adversaries of Yahweh. They even go so far as to call them "oppressors" (*sorerim*) of God, so natural is it to identify the two causes. See Ps. 65: 7; 67: 7, 19; 8: 3.

[128] Ps. 72: 15.

[129] Matt. 9:10; 11: 19; Luke 6: 34. "Sinners" here denotes, as is evident from the association "publicans and sinners," a real social category. The distinction between the *saddiqim* and the *recha'im,* the just and the impious, of post-exilic Judaism, already was tending in that direction. Cf. K. H. Rengstorf, in *Theologisches Wörterbuch,* Kittel, I, pp. 324–325.

[130] Cf. A. Feuillet, *Le verset 7 du Miserere,* in *Science Religieuse* (=*Recherches de Science religieuse*), 1944, p. 13.

[131] Fr. J. Cales, (*Le Livre des Psaumes,* Paris, 1936, I, pp. 518–519) thinks that this tradition is serious and sees no reason why the points of contact of the psalm with subsequent writers could not result from their borrowing. See, for the other viewpoint, the article by M. Feuillet.

132 Ps. 142: 2; cf. 13: 3; 102: 10, 14; 115: 11; Job. 4: 17; 9: 2; 14: 1–4; 15: 14–16; 25: 4–6; Prov. 20: 9.

133 Ps. 129: 3.

134 Ps. 50: 7. There is "among the Jews, even the very pious ones, the conviction that they belong to a sinful race, and, for this reason, that they had sinned long before being able to sin personally, from the first moment of their existence." A Feuillet, *art. cit.*, p. 22.

135 Deut. 32: 5, 20.

136 Matt. 12: 39; 16: 4; Mark 8: 38.

137 Matt. 23: 35–36; Luke 20: 50–51.

138 Luke 17: 25.

139 Ps. 94: 9.

140 Matt. 12: 38; Luke 11: 30. The absolute refusal mentioned by Mark (8: 12): "A sign shall not be given," contradicts only in appearance the text of Matthew and Luke. The "sign of Jonas" will be perceptible only to those who are faithful to the crucified Messias. The others will ignore it, and it will be their condemnation: their blindness was complete.

141 Matt. 24: 34; Mark 13: 30; Luke 21: 32.

142 Jer. 7: 29.

143 Mark 8: 38.

144 Matt. 10: 33; Luke 12: 9.

145 Luke 16: 8.

146 Fr. Huby translates "in their relationships" and comments "with their contemporaries." Loisy translates "with regard to their equals."

147 "This generation": 1 Cor. 1: 20; 2: 6, 8; 3: 18; 2 Cor. 4: 4; Rom. 12: 2; "this world": 1 Cor. 3: 19; 5: 10; 7: 31.

148 John 8: 23; 9: 39; 11: 9; 12: 25, 31; 13: 1; 16: 11; 18: 36.

149 John 1: 10.

150 John 14: 31.

151 John 9: 39; 12: 31; 16: 8.

152 Acts 2: 40.

153 Phil. 2: 15. The text continues: "you shine like stars in the world." Fr. Huby interpets it of the universe, Lightfoot, of the sinful world.

154 John 17: 6.

155 John 15: 19.

156 John 17: 14, 16.

157 Cf. A. George, "Fautes contre Yahweh dans les Livres de Samuel," in *Revue Biblique,* 1946, pp. 161–184.

158 1 Kings 14: 31 ff.

159 1 Kings 14: 24–30, 36–45.

160 1 Kings 14: 37.

161 2 Kings 6: 6–7.

162 A. Loisy, *La religion d'Israël,* 3rd ed., Paris, 1933, p. 107.

163 The reservations of E. Dhorme (*L'évolution religieuse d'Israël,* vol. I, *La religion des Hébreux nomades,* Brussels, 1937, p. 302), for whom impurity is defined by its nefarious natural effects, seem to arise from confusion. If it belongs to experience to discover cases of impurity from their effects, the notion of impurity itself, with the supernatural forces which it implies, is, as Loisy puts it, "magico-rational, not properly-speaking moral nor rationally utilitarian." *Op. cit.*, p. 107.

164 Fr. Lagrange has brought to light, against the current dominant theories, the distinction between the sacred and the impure (*Études sur les religions sémitiques,* 2nd ed., Paris, 1905, pp. 144–158). See also E. Dhorme, *op. cit.*, pp. 297–311.

165 A. George, *art. cit.*, p. 169.

166 A. George, *art. cit.*, p. 168.

167 A. George, *art. cit.*, pp. 182–183.

168 Is. 6: 1–8.

[169] Cf. 3 Kings 8: 10.

[170] Is. 6: 5.

[171] The components of the root *tm'* constitute one of the key series of the writings called sacerdotal. The cadaver is impure along with whoever touches it (Lev. 11: 24 ff.; Num. 6: 12; 19: 20), the leper and everything he touches (Lev. 13–14), man and woman after sexual relations (Lev. 15).

[172] Cf. Jer. 1: 9.

[173] Is. 6: 7.

[174] Ex. 33: 20; Judg. 6:22; 13:22.

[175] Is. 4: 4; cf. 1: 15.

[176] Is. 4: 4; cf. 28: 8; 36: 12.

[177] Jer. 2: 22.

[178] Jer. 2: 23.

[179] Jer. 3: 1–3, reading verse 1 as in the Septuagint and the Vulgate.

[180] They are found again in a text of Num. 35: 33–34, attributed to P: "You shall not desecrate [*hnp*] the land where you live. Since bloodshed desecrates [*hnp*] the land . . . . do not defile [*tm'*] the land in which you live and in the midst of which I dwell." The word *haneph* becomes one of the favorite words of the Book of Job to denote sin. Cf. P. Dhorme, *Le Livre de Job*, Paris, 1926, p. 107. It is no doubt borrowed from the prophetic tradition.

[181] Gen. 46: 34.

[182] Gen. 43: 32.

[183] Ex. 8: 22.

[184] Is. 1: 13.

[185] Jer. 6: 15 = 8: 12.

[186] Jer. 7: 10–11.

[187] Ezech. 16: 25.

[188] Osee 5: 12.

[189] Cf. A. Van Hoonacker, *Les douze petits prophètes*, Paris, 1908, pp. 59–60.

[190] Osee 5: 13.

[191] Lev. 5: 20–26.

[192] To distinguish *'acham* from *hattat*, the former is often translated "sacrifice for the crime," and the latter "sacrifice for the sin," thereby giving the latter a seriousness in excess of that of the simple misdemeanor. The explanation of M. Dussaud, for whom "the sacrifice called *hattat* aims at the expulsion of sin resulting from the non-observance of the divine law," while the *'acham* expiates an offense which concerns the community more particularly, such as theft," seems to recognize the difference between the victims offered up, more precious in the case of the *'acham* than in the case of the *hattat*. Cf. R. Dussaud, *Les origines cananéenes du sacrifice israélite*, 2nd ed., Paris, 1941, pp. 126–27.

[193] M. Dhorme found, in the ritual of Ras Shamra, the *'acham* of the Israelite ritual. There, too, the same word no doubt denotes both sin and the sanction which it involves. Cf. *Revue Biblique*, 1931, p. 53.

[194] Num. 32: 23.

[195] Is. 30: 13.

[196] Is. 30: 14.

[197] Jer. 4: 16, 18.

[198] Jer. 10: 19.

[199] Prov. 22: 8.

[200] Job. 4: 8.

[201] Osee 10: 13.

[202] Prov. 5: 22.

[203] Osee 13: 12.

[204] Prov. 10: 24.

[205] Is. 66: 4.

[206] Osee 4: 9.

[207] Jer. 2: 19.

[208] Jer. 14: 16.

[209] Is. 32: 15; Ezech. 39: 29; Zach. 12: 10; Joel 3: 1.

[210] There is a similar image in Ezechiel, where the sentence: "I will lay upon thee all thy crimes" (7: 8), corresponds to the threat "bear also thy wickedness and thy fornications" (23: 35). See also Osee 4: 9: "I will visit their ways upon them."

[211] Jos. 7: 7; Judg. 2: 14; 3: 8; 4: 2; 6: 1; 10: 7; 13: 1; 1 Kings 12: 9; Mich. 5: 2; Jer. 20: 4, 5; 21: 10; 22: 25; cf. Is. 36: 15.

[212] Ezech. 23: 9–10; cf. 23: 28–29; Jer. 4: 30.

[213] Is. 64: 7, reading *temaggenenu* with the Septuagint, the Targum, and the Syriac.

[214] Rom. 1: 24, 26, 28. Cf. Rom. 7: 14: "I . . . am sold into the power of sin."

[215] Rom. 1: 23.

[216] Jer. 2: 11. Perhaps it is already present in Osee 4: 7. Cf. A. Van Hoonacker, *Les douze petits Prophètes*, Paris, 1908, pp. 45–46.

[217] Ps. 105: 20.

[218] Ps. 105: 40–43. Cf. Osee 4: 9 after 4: 7.

[219] Rom. 6: 23.

[220] Ezech. 16: 34. Cf. Mich. 1: 7.

[221] Is. 64: 5.

[222] Rom. 3: 23.

[223] Mark 8: 12.

[224] Ps. 94: 10–11. Cf. Lagrange, *Saint Marc, in loc.*

[225] Matt. 17: 16; Mark 9: 18; Luke 9: 41.

[226] Ex. 33: 3.

[227] Deut. 12: 31; 17: 1; 18: 12; Prov. 3: 32; 11: 1, 20; 12: 22; 15: 8, 9, 26, etc.

[228] Cf. Rom. 6: 21; Heb. 10: 28–29.

Chapter V

THEMES OF DAMNATION

1. THE SATANIC POWERS

The first sin committed on earth, that of Adam and Eve, is described by Genesis in such depth that this scene, which seems to bring us back to some fabulous bygone time, still appears as the authentic type of our daily sins. It seems like a sin of children, described by a child, but these children have a very enlightened sense of God and a most lucid awareness of sin. How many men there are whose lives have been determined by a decisive act which they performed in their childhood! The adult cannot be satisfied with the religion of his childhood, but the religion he has to build for himself is no different from that of his youth. Thus, Adam's sin has all the traits of the everlasting sin.

Genesis, first of all, indicates that there is something seductive in sin. Becoming like God is doubtless a monstrous pretension, and ridiculous besides, but it is quite natural. The irony of the account brings out this ridiculous aspect perfectly, but without failing to understand the tragic seriousness of the ambition. Sin is presented as an absurdity, but the absurdity of a reasonable being.

137

Man alone cannot explain sin. Behind him, more intelligent than he, more guilty than he, Genesis places a mysterious animal, the serpent. This serpent is no ordinary animal. People have conjured up a marvelous dragon, the chief of the animals, capable of seducing Eve, which became, through God's curse, a creeping and hideous beast.[1] This hypothesis would have the advantage of making Eve's fall more natural. But, while extending the role of the marvelous, it is injurious to the sacred part of the mystery which is so manifest on every line of these pages. The serpent remains a serpent. A biblical tradition couples the animal with temptation:

> Look not on the wine when it is red,
>   when it sparkles in the glass.
> It goes down smoothly;
> But in the end it bites like a serpent,
>   or like a poisonous adder.
> Your eyes behold strange sights,
>   and your heart utters disordered thoughts;
> You are like one now lying in the depths of the sea,
>   now sprawled at the top of the mast.[2]

The serpent here is but an image. The one in Genesis has a different reality. What is it? It conceals behind itself a power which is not that of man and which goes beyond the animal, no matter how marvelous the latter might be. This power has no name, for it is not a distinct being which the author imagines or conceives. It seems to be the "agent," the spokesman of this power.[3] But this agent is not the delegate of some other personage, who remains concealed but could come forward. There is no hidden personality, there is instead a power, a power superior to man's, more conscious in its intentions, more subtle in its activities. It knows the heart of man, and knows how to reach it, but its penetration is not the product of love. It is a jealous and evil power, and it is difficult to believe that it is not also God's enemy. Why else should it so soon attack His finest creation?

138

If we must give a name to this power, the most accurate name would perhaps be "the tempter." Temptation is a reality of our world, a reality that the biblical author knew quite well, to have described it with such perfection. But he was not acquainted with our abstractions. He only knows the tempter. In so doing, he is more faithful to reality than we are: in giving this power an abstract name, we reduce it to nothingness.

No book of the Old Testament dares give as sinister an image of this unknown tempter as does the ancient account of Genesis. We do pick up his trail in following through the Bible, but his features seem to soften. One might think him domesticated.

In sin, crouched at Cain's door to drag him to evil,[4] we rediscover the tempter's mysterious origin, mingled with the earth, with the nether forces, and its immense hatred. It is no longer an animal; it rather resembles a spirit. But it is frightening only to the lazy soul who refuses to fight.

The spirits which seize man brusquely and throw him into deadly conditions where he seems abandoned to evil are also tempters. Spirit of jealousy,[5] wicked spirit,[6] spirit of prostitution,[7] spirit of giddiness,[8] spirit of lethargy,[9] spirit of impurity[10] —they are almost always sent by God Himself,[11] most of the time in punishment of sin. Their power is unfailing, but it is at God's orders.

The tempter by trade in the Old Testament is Satan.[12] Before being a proper noun denoting a person, this word was a common noun. It denoted an adversary, generally one who rose up in an unforeseen manner, such as the angel of Yahweh before Balaam and his ass,[13] such as David turning in full combat against his masters the Philistines,[14] or Abisai interfering in order to bring to naught David's considered clemency.[15] "Satan" is the unexpected obstacle, the sudden intervention which threatens plans and thwarts calculations.[16] The gesture of Jesus, "Get thee behind me, Satan," pushing aside Peter who would have restrained Him from the path of Calvary, evokes the same image.[17]

139

This common noun became the proper name of an individual, designating this person primarily by the role he plays: that of "Adversary" before the tribunal of God.[18] The adversary is a pleader of cases. Standing at the right hand of the accused, next to the lawyer charged with directing the accused in his defense, he represents the accuser, who watches over the debate in order to pose, at a given moment, the embarrasing question, to provoke the decisive revelation which brings on the condemnation.[19]

There is a continuous judgment going on in God's presence. The entire world appears before Yahweh.[20] Like the whole of Israel's history, the existence of each man unfolds before the tribunal of God. At every instant, we might say, this existence is receiving the divine verdict which rules on its real worth. This judgment involves a system similar to that in earthly trials. There is an accuser; he too is a "satan."[21] The Septuagint translated his name as διάβολος, but he does not as yet have the definitive traits of the devil in the Gospels. His role is indispensable for the proper proceeding of the trial: he must preserve God's justice in its purity, prevent it from being degraded in indulgent compromises. He will spare nothing to lay bare the evil of the human heart and to confound its apparent justice.

In the Book of Paralipomenon, this role is barely developed. Satan only figures therein to fill the place which the original account assigned to Yahweh's wrath.[22] The ancient faith in Yahweh, permeated with the mysterious grandeur of a God at once beneficent and terrible, was not astonished to see Him inspire sin, in order to punish it severely afterward.[23] More sensitive to scandal, the author of Paralipomenon imputes to Satan the temptation of David. Unceasingly lying in ambush against Israel, waiting for the opportunity to do it harm, Satan sees in David's sin the means of unleashing the disasters of which he dreams. He seems rather to seek to do harm than to make anyone sin.

140

The Satan of the Book of Job, on the other hand, has sworn to make his victim sin. But the more his intentions seem formidable, the more the Bible stresses his dependence on God. He is the instrument of Yahweh to make His merit and His glory shine forth. If Yahweh lets fall upon Job all the resources of an adversary who disposes all the forces of nature and a superior intellect for the sole purpose of tarnishing Yahweh's justice, it is because the justice of His servants is priceless in His eyes. To be served by a Job is the most beautiful testimony God can give of what He deserves. He is prepared to pay dearly for such a one, to allow even a Satan in His presence.

Thus the Book of Job, which develops so thoroughly the role of Satan, brings to light one of the essential aspects of the tempter and of temptation. It is a trial of fidelity, and God would not do without it. Also, the tempter is, from this viewpoint, a direct agent of God's providence. The stage settings of the Old Testament do not falsify reality.

They do, however, permit us to suspect more sinister depths. Satan may well be an instrument, but he is a balky instrument. "He is an evil presence among the children of God. He is always against things. We might say, the Judas among the Twelve."[24] He is restrained more than submissive. His role in the Book of Job ends in defeat, and he disappears, not only because his game is up, because God has been justified, but because he is conquered. He is therefore not only man's adversary, but he is also opposed to God. Here the other face of the tempter reappears. The account of Genesis is doubtless more somber. At the close of the Book of Job, the trial is finished. Even if the tone is different from that of the earlier poems, it has continuity with them. God being victorious, perfect peace reigns. The intervention of Yahweh after the sin of Adam assured His sovereign power, but left evil, established in the world, to work destruction there. Still, the Satan of Job already gives us a glimpse of the fallen angel.

Also, it is natural that the Book of Wisdom should come to identify Satan with the tempter of Genesis: "By the envy of the devil, death entered the world."[25] Written in Greek, in a Greek environment, the Book of Wisdom is nevertheless permeated with the tradition of Israel. It seems to relegate to the sidelines the clearly-drawn role of Satan, accuser before God's tribunal. Still, it remains faithful to these perspectives. When it describes sinners taken by death and appearing before God, and seeing that their "transgressions shall convict them to their face,"[26] it has these terrifying figures playing the very role of Satan.

In giving a name to the tempter who, from his origins, has been working against man, in fixing his place among fallen creatures cursed by God,[27] it seems that the Old Testament has set the stage for the decisive encounter between Jesus and His adversary. Jesus, indeed, recognizes and names him.[28] He sees "Satan fall as lightning from heaven."[29] But this expression proves that He is not thinking simply of Job's adversary. He who fell from heaven like lightning was the King of Babylon. In one of the most dramatic poems of the Book of Isaias, Israel celebrated the sudden death of its most cruel enemy, the almighty monarch:

> How art thou fallen from heaven, O Lucifer, who didst rise in the morning? How art thou fallen to the earth, that didst wound the nations?
> And thou saidst in thy heart: I will ascend into heaven. I will exalt my throne above the stars of God.
> But . . . thou shalt be brought down to hell, into the depth of the pit.[30]

Thus Jesus sees in the King of Babylon, the most formidable opponent of Yahweh in all history, the figure of His own adversary.

The King of Babylon is only the most ferocious of Israel's enemies. He is the heir of a long series of adversaries and oppressors. Calling down upon these tyrants the divine curse is a constant theme of the prophets. This persistence is no doubt explained by the constant repetition of analogous circumstances, arousing identical reactions; to which must be added

142

literary influences: the messages of the prophets were handed down, and they inspired successors. In this way, a type of enemy of Israel had been created; the first representative thereof is Pharaoh; then the Philistines, the Assyrians and the Chaldeans, and, finally, Antiochus Epiphanes.

These great devastators unleash on the world catastrophes beyond human bearing. We might say that the monsters of the primal chaos, tamed for a time, have regained their liberty. All the prophets described the onslaught of these invasions in terms of a catastrophe bringing the world to an end.[31] For Amos, it is an army of locusts,[32] and the mechanical cruelty of this world of insects, its methodical organization of the devastation, the very physical appearance of these literally monstrous organisms, all armed and armored, furnishes Joel with a properly apocalyptic theme.[33] Isaias hears the gathering, from all parts of the world, of an army invulnerable to fatigue and to blows.[34] Jeremias sees, coming down from the north, sowing destruction everywhere, a monstrous invasion,[35] the hordes of Gog and Magog foretold by Ezechiel.[36] All these scenes of carnage and terror are something other than descriptions made feverish by panic. They announce the annihilation of the world, its return to chaos. Are we to call these monstrous forces satanic?[37] Properly speaking, the Bible sees in these formidable beings, not so much the enemies of God as the adversaries of the world, the princes of disorder and ruin. If they are opposed to God, it is through the unconscious movement which naturally arrays disorder and chaos against light and life, and not through hatred.

But from the day in which God, by choosing a people for Himself, in entering upon a dialogue with it, in establishing for it a future and an expectation, manifests that He has designs upon the earth and that He expects fruit from the history of the world; from this day, the enemies of His people become His personal enemies. Except that now, the real enemies of Israel are no longer the old forces which are always ready to descend upon mankind—pestilence, famine and war. These enemies are only natural forces and God is their master. While He does not hesitate to deliver His people up to the attacks of these forces, it is in order to force them to return to Him.[38] Simple instruments in His hands, these forces do not even have the controlled initiative of Satan that He allows Job to experience.

The authentic enemies of Israel are not these blind forces, but rather, those which attack its vocation. In practice, these forces are often the same. But the prophets are able to distinguish, in the blows struck against Israel by the kings of Assyria and of Babylon, between the simply human part, the fatal play of alliances and politics, and the more sinister element, hatred for God. The latter is the power of seduction and demoralization which, above and beyond the chosen people, strikes out at the very holiness of God Himself. In these inhuman paganisms, albeit crowned with the prestige of power and luxury, the prophets denounce the "lovers," the perpetual tempters of Israel. The same words, prostitution, and sacrilege, define, in the Book of Kings, the seduction of the paganism propagated by Jezebel, and, in Nahum, the sinister influence of Niniveh.[39]

These centuries of temptations find a unity in the Apocalypse of Daniel. One of the laws of the apocalyptic form is the synthesis of history into global visions. Daniel sees in the succession of empires the work of a unique architect. The monumental statue made of clay, iron, bronze, silver and gold, which Nabuchodonosor sees in a dream, gathers together all these materials, each of which represents an empire, into one gigantic mass, in a unified kingdom which rises up against God.[40] The Book of Daniel does not know Satan, but the architect of this monstrous statue is the "prince of this world."

What gives Daniel's visions their true religious sense, what raises his sinister interpretation of a world dominated by evil above the mere exaltations of nationalism, is the fact of martyrdom. Daniel is the witness of the era in which the Jews, in order to remain faithful to God, had at times to choose death in preference to idolatry. Israel is no longer threatened in her national independence. The Jerusalem of 587 B.C. was still an important pawn in the chess game of the great powers, and its destruction a political act, to the point where Jeremias is called upon to preach submission to the conqueror. Under the Seleucids, on the other hand, Jerusalem is subjugated. There is no longer a Jewish state. The measures taken by Antiochus constitute a real persecution and betray a hatred which is authentically religious. From the moment that King Antiochus and God are opposed, a choice is imposed with death as the stake. The struggle between them must be without mercy, the abyss bottomless. Evil openly becomes God's adversary, the true face of Satan is revealed; not, we must note, in the hatred of a people reduced to despair—many Jews adapted themselves quite readily to Greek ways—but in the light of faith.

Under the features of the pagan capitals and the persecuting kings, Satan is still hidden; he was much closer in the serpent, his voice there really being that of the tempter. But in order to unveil his face, more was required than all the prophets together; to uncover the source of injustice, the source of justice was needed. To reveal the power of darkness, the Light had to appear. Jesus alone unmasks Satan.

He unmasks him by naming him. He casts out devils, but His target is Satan. His adversaries, to explain His miracles, invoke Beelzebub, some more-powerful demon among the multitude of those that the Judaism of the time had assembled. He pays no attention to these underlings; His opponent is Satan.[41]

He unmasks him even more directly. The temptation of Jesus in the desert puts Christ face to face with His enemy in his most personal form. No detail of the Gospels allows us to draw a portrait of this figure whom Jesus alone was able to see. But His dialogue with the devil reveals the real action of Satan in the world. If Jesus is led by the Spirit into the desert "to be tempted,"[42] it is, as we have seen, in order to take up, in His own turn, the itinerary of His people, but it is also for the purpose of revealing the meaning of those forty years. They had been forty years of temptation;[43] Jesus is tempted for forty days. Still, there is a major difference: Yahweh was tempting His people, but Jesus is tempted by Satan. The difference is explained by the twofold aspect of temptation, the trial willed by God, but by a God who uses as His instrument His adversary, the tempter. The Old Testament could not plumb the depths of evil, to discover therein this figure which was too formidable for it. Jesus establishes it and reveals it to us. His encounter with Satan gives its true meaning to the temptation of His people. Where the biblical author saw only the stiff neck of the Hebrews, the baleful remembrance of Egypt, Jesus reveals a hidden personality with supernatural power. It was the latter that was behind the scenes of covetousness, of revolt, or of apostasy, described in Exodus. The Adversary of God, the perennial Adversary, was therefore not Antiochus or Nabuchodonosor; it was in the very midst of Israel, accompanying it at every stage. Jesus finally unmasks it.

Unmasked, Satan is reduced to impotence.[44] The New Testament, which uncovers the power of Satan, "the prince of this world," revealing his ravages in the world and the depths of his hatred, also announces his defeat. Alongside this terrifying figure, the Satan of Job appears harmless, and his defeat, too, was only a false start. The Satan of the Gospels is thrown down from heaven,[45] driven from his kingdom.[46] The Apocalypse of John, the history of the fury of the monster against the saints, is at the same time the triumphal chant which celebrates their victory over the Beast. This Beast is:

The ancient serpent, he who is called the devil and Satan, who leads astray the whole world.[47]

His capital is Babylon, "the great harlot who sits upon many waters."[48] Thanks to the revelation of Jesus, biblical history is illuminated, the tempter has found his name. The themes of the Old Testament are put in order and clarified. Between the tempting serpent, the accusing Satan, the seductive capitals, the persecuting kings, there is revealed a profound kinship. Piercing the shadows which concealed them, the sovereign look of Jesus sheds light on these confused shapes, the tentacles of a unique monster struck dead.

2. THE ACCURSED PLACES

Our word hell derives from the Greco-Roman representations of the world of death. The *infernus* of the Latins, the *Hades* of the Greeks were the subterranean regions where the dead, reduced to the state of formless shadows, led a desolate and pointless existence in an unending night. The Hebrew beliefs are rather similar to these representations. True, they ignore all the pagan fantasies that conjure up a kingdom of the dead subject to the government of infernal gods—Pluto and Proserpine in Greece, Nergal and Erechkigal in Babylon—surrounded by a numerous staff of functionaries, judges, guards, and monsters. In Israel, God alone is the master of sheol.[49] Still, once paganism was driven out, the lot of the dead as Israel imagined it is similar to that described in the Babylonian texts.[50] The dead, flaccid[51] and impalpable, their voices reduced to a whisper,[52] descend to the "destined place of everyone alive."[53] It is a sort of well,[54] a common grave given over to dust[55] and to worms,[56] in the depths of the earth,[57] as opposed to the heavens above. It is a place of darkness,[58] and of desolation. One enters therein stripped of everything that made life worth living,[59] even of one's memories,[60] and there is no leaving: the gates of sheol are forever shut.[61]

The worst part of sheol is the absence of God. He has no interest in its depths.[62] Not that He is unaware of what goes on there.[63] His vengeance would be able to pursue anyone who thought he could hide from it.[64] However, He does not hear the prayers from that place,[65] He performs no miracles there;[66] no one honors Him, no one thinks of Him in the land of silence and oblivion.[67]

Still, sheol is not hell. Its inhabitants are not the damned. Neither just nor sinners, they are formless shadows. The most accurate image of the real substance of this place would seem to be, not a place of sin, but a void where human existence ends; according to the definitive phrase of Ecclesiastes, vanity of vanities.[68]

But this conclusion of the disillusioned wise man does not have the sound of triumph. For, if death is the last word of human life, that is because man is a creature of weakness and sin. A fundamental conviction in Israel associates death with sin. Without having St. Paul's definitive clarity of formulation, the key phrase: "sin entered into the world and through sin death,"[69] nevertheless expresses a theme which is constant in the Bible.

Beginning with the most ancient accounts of Genesis, the association is a consecrated one. Yahweh's threat to Adam: "Thou shalt die," expresses it with the rigor of a sentence that cannot be appealed. The entire story is built up on the fatality which vows the sinner to death. Refusing its fecundity to man, the earth is covered over with nettles and thorns, and it will be necessary, in order to produce, to suffer and to sweat. Refusing its generosity to woman, life will be born of her only at the price of agony. In these two sources, the fecundity of the woman and the fertility of the earth, man's most precious wealth, the central object of all the nature-religions, life itself, is half-sterilized from its very origins and condemned to disappear beneath the triumphant blows of death.

From the beginning, too, the death which sin brings with it is not simply a natural death at the end of a life filled with days. It is violent death, crime born of hatred. The corpse of Abel

148

gives a sinister meaning to "Thou shalt die." But this crime has its proper location. The earth, cursed after the sin of Adam, of itself brings forth only a rebellious vegetation, but man can, by dint of labor, make it bring forth fruit. The region where Cain buries himself, without fire or abode, is a land abandoned by Yahweh, subject to the laws of the jungle.

The account of the Deluge pursues the association of sin with death. It sees in the moral corruption of mankind the cause of its punishment, the material corruption of death:

> The earth was corrupt [*chahat*] in the sight of God, and it was filled with violence. God saw that the earth was corrupt [*chahat*]; for all men lived corruptly [*chahat*] on the earth. And God said to Noe "The end of all creatures of flesh is in my mind. . . . I will destroy [*chahat*] them with the earth.[70]

There is perhaps something a bit affected about this determination to play on the root *chht*, but the intent is a good expression of the substance of the account: God is only pursuing to its conclusion the devastating action of sin. The Deluge is a return to the primal chaos.

The episode of Babel indicates a precise point where the curse of God fell upon sin. In describing this tower, the author was presenting a picture of the ruination of the most impressive achievements of Babylonian paganism, the superb multi-storied temples. Thus had ended the most audacious attempt ever made against God.

The fate of Sodom and Gomorrha, if one may say so, placed hell at the very doors of the promised land. By an astonishing coincidence, nature set aside for Israel one of the most extraordinary sites in the world, the Dead Sea and its borders, desolate places where the salt sterilizes all life, frightening symbols of the divine curse. Throughout its history, the people of Palestine had before its eyes this image of sin. At the very foot of Jerusalem, Yahweh's city, stretched the plain where Sodom and Gomorrha had committed their abominations. The prophets never cease recalling this terrible example.[71] They threaten the holy city with the same fate. Not that Yahweh has changed, He is always the one who forgives:

> Go about through the streets of Jerusalem, and see and consider, if you can find a man that executeth judgment and seeketh faith: and I will be merciful unto it.[72]

Alas,

> The iniquity of the daughter of my people is made greater than the sin of Sodom.[73]

Jesus said no more than this.[74] But he hurled His curse on Bethsaida and Capharnaum as more guilty than Sodom.[75] He revealed Himself the equal of Yahweh, the visitor received of yore by Abraham and insulted by the people of Sodom.[76]

The fate of Sodom, more than just ordinary death, is the real punishment of the sinner:

> He rains upon the wicked fiery coals and brimstone;
>   a burning blast is their allotted cup.[77]
> May he rain burning coals upon them;
>   may he cast them into the depths, never to rise.[78]

Sodom, nearby, was nevertheless not Jerusalem. But sin entered the holy city. At once, the latter finds itself joined to the cursed regions. Sheol, the subterranean monster, suddenly appears, as it had arisen to engulf Core, Dathan and Abiron, which had revolted against Moses.[79] In the heart of the city it comes to open its jaws:

> Therefore hath hell enlarged her soul and opened her mouth without any bounds: and their strong ones and their people and their high and glorious ones shall go down into it.[80]

This redoubling of the activity of sheol, this excess of fury, enables us to see that, while death is the common lot, it can keep its violence for sinners.

The true place of sin in the Bible is gehenna. Now gehenna is located in the heart of Jerusalem. The ravine of Hinnon is not, like the site of Sodom, a place of horror. It is, on the contrary, at the very gates of the city, amid the well-watered gardens, a charming spot.[81] But, in this smiling green corner, idolatry had set up a monstrous rite, the sacrifice of children:

> . . . the children of Juda have done evil in my eyes, saith the Lord.
> . . . they have built the high places of Topheth, which is in the valley of the son of Ennom, to burn their sons and their daughters in the fire, which I commanded not nor thought on in my heart.[82]

Isaias was the first to curse these abominations, and predicted that this miserable fire would draw down on itself quite another fire, the wrath of Yahweh:

> For Topheth is prepared from yesterday, prepared by the king, deep and wide. The nourishment thereof is fire and much wood: the breath of the Lord as a torrent of brimstone kindling it.[83]

The flames are no longer natural ones. Already we have a glimpse of the inextinguishable flames lighted by the eternal God.

The prophecies addressed to the exiles enlarge the scene. They end up in the vision of the final judgment to which Yahweh will subject all of mankind. This judgment inaugurates the new age. Jerusalem remains the center of this transfigured world. But all the nations which go up to the holy mountain to adore the glory of Yahweh, file by, in passing, the site of Topheth:

> And they shall go out and see the carcasses of the men that have transgressed against me. Their worm shall not die and their fire shall not be quenched: and they shall be a loathsome sight to all flesh.[84]

To flames, corruption is added here. One more aspect of hell is delineated, that of disintegration.[85] Thus appears one of the evangelical formulas for hell.[86] Moreover, the guilty ones are not only the unnatural parents who sacrifice their children to an idol, they are all the "rebels," all sinners. The sin of Jerusalem becomes that of mankind. In its turn, the Book of Judith, which promises gehenna to the enemies of Israel, strips this cursed place of every geographic factor:

151

Woe be to the nation that riseth up against my people: for the Lord almighty will take revenge on them. In the day of judgment he will visit them.

For he will give fire, and worms into their flesh, that they may burn, and may feel for ever.[87]

The threats of the prophets bore their fruit. As Israel saw disasters descending upon it, it became aware that the cause thereof was its own sin. Deuteronomy, in a sinister tableau which gathers together all the disasters of nature and of history, depicts the curse reserved for sin.[88] It is death, but not the serene death of the patriarch who "died at a good old age, an old man, after a full life, and was gathered to his kinsmen";[89] it is death from famine and terror, in horror and despair.

Israel experiences this kind of death. In 587 B.C. Jerusalem is taken by storm, its king carried away as a prisoner, its Temple profaned, the elite of its populace reduced to slavery and taken into exile. The lesson then is brought home. Ezechiel hears people around him repeat:

Our iniquities and our sins are upon us and we pine away in them. How then can we live?[90]

No doubt there was, in such avowals, a facile resignation, a very human haste to throw the responsibility onto others. There was an old proverb:

The fathers have eaten sour grapes and the teeth of the children are set on edge.[91]

But the prophet brings everyone up short before his own responsibilities:

The son shall not bear the iniquity of the father, and the father shall not bear the iniquity of the son. The justice of the just shall be upon him, and the wickedness of the wicked shall be upon him.[92]

For Yahweh, who has made Israel perish, will recall it to life, will give new spirit to the already putrescent dry bones.[93] It is up to each person to participate in this resurrection, to adhere to the new Israel.[94] Yahweh, the living God, says: "I desire not the death of the wicked."[95] On the contrary, He wants to snatch him away from this natural fatality and bring it to pass that "the wicked turn from his way and live."[96] But the restoring of the initiative to individual responsibility, far from breaking up the combination of sin and death, rather consecrates the absolute value of the old law; the prophet's mission is to repeat to the sinner the warning given of yore to Adam: "You must die":[97]

The justice of the just shall not deliver him in what day soever he shall sin: and the wickedness of the wicked shall not hurt him in what day soever he shall turn from his wickedness.[98]

The soul that sinneth the same shall die.[99]

Just as life promised to the just man is life in a resurrected and renewed people, the death reserved to the sinner is not simply natural death: it is a death which will involve him in the catastrophe that has engulfed his people,[100] a death in fright, under the terror of Yahweh's wrath. Ransom of a privileged destiny, it is, in one sense, a supernatural death.

Time was needed for the reflection of Israel to extract all the meaning from the lesson of the prophets, and to understand the nature of the death promised to the sinner. Traditional wisdom was restricted in general to repeating, like a trite phrase, the old association between sin and death:

> Ill-gotten treasures profit nothing,
>   but virtue saves from death.[101]
> Virtue directs toward life,
>   but he who pursues evil does so to his death.[102]
> In the path of justice there is life,
>   but the abominable way leads to death.[103]

The same popular wisdom inspires the maxims regarding the necessity of a firm education:

> Withhold not chastisement from a boy;
>   if you beat him with the rod, he will not die.
> Beat him with the rod,
>   and you will save him from the nether world.[104]

Job's friends brought out the same conviction in images that are more vivid, although inspired by the same source:

> Truly, the light of the wicked is extinguished;
>   no flame brightens his hearth.
> The light is darkened in his tent;
>   in spite of him, his lamp goes out.
> On every side terrors affright him;
>   destruction is ready at his side.
> The first-born consumes his limbs;
>   terror conducts him to the king.
> He is plucked from the security of his tent;
>   over his abode brimstone is scattered.[105]

The naive assurance of these maxims is disconcerting to us. Is it possible that the Hebrews believed that death struck the sinner and spared the just? First of all, we must be careful not to take literally all the biblical expressions about death and even about sheol. We must take into account the need, very Hebraic and very popular, of vigorous and full expression.[106] We must also re-discover this "sense of totality" which dominates the Hebrew mentality and which Pedersen presupposes:

The sinner descends into sheol but, in reality, he is already there. Just as the desert encroaches on man's land and establishes itself wherever evil gets a foothold, so too the nether world, once it has become the sojourn of the wicked man. Where obscurity reigns, one is in the nether world; for the nether world is rediscovered wherever one of its elements appears. He who is struck down by some evil, by misfortune, by sickness, or some other tribulation, is in reality in sheol, and when he leaves misery behind and returns "to the light," he has actually escaped from sheol. If this thought comes so naturally to an Israelite, it is because he always obeys the law of totality. If he feels within himself one of the elements of sheol, he feels himself completely immersed therein. He experiences the desolation of the tomb, the oppression of darkness, and even the buffeting of the waves of the abyss.[107]

One must know this mentality in order to give true scope to the prayers of the psalms, in which the author already seems in the depths of sheol,[108] or else thanks God for having drawn him out of it,[109] and, also, in order to understand the curses which assign his enemies to sheol.[110]

154

To give the true scope to these texts will mean, for one thing, to minimize their tragic violence. An analysis of the literal sense often shows that the hell in question amounts to a grave illness, to pursuit by bitter enemies, to a condemnation at law, even to a perilous crossing of the sea or of the desert. Giving these texts their true bearing will also mean—if we respect the Hebrew sense of "totality"—placing them in the constant perspective of the Old Testament which never ceases associating sin with death and with sheol. Throughout the entire Bible there runs a conviction: evil, in all its forms, is a harbinger of death, but also a sure sign of sin; sin can only give birth to evil and, ultimately, to death.

Experience, however, was continuously giving the lie to this conviction. Applied to a people, the doctrine of temporal retribution is borne out in an overall way: the healthy nations are the happy nations. But the law does not hold for individual cases. How many sinners enjoy, in a full old age, the fruit of their injustices! How many just men are struck down before their time! Could people close their eyes to this evidence?

The Old Testament did not escape the problem. The Book of Job is an anguished protest against the accepted view:

> One dies in his full vigor,
>   wholly at ease and content;
> His figure is full and nourished,
>   and his bones are rich in marrow.
> Another dies in bitterness of soul,
>   having never tasted happiness.[111]

It is not true that death is reserved for the sinner. Job suffered enough to reject all the classical justifications his friends have offered him; he dared to provoke God:

> Though I am innocent, I myself cannot know it;
>   I despise my life.
> It is all one! therefore I say:
>   Both the innocent and the wicked he destroys.
> When the scourge slays suddenly,
>   he laughs at the despair of the innocent.[112]

155

God responds to this upbraiding by manifesting His presence, and that suffices for Job, face to face with His grandeur and His mystery, to admit his defeat and his satisfaction:

> I know that you can do all things,
>> and that no purpose of yours can be hindered.
> I have dealt with great things that I do not understand;
>> things too wonderful for me, which I cannot know.
> I had heard of you by word of mouth,
>> but now my eye has seen you.
> Therefore I disown what I have said,
>> and repent in dust and ashes.[113]

The problem had been poorly set forth: man's destiny is too mysterious to be expressed in a simplistic formula: death to the sinner. The Book of Job ends on this mystery, on recourse to God alone, in naked faith. This is truly the correct direction, the one which will lead to light, but here it is still night.

Psalm 72 expresses the same scandal and finds the same answer for it: God's presence, attachment to God alone:

> Whom else have I in heaven?
>> And when I am with you, the earth delights me not.
> Though my flesh and my heart waste away,
>> God is the rock of my heart and my portion forever.[114]

As at the conclusion of Job, the psalmist finds, along with peace, the traditional formulas, the equivalence between sin and death:

> For indeed, they who withdraw from you perish;
>> you destroy everyone who is unfaithful to you.[115]

Taken literally, in the obvious sense of the words, these formulas are false, and the poet knows this: his scandal is precisely that of finding them constantly at fault. Still, if he restates them, in concluding his prayer, it is because now they take on for him a new savor. In contact with God, in the stripping away of all human desire, the sinner's death can no longer simply mean quitting the earth. It is primarily separation from God. The author of the psalm could not think of hell, of the "second death"; he knew only the death common to us all. But when he speaks of the annihilation of the sinner by God, he introduces a horror much greater than the ordinary lot of man. Light has not yet come, but already faith is affirming it.

Only exceptionally religious souls were capable of acceding to this faith. One could remain a good Israelite without perceiving these depths. The testimony of Ecclesiastes is a proof of this. Believing sincerely, his spirit is free and his vision clear. Without bitterness, but without excessive precaution, he criticizes some of the truths which pass as the most solid because they are the most frequently repeated. Of this number is the old maxim: death to the sinner. It is clearly false:

Love from hatred man cannot tell; both appear equally vain, in that there is the same lot for all, for the just and the wicked.[116]

I have seen all manner of things in my vain days: a just man perishing in his justice, and a wicked one surviving in his wickedness.[117]

There is no question that the critique of Ecclesiastes was needed to give to the traditional equation "sin=death" its true meaning.[118] In forcing a realistic view of the human condition, it made it necessary to become aware that death did not automatically correspond to sin. There was still no affirmation of any other kind of death, but it was necessary, in order to make clear the real meaning of the great threat of death that the Bible poised over sinners, to show first that natural death did not suffice to carry out this threat.

Traditional wisdom ran into an impasse. The old maxims only had an approximate truth. Moreover, the purest hearts went beyond them, but their experiences, in the darkest night of faith, remained indecipherable. Still, light progressed by a reflection based on the destiny of Israel.

Among the wise men, certain ones were not content to collect and to enrich the maxims through which a believing people expressed its attitude in the face of human destiny. Some wise men had filled themselves with the prophetic teachings and

157

thought that they would spread these lessons according to the rhythms and images familiar to current wisdom. In this way, they edited a sort of cathechism, transposing into an accessible language, close to daily life, the message of the great prophets. One of these authors composed the first nine chapters of the Book of Proverbs, shot through with recollections of Deuteronomy and the prophets.[119] While it knows and carries on the tradition which associates sin with sheol, the sin which the book describes takes on special coloration. It is proposed by the temptress, Folly, whose

. . . house is made up of ways to the nether world, leading down to the chambers of death.[120]

Through her wiles, she manages to lead into this cursed dwelling the foolish, blind, man:

Little he knows that the shades are there,
that in the depths of the nether world are her guests![121]

The fact is, that in yielding to Folly, the sinner lacks Wisdom, and this fault is his condemnation:

He who misses me harms himself.[122]

Is there, in these formulas, something more than just metaphors, deliberately exaggerated expressions of the fate reserved to the sinner? Does not the whole thing need literary analysis?

It is, in point of fact, a question of literary analysis, but, to determine in what sense this is so, it is necessary to take an over-all view of these nine chapters. With a subtle faithfulness, they take their inspiration from the entire prophetic tradition, but particularly that of Jeremias and the end of the Book of Isaias. It is a perpetual transposition of their teachings, an application to individual life of the appeals addressed to the community of Israel. Thus, the first chapter of Proverbs puts into the mouth of Wisdom, speaking to sinners, the verdict of condemnation which, in the final poem of Isaias, is rendered by Yahweh upon His people:

158

Because I called and you refused,[123]
    I extended my hand and no one took notice;[124]
Because you disdained all my counsel,
    and my reproof you ignored—
I, in my turn, will laugh at your doom;
    I will mock when terror overtakes you;[125]
When terror comes upon you like a storm,
    and your doom approaches like a whirlwind;
    when distress and anguish befall you.[126]
Then they call me, but I answer not;[127]
    they seek me, but find me not.[128]

In the preaching of the prophets, terror, anguish and distress had a very clear meaning: they were disasters about to befall the people.

In threatening the sinner with the catastrophes which the prophets had foretold for the guilty people, the first collection of Proverbs does more than make use of a literary device. It is teaching the Israelite that his personal destiny is not only dependent on the lot of his nation, but, what is more, that it is, in some way, the reproduction of the latter on an individual scale. This had already been taught by Ezechiel: it behooves every son of Israel to undergo the death that has just struck down his people, or to avoid it by conversion. The wise man exploits this idea in depth: the experience of the sinner is that of exile, the death which threatens him is that which has been unleashed during these days of terror. Even more, it is the terrifying power whose savage presence is seen outlined behind the great historic calamities, throughout the prophetic tradition. It is more than a force of nature, it is a monster.

Thus, sheol is the insatiable beast whose gaping jaws Isaias saw opening to swallow Jerusalem, with its confusion and luxury.[129] Perhaps these features evoke some old mythical representations[130] analogous to the informal legends of the Greek world; but while myths furnished the images, history fulfilled them. The history of Israel demonstrates the fate that Yahweh reserves for His enemies. The more powerful they are, the

159

greater is their fall, the more terrible their lot. The sheol in which Ezechiel sees Pharaoh falling is a sheol of the uncircumcised, a heathen sheol reserved for those who have risen up against God.[131] The King of Babylon, "the brilliant star, son of the dawn," is cast into the depths of horror, while the shadows, awakened for this unique spectacle, hurry so as not to miss any part of his fall.[132]

Do these superb pages reveal a belief? Old myths, rejuvenated by a powerful imagination, surely do not suffice to establish that Israel ever distinguished a pagan sheol more sinister than the common sojourn of the faithful of Yaweh. It is not a question of conferring upon these expressive scenes a true dogmatic value. But it is not to enlarge their scope to recall that these descriptions, in which imagination takes such a fine part, are the poetical transcription of uncontested facts: one after another, the great empires that had terrified Israel were to crumble, while Yahweh's people remained. These reverberating ruins where God's power shone forth, were, for the Hebrews, a clear vision of one of the most impressive aspects of sheol. It is quite natural that these visions remained vivid, and that they continued to be linked with the final destiny of sinners. This is the use that Jesus made of the poem concerning the King of Babylon: "I was watching Satan fall as lightning from heaven."[133]

With the persecutions, these images become beliefs. It was inconceivable that the martyr dying in torment should, in the hereafter, be mixed in with his tormentors. One of the themes of the Book of Daniel is to show the sinner undergoing the suffering he was preparing for the just man. The denunciators of the three youths are devoured by the flame they were kindling for their victims;[134] Daniel's adversaries are thrown in his place into the lions' den;[135] the old men who calumniated Susanna receive, at the hands of the outraged crowd, "as they had maliciously dealt against their neighbor."[136] All these miracles

160

are the signs of the truth discovered at that time in Israel and formulated in explicit terms:

And many of those that sleep in the dust of the earth shall awake; some unto life everlasting, and others unto reproach, to see it always.[137]

The fourth of the seven brothers martyred in Jerusalem under Antiochus Epiphanes, bears witness to this truth in the midst of tortures:

It is better, being put to death, by men, to look for hope from God, to be raised up again by him: for, as to thee thou shalt have no resurrection unto life.[138]

Once this truth has been acquired, at the price of blood, it finally gave to the traditional maxims a satisfactory meaning, and resolved the difficulties raised by the frankness of Ecclesiastes. In fact, in the Book of Wisdom, we find sentences similar to the customary proverbs:

A stealthy utterance does not go unpunished,
    and a lying mouth slays the soul.[139]

Court not death by your erring way of life,
    nor draw to yourselves destruction by the works of your hands.[140]

Out of context, these formulas would have only a metaphorical value, like their traditional models. But the text goes on:

It was the wicked who with hands and words invited death,
. . . .
. . . they deserve to be in its possession.[141]

For they said among themselves, thinking not aright:
. . . .
. . . our lifetime is the passing of a shadow;
    and our dying cannot be deferred
. . . .
Come, therefore, let us enjoy the good things that are real,
. . . .
Let us beset the just one, because he is obnoxious to us;
. . . .
Let us condemn him to a shameful death;
    for according to his own words, God will take care of him.[142]

The cry of the impious was that of the pagan nations throwing themselves upon Israel, that of the persecutors determined to rid themselves of a religion which went against their policy. These pagans now have heirs in the very midst of the people, who cannot bear the living reproach of their compatriot who has remained faithful to God:

> To us he is the censure of our thoughts;
> merely to see him is a hardship for us.[143]

They are reassured when they see that his justice, far from making him happier, brings misfortune down upon him, and death, despite beautiful words, claims him faster and more cruelly than the impious man:

> These were their thoughts, but they erred;
> for their wickedness blinded them.[144]

> For they see the death of the wise man
> and do not understand what the Lord intended for him,
> ....
> They see, and hold him in contempt;
> but the Lord laughs them to scorn.[145]

just as Yahweh, in the last chapter of Isaias, laughed at the enemies of His chosen ones,[146] just as, in the Book of Proverbs, Wisdom predicted to the foolish:

> I, in my turn, will laugh at your doom.[147]

The finale of the Book of Isaias, in the guise of the restoration of Israel and the punishment of the nations, prophesied the final judgment, the separation of the good and the wicked:

Behold my servants shall eat, and you shall be hungry: behold my servants shall drink, and you shall be thirsty. Behold my servants shall rejoice, and you shall be confounded.[148]

The Book of Wisdom describes, in slightly different images, a similar scene. It shows the meeting of the just man "with great assurance,"[149] and his persecutors, who shall come, "fearful . . .

162

at the counting up of their misdeeds,"[150] to undergo the vengeance of God:

> And they shall afterward become dishonored corpses[151]
> and an unceasing mockery among the dead.
> For he shall strike them down speechless and prostrate
> and rock them to their foundations;
> They shall be utterly laid waste
> and shall be in grief
> And their memory shall perish.[152]

The hell of the Book of Wisdom is therefore no longer the natural sheol, the common grave of mankind. It is a more shameful death, more complete than ordinary death. This belief, if it is now expressed with a new clarity, nevertheless presupposed all the history of Israel. This past, made up of exceptional, miraculous, divine initiatives, and of catastrophes, also divine, had introduced among the peoples a destiny surpassing the horizons of history. Moreover, in this destiny, all the neighbors of the chosen people participated, all those who, at one time or another, had gotten in their way. Edom, Emalec, Madian, Moab, the Philistines and the Ammonites, Tyre, Sidon, Damascus, the Egyptian Pharaoh and Cyrus the Persian, Assyria and Babylon, even the fabulous Gog, King of Magog—all played a part in the adventure of Israel, all will be judged by Yahweh according to their behavior toward His chosen one, His son. All will then know that their actions had a bearing that they did not suspect, that the strategems of war and of politics had drawn them into an unknown land where suddenly they were to awaken in the presence of God, to hear His sentence "As long as you did it for one of these, the least of my brethren, you did it for me."[153]

Such had been the prophets' message, the meaning of all those oracles against the nations, which seem to us to hold such a disproportionate place in the Old Testament. The judgment which is to strike them is the announcement and the sign of the judgment God reserves for those who oppose His designs. The mission of the prophets had been to reveal to Israel, in the events of history, the sovereign hand of Yahweh. The role of the wise men was to show each Israelite that his destiny also went beyond the visible horizons, to give a new meaning to the common maxims of morality, to prepare it to meet God.

There is continuity from one level to the other. It is not through reflection on the nature of man that the wise man comes to conceive his destiny, but rather by a reviewing of God's actions in history. The author of Wisdom sees, in the darkness spread over Egypt, in this "night, powerless though it was, that had come upon them from the recesses of a powerless nether world,"[154] and in the horror of which the Egyptians saw discovered "their secret sins" which they "supposed . . . were hid under the dark veil of oblivion,"[155] the image of "the darkness that next should come upon them."[156] The miracles of Israel's history are the signs of the divine meaning of the human destiny.

Supernatural hell, the prophetic hell, this hell is still not the Christian hell. What is missing is not certainty in affirmation; it is not even preciseness in details—the Gospels will not add any new ones. It is this: that hell is to be a purely divine punishment. It is, to be sure, the place of the wrath of God which finally wreaks its vengeance on His enemies, but this triumph is not pure. It is mixed up with the national vengeance of Israel, the human revenge of the just man who rejoices at the reversal of roles. It is impossible that this triumph be that of heaven, that the pain of the damned be reduced to seeing the joy of their victims.

True, the hell of the Old Testament is still partly a dream of revenge. In order for it to be stripped of all impurity, it is necessary that this impurity be revealed by Him who dies pardoning all. For while Jesus is indeed the heir of the persecuted ones of Israel, the just man "who boasts that God is his father,"[157] He whom the impious condemn to "a shameful death; for,

164

according to his own words, God will take care of him,"[158] and while He repeats the lament of those unhappy ones:

> My God, my God, why hast thou forsaken me?[159]

> They put gall in my food,
>   and in my thirst they gave me vinegar to drink,[160]

He is not heard to carry on to the point of cursing, as they did:

> Heap guilt upon their guilt,
>   and let them not attain to your reward.
> May they be erased from the book of the living,
>   and not be recorded with the just![161]

And yet these curses will be carried out, and He shall say: "Depart from me, accursed ones!"[162] This word, indeed, is a total rupture because it emanates from Him who thinks only of forgiving, but whose love, powerless to force a heart which is closed, is aware of this uncrossable abyss. No shadow of resentment alters the generosity of the Crucified. He is love, pure and perfect. But whoever shuts himself off from Him can find only a curse. Jesus did not repeat the appeals of the psalms calling down the divine curse, for God "did not send his Son into the world in order to judge the world, but that the world might be saved through him."[163] Still, Jesus has seen the sinner's sin return to him as a curse, for "he who does not believe is already judged."[164] The curses of Scriptures are fullfilled to the last iota.[165]

Thus, the "sign of the Son of Man" marks the frontier between heaven and hell. The Christian hell continues to be localized, but outside of a place, so to speak, localized with respect to the Kingdom of God. Sheol, in the depths of the earth, was at the opposite pole from heaven and from the light. The land of Sodom and Gomorrha, an even closer figure of hell, was visible from the heights near Jerusalem. Gehenna was established at the very gates of the Holy City, and when the city of Yahweh is opened to the chosen of all nations, their columns, going up to the Temple of God, pass by the place where the cadavers

165

of sinners are tormented. Hell is, in the Old Testament, the sinister region where men throw the excrements and refuse of the Holy City.

The Gospels, which abolish the privilege of Jerusalem,[166] also stress the proximity between the place of sin and that of the elect. The Apocalypse throws Satan headlong into "the pool of fire that burns with brimstone,"[167] the replica of Sodom near the heavenly Jerusalem. Hell is, in the Gospels, the "darkness outside,"[168] on the other side of the door which opens on the feast where God unites His own into His joy.[169] Theological reflection has distinguished in the punishment of sin, the pain of sense and the pain of damnation, and has demonstrated that the latter infinitely surpasses the former in horror. Always concrete, the biblical tradition keeps these two aspects united: the place of sin is contiguous to the abode of God.[170] There is only one door between the two, but it has been closed forever.

NOTES

[1] P. Joüon, "Le grand dragon, l'antique serpent," in *Recherches de Science religieuse*, 1927, pp. 244–246.

[2] Prov. 23: 31–34, according to A. Lefèvre, *Études Carmélitaines*, 1948, *Satan*, p. 24.

[3] M.-J. Lagrange, "L'innocence et le péché," in *Revue Biblique*, 1897, pp. 350, 365.

[4] Gen. 4: 7.

[5] Num. 5: 14, 30.

[6] Judg. 9: 23.

[7] Osee 4: 12; 5: 4.

[8] Is. 19: 14.

[9] Is. 29: 10.

[10] Zach. 13: 2.

[11] Exceptions: Osee 4: 12; 5: 4. Zach. 13: 2. Even in these cases, nothing offers any grounds for believing that these spirits emanate from a power opposed to God.

[12] Satan is never called spirit by the Old Testament. But, being one of the "children of God," he belongs to His court, where the spirits are also present. His features, in the prologue of the Book of Job (Job 1: 1–11), are exactly those of the spirit who comes down to lead astray the prophets of Achab in 3 Kings 22: 19–23.

[13] Num. 22: 22, 32.

[14] 1 Kings 29: 4.

[15] 2 Kings 19: 23.

[16] Cf. 3 Kings 5: 18; 11: 14, 23, 25.

[17] Matt. 16: 23.

[18] The three texts in which Satan figures as a personal being (Zach. 3: 1; Job 1: 1–11, 10; 1 Par. 21: 1), are all more or less recent, but the prologue of Job, where these features are

most clearly developed, is certainly inspired by an ancient popular composition (cf. P. Dhorme, *Le Livre de Job*, Paris, 1926, pp. 14, 63–65).

[19] It is quite possible that the term "provoker of crime," *mazkir 'awon*, denotes, by means of an expressive formula, the function of Satan. Cf. von Rad, in Kittel, *Theologisches Wörterbuch*, II, p. 71.

[20] Ps. 9: 9.

[21] He only obtains a proper name in Zach. 3: 1, and 1 Par. 21: 1. In Job, he has the name of the role he plays.

[22] Compare 1 Par. 21: 1, with 2 Kings 24: 1.

[23] Fr. Dubarle notes very properly, in this "apparently inferior conception of God's justice," the seed of profound religious perceptions. "Some sacred authors have preferred to place God's justice on trial rather than close their eyes on all the tragedy inherent in the human condition" (*Les Sages d'Israël*, Paris, 1946, p. 71).

[24] A. Lefèvre, *Études Carmélitaines, Satan*, Paris, 1948, p. 24.

[25] Wis. 2: 24.

[26] Wis. 4: 20.

[27] Regarding the belief in the fallen angels in Judaism, cf. A. Lods, "La chute des anges, origine et portée de cette spéculation," in *Revue d'Histoire et de Philosophie religieuses*, 1927, pp. 295–315.

[28] Matt. 4: 10.

[29] Luke 10: 18.

[30] Is. 14: 12–15. According to the actual title, this canticle is directed at the King of Babylon without specifying his name. Many Assyriologists, struck by the close points of contact with the fate of Sargon, the greatest and most terrible of the Assyrian conquerors, ask whether it might not be a question of some "ancient lament over the death of Sargon, collected in a more recent selection" (P. Dhorme, "Les pays bibliques et l'Assyrie," in *Revue Biblique*, 1910, p. 389, note 3). Similar testimony cited by O. Procksch, *Jesaia I*, Leipzig, 1930, p. 194.

[31] Cf. H. Gressmann, *Der Messias*, Gottingen, 1929, pp. 94–148; W. Staerk, *zu Hab.*, I, 5–11, in the *Zeitschrift für die alttestamentliche Wissenschaft*, 1933, pp. 1–28.

[32] Amos 7: 1.

[33] Joel 1: 4; 2: 2–11.

[34] Is. 5: 26–28.

[35] Jer. 4: 6–7; 5: 15–17; 6: 1–5, 22–26.

[36] Ezech. 38 and 39.

[37] W. Staerk does so in the article cited above: "Myth of the Antichrist," p. 6; "satanic power," p. 8; "demoniacal grandeur," p. 11; "demoniacal army," p. 13; "power struggling against God," p. 19; "kingdom of Satan," p. 21; "satanic sovereign," p. 26.

[38] Jer. 15: 2; 21: 7, 9; 24: 10; 27: 8, 13; 29: 17; 32: 36; 34: 17; 38: 2; 42: 17, 22; 44: 13.

[39] 4 Kings 9: 22; Nah. 3: 4.

[40] Dan. 2: 31–45.

[41] Matt. 12: 24–29. Cf. W. Foerster, in Kittel, *Theologisches Wörterbuch*, I, p. 615.

[42] Matt. 4: 1.

[43] Deut. 8: 2; cf. *supra*, p. 15, 16.

[44] Cf. St. Ignatius, *Spiritual Exercises*, "Discernment of spirits," rule no. 13.

[45] Luke 10: 18.

[46] John 12: 31.

[47] Apoc. 12: 9.

[48] Apoc. 17: 1.

[49] Cf. 1 Kings 2: 6. Even if there subsist traces of a cult of the dead (cf. 1 Kings 28: 13), not a single rite can be found directed toward the dead.

[50] Cf. P. Dhorme, "Le séjour des morts chez les Babyloniens et les Hébreux," in *Revue Biblique*, 1907, pp. 59–78.

[51] This is the probable meaning of the root which has furnished one of the names given to the shadows: the *repha'im* (Is. 14: 9; 26: 14, 19; Ps. 87, 11.)

[52] Is. 29: 4.

[53] Job 30: 23.

[54] Ps. 29: 4; 87: 7.

[55] Job 17: 16; Ps. 21: 30.

[56] Is. 14: 11.

[57] Deut. 32:22; Ps. 85: 13.

[58] Ps. 87: 7, 13, 19; Job 10: 22.

[59] Ps. 48: 18; Job 1: 21; Eccl. 5: 14.

[60] Ps. 87, 13; Eccl. 9: 10.

[61] Ps. 87: 9; Job 38: 17; cf. Wis. 16: 13.

[62] Ps. 87: 11.

[63] Prov. 15: 11; Job 26: 6; Ps. 138: 8.

[64] Amos 9: 2.

[65] Ps. 142: 7.

[66] Ps. 87: 11.

[67] Ps. 6: 6; 29: 10; 114: 17.

[68] Eccl. 1: 2; 12: 8.

[69] Rom. 5: 12.

[70] Gen. 6: 11–13.

[71] Amos 4: 11; Osee 11: 8; Is. 1: 9; Jer. 50: 40.

[72] Jer. 5: 1.

[73] Lam. 4: 6; cf. Ezech. 16: 46–58.

[74] Matt. 10: 15.

[75] Matt. 11: 23–24.

[76] Gen. 18–19.

[77] Ps. 10: 6.

[78] Ps. 139: 11.

[79] Num. 16: 32–33.

[80] Is. 5: 14.

[81] Regarding the name and the location of the ravine of Ben-Hinnom, see H. Vincent, *Jerusalem,* vol. I, Paris, 1912, pp. 124–234.

[82] Jer. 7: 30–31; cf. 19: 5; 32: 35. Regarding the sacrifices to Moloch, cf. the summary by R. de Vaux, *Revue Biblique,* 1936, pp. 278–282, of O. Eissfeldt, *Molk als Opferbegriff,* Halle, 1935.

[83] Is. 30: 33.

[84] Is. 66: 24.

[85] Cf. Jer. 7: 32; 19: 6.

[86] Mark 9: 43, 45, 47.

[87] Judith 16: 20–21.

[88] Deut. 28: 15–57. If Deuteronomy is generally cited in these pages concerning the prophets, it is not at all to conceal the very important role of customs and ancient ideas which push its roots back so far in the traditions of Israel. It is simply that these researches into vocabulary and style made it necessary to put this book in its most approximate literary environment, that of the prophets.

[89] Gen. 25: 8, 17; 49: 29, 33.

[90] Ezech. 33: 10.

[91] Ezech. 18: 2.

[92] Ezech. 18: 20.

[93] Ezech. 37: 12.

[94] Ezech. 18: 1–32.

[95] Ezech. 33: 11.

[96] *Ibid.*

168

[97] Ezech. 3: 18; cf. Gen. 2: 17.

[98] Ezech. 33: 12.

[99] Ezech. 18: 20.

[100] J. Hempel, *Das Ethos des Alten Testaments,* Berlin, 1938, p. 39.

[101] Prov. 10: 2.

[102] Prov. 11: 19.

[103] Prov. 12: 28.

[104] Prov. 23: 13–14.

[105] Job 18: 5–6, 11–15.

[106] Cf. the popular American expression for death, "to croak."

[107] J. Pedersen, *Israel, its Life and Culture,* I-II, London-Copenhagen, 1926, pp. 466–467.

[108] Ps. 27: 1; 29: 10; 68: 16; 142: 7; cf. Gunkel-Begrich, *Einleitung in die Psalmen,* Gottingen, 1933, pp. 185 ff.

[109] Ps. 9: 14; 29: 4; 59: 3; 40: 5–10; 70: 20; 102: 4; 106: 18; 115: 3; Is. 38: 10; Jon. 2: 3–7; Job 33: 28; Ecclus. 51: 6–12.

[110] Ps. 30: 18; 48: 15; 54: 16.

[111] Job 21: 23–25.

[112] Job 9: 21–23.

[113] Job 42: 2–6.

[114] Ps. 72: 25–26.

[115] Ps. 72: 27.

[116] Eccl. 9: 2.

[117] Eccl. 7: 15.

[118] Regarding this role of clarification played by the critique of Ecclesiastes, see the Introduction by R. Pautrel to his translation: *La Sainte Bible . . . de Jerusalem,* Éditions du Cerf, Paris, 1948, pp. 10–11.

[119] A. Robert, "Les attaches littéraires de Proverbes," I-IX, in *Revue Biblique,* 1935, pp. 344–365.

[120] Prov. 7: 27.

[121] Prov. 9: 18.

[122] Prov. 8: 36.

[123] Cf. Is. 65: 12; 66: 4.

[124] Cf. Is. 65: 2.

[125] Cf. Is. 66: 4.

[126] Cf. Is. 65: 13–14.

[127] Cf. Is. 65: 24.

[128] Prov. 1: 24–28.

[129] Is. 5: 14.

[130] H. Schmidt, *Die Grossen Propheten* (*Die Schriften des A.T.,* Ed. II, Bd. 2) p. 45.

[131] Ezech. 32: 18–32.

[132] Is. 14: 4–20.

[133] Luke 10: 18.

[134] Dan. 3: 48.

[135] Dan. 6: 25; cf. 14: 41.

[136] Dan. 13: 61.

[137] Dan. 12: 2.

[138] 2 Mac. 7: 14.

[139] Wis. 1: 11.

[140] Wis. 1: 12.

[141] Wis. 1: 16.

[142] Wis. 2: 1, 5, 6, 12, 20.

[143] Wis. 2: 14.

[144] Wis. 2: 21.

[145] Wis. 4: 17–18.

146 Is. 66: 4.

147 Prov. 1: 26.

148 Is. 65: 13, 14.

149 Wis. 5: 1.

150 Wis. 4: 20.

151 Cf. Is. 66: 24.

152 Wis. 4: 19.

153 Matt. 25: 40.

154 Wis. 17: 14.

155 Wis. 17: 3.

156 Wis. 17: 21.

157 Wis. 2: 16.

158 Wis. 2: 20.

159 Matt. 27: 46=Ps. 21: 2.

160 Ps. 68: 22; cf. Matt. 27: 48.

161 Ps. 68: 28–29.

162 Matt. 25: 41.

163 John 3: 17.

164 John 3: 18.

165 Matt. 5: 18.

166 John 4: 21–23.

167 Apoc. 19: 20; 20: 9, 14, 15; 21: 8.

168 Matt. 8: 12; 22: 13; 25: 30.

169 Matt. 25: 11–12; Luke 13: 28.

170 Even the impassable abyss which separates the poor Lazarus from the wicked rich man does not prevent the latter from seeing "afar off" Abraham and Lazarus, and from measuring his misery in terms of their happiness. Luke 16: 23–24.

Chapter VI

THEMES OF HOPE

The religion of Israel is sometimes considered as one whose morality rests on the strict application of a quasi-commercial contract: quid pro quo. This view is not entirely false, but it is very superficial.

One sign first alerts us: the almost total absence of a "reward" vocabulary. There is no technical word for "merit," the reward of a good action. The word which denotes salary, *sakar*, is very rarely used to indicate a moral recompense.[1] It always understood metaphorically. While it keeps in bold relief its original meaning of compensation for effort expended[2] it is far from suggesting computations and accounting. Booz' prayer to Yahweh on behalf of Ruth:

May the LORD reward what you have done! May you receive a full reward [*maskoret*],[3]

reflects the admiration of a noble heart in the presence of the disinterested generosity of Ruth. And Yahweh's promise to Abraham: Fear not . . . I am thy shield; your reward [*sakar*] shall be very great,"[4] far from offering lucrative compensations, is an invitation to a hope as devoid as possible of human dreams.

In truth, the idea of retribution is frequent in the Bible, but it is only very rarely that there is question of rewards. Most of

171

the time, it is sinners who must receive the punishment for their faults, the enemies of Israel who must expiate their conduct toward God's people:

Take courage, and fear not. Behold, your God will bring the revenge of recompense. God himself will come and will save you.[5]

Such is Yahweh, the "Lord who is a strong revenger,"[6] the God who "showest mercy unto thousands and returnest the iniquity of the fathers into the bosom of their children after them."[7] There is a very clear-cut opposition between the gratuitousness of pardon and the almost mathematical repayment for sin. Toward those whom He punishes, God makes careful computations, but He does not keep accounts with those whom He loves.

Still, for a Hebrew, virtue must find its reward. And everything seems to indicate that this reward is not to be expected in some other world, but to be pursued here on earth.

1. LIFE

The proper reward for virtue is life, and this life is, without doubt, the present life. It is enough to leaf through the collection of Proverbs to penetrate the Hebrew mentality quite thoroughly. The phrases accumulate quickly:

> The just man's recompense leads to life,
>   the gains of the wicked, to sin.[8]
> The fear of the Lord prolongs life,
>   but the years of the wicked are brief.[9]
> Virtue directs toward life,
>   but he who pursues evil does so to his death.[10]

One could easily collect twenty maxims in this vein.[11] This is the wisdom of the Hebrew, not only of what we might call the average Hebrew, but also of the pious Israelite.

At the basis of this mentality, there is something other than the naive belief that the just man lives longer than the wicked man. Experience would quickly give the lie to this illusion.[12]

172

There is here a profoundly moral conviction: that sin is, in man, a principle of corruption, an evil which undermines his well-being. The sinner may appear prosperous, but this is an illusion. At bottom, he is a sick man whose equilibrium has been affected.[13] Life, the lot of the just man, is not simply the multiplication of days;[14] it is, especially, a feeling of security that evil cannot shake. Much more than with mere promises of longevity, the Book of Proverbs is filled with images exalting the security in which the good man lives, and opposes this to the downfall and ruin which are the fatal destiny of the wicked.[15]

These convictions are not proper to Israel alone. In the neighboring cultures, in Egypt and Babylon, life appears equally to be the assured portion of the just man.[16] In fact, these convictions are what the moral sense normally rests on; they are the sign of a healthy conscience, capable of preferring the austere joys of human duty to the seductions of caprice or of passion. They are not the reactions of heroism, but they are the solid habits which make vigorous races and happy homes. The popular morality of Israel, that which ruled daily life, could not ignore these natural virtues, nor could it give them other rewards than their natural sanctions, the peace of a society faithful to the great human laws. Without this "natural" morality, Israel would have remained a mythical people, without roots in mankind. Its history would have been only a collection of fairy tales. If the Bible, in its legislative and sapiential writings, and in a large number of the psalms themselves, has preserved for us so considerable a portion of beliefs and spontaneous reactions, it is because the chosen people had, first of all, to be a people of the flesh, as Peguy used to say.

But God was reserving a particular destiny for His people, and that is why He promises them a unique fate. To the common laws which are incumbent upon all peoples, Yahweh adds the prescriptions of His personal law, and the hope of a life more beautiful than the normal existence of mankind. The life which awaits the Israelite who is faithful to Yahweh is not indeed, just any life: it is life in the promised land, that land of marvels "flowing with milk and honey."[17]

... a land with streams of water, with springs and fountains welling up in the hills and valleys, a land of wheat and barley, of vines and fig trees and pomegranates, of olive trees and of honey ... a land whose stones contain iron and in whose hills you can mine copper.[18]

For someone who is acquainted with the lands of the Beauce or the green pastures of Normandy, for the man who has seen the valley of the Nile, Palestine seems miserable, and this enthusiasm a bit childish. But the patriotism which inspires it is not illusory. It is not paradise which this text is describing, it is the real Palestine, its products and its countryside.

Besides, if the ancient texts are sober, contenting themselves with repeating the formula "flowing with milk and honey," which seems especially to refer to Palestine—much poorer than Egypt—as a land of pasturage suitable for sustaining semi-nomadic tribes, the brilliant images of Deuteronomy are aimed less at the country itself than at the existence promised to the faithful Israelite. The typical expression of his reward is: "that you may have a long life in the land which the LORD, your God, is giving you."[19] Not that this land is without importance. Quite the opposite, there is no true life except in Palestine. Already the old Decalogue associated possession of the land with observance of the law.[20] But these indications are colorless. Deuteronomy likes to describe the delights of this life in order to bring its readers to "choose life." Such is the objective which is admirably summed up in its solemn conclusion:

I call heaven and earth today to witness against you: I have set before you life and death, the blessing and the curse. Choose life, then, that you and your descendants may live, by loving the LORD, your God, heeding his voice, and holding fast to him. For that will mean life for you, a long life for you to live on the land which the LORD swore he would give to your fathers Abraham, Isaac and Jacob.[21]

In the abundance of detail to which Deuteronomy abandons

174

itself, three essential actions constitute the life promised to the just man: to plant, to build, and to marry. Fields, home, love, is this not the whole of man's life? It is quite naturally the Israelite ideal of happiness. The curse which is the destiny of the sinner is to see his home, his vineyard, and his wife, everything to which his instinct of possession attaches itself, being lost to him:

Though you betroth a wife, another man will have her. Though you build a house, you will not live in it. Though you plant a vineyard, you will not enjoy its fruits.[22]

Also, whoever has just become engaged, planted a vineyard, or built a house, is dispensed from combat:

Is there anyone who has built a new house and not yet had the housewarming? Let him return home, lest he die in battle and another dedicate it. Is there anyone who has planted a vineyard and never yet enjoyed its fruits? Let him return home, lest he die in battle and another enjoy its fruits in his stead. Is there anyone who has betrothed a woman and not yet taken her as his wife? Let him return home, lest he die in battle and another take her to wife.[23]

This is knowledge of the human heart, but also concern to maintain an almost idyllic atmosphere in the land where justice must reign. That, for Deuteronomy, is life: a world which no longer belongs to earth. A childish illusion, but also the naive expression of a correct belief: that, without sin, earth would be a paradise. These hopes could obviously be interpreted in a purely earthly sense by a "carnal" people, as Pascal was aware. But this could only be at the price of a deviation. Taken literally, as sanctions for irreproachable conduct, these hopes had rather to sustain the expectation of a paradise-like world.

Israel did not find this paradise, but that was not its vocation. Its vocation, on the contrary, was to develop the awareness that it was sin which kept paradise out of this life. Such, in St. Paul's testimony, is the role of the Law.[24] And to preach this message was the mission of the prophets.

The prophets speak little of life. They scarcely proclaim anything but ruin and devastation. Life, concretely, is for them a salvation: it is to escape the catastrophes which the wrath of Yahweh brings down upon the people. This is the message of Amos:

> Seek ye good and not evil, that you may live.[25]
> For thus saith the Lord to the house of Israel: Seek ye me, and you shall live.
> But seek not Bethel and go not into Galgal, neither shall you pass over to Bersabee: for Galgal shall go into captivity and Bethel shall be unprofitable.
> Seek ye the Lord and live, lest the house of Joseph be burnt with fire; and it shall devour, and there shall be none to quench Bethel.[26]

But because Israel is unfaithful, the curses of Deuteronomy fall upon it:

> Therefore because you robbed the poor and took the choice prey from him; you shall build houses with square stone and shall not dwell in them: you shall plant most delightful vineyards and shall not drink the wine of them.[27]

In the background of these threats there still remains hope. Life will triumph over death:

> I will bring back the captivity of my people Israel: and they shall build the abandoned cities and inhabit them: and they shall plant vineyards and drink the wine of them.[28]

For Osee, even more clearly than for Amos, life is not only the safe life, life spared by disaster; the devastation will be total but it will make the converted people return to Yahweh:

> Come, and let us return to the Lord:
> For he hath taken us, and he will heal us: he will strike, and he will cure us.
> He will revive us after two days: on the third day he will raise us up and we shall live in his sight.[29]

To live is to live again, to be reborn. A miracle is required. The laws of nature are abolished:

> I will deliver them out of the hand of death. I will redeem them from death. O death, I will be thy death; O hell, I will be thy bite.[30]

This new life is a redeemed life. It is also a transfigured life. To live again is no doubt, primarily, to find one's field and home again, but it is more. It is to "live in His sight." This presence is an assurance of peace but also entrance into a mysterious intimacy. What follows confirms this:

We shall know and we shall follow on, that we may know the Lord.[31]

The Book of Osee ends with a passage in which we think we have found, through the obscurities of a difficult text, the image of a divine garden having as its center a great tree.[32] It is a vision quite similar to that of the garden of Eden surrounding the Tree of Life, at the beginning of Genesis.[33] Israel's salvation seems to signify the return to the lost paradise, to the land which knows not death. What is the nature of this new life? The literary form of this passage excludes any indication which is too detailed. We must avoid both a wholly spiritual transposition, and also a literal interpretation of the descriptions of an existence that still has worldly features. The prophet makes use of poetical traditions in order to interpret a properly religious hope. Thus the essential feature of this life is that it comes from God.

Isaias, by a direct reference to the "plantation of the Lord," also evokes the new life which God must bring forth from the earth at the end of time:

In that day, the bud [i.e. garden] of the Lord shall be in magnificence and glory, and the fruit of the earth shall be high and a great joy to them that shall have escaped of Israel.[34]

This new garden of God is not located in some fabulous Orient. It belongs to the capital of Israel:

Every one that shall be left in Sion, and that shall remain in Jerusalem, shall be called holy: everyone that is written in life in Jerusalem.[35]

Elsewhere in the Old Testament we find mention of a "book of life."[36] It is the great volume in which God inscribes the days allotted to each man. On the day when a name is erased, the holder disappears. The book in question here, however, is a different one. It is a special register in which God inscribes the citizens of the new Jerusalem. He will not erase them from it, for they are "inscribed for life." The prophet does not give any description of this new existence.[37] He promises it to the "remnant of Israel," they "that shall be left in Sion," that is, to the little nucleus which, renouncing human points of view, shall have held fast in the faith and passed the divine judgment unscathed.[38] This life is already a life beyond death. Jerusalem will be regenerated only through a catastrophe which will wipe away all human constructions.

The prophecies addressed to the exiles do not mention the theme of life directly. But they speak only about the new life that Yahweh will give as a gift to His restored people. In the midst of exile and death, the prophet announces with certitude regeneration. Life appears primarily as a liberation, a salvation, but also a new creation. The Lord redeems His people because He created them.[39] The word which had, up to that time, denoted the action by which God made heaven and earth,[40] the word reserved for expressing His sovereign power over the world,[41] now denotes another divine action, a second creation, the salvation of the people:

> Drop down dew, ye heavens, from above: and let the clouds rain the just. Let the earth be opened and bud forth a Savior: and let justice spring up together. I, the Lord, have created all these things.[42]

This creation is, literally, a new world. The curse which has weighed upon the earth since Adam's sin is lifted:

> Instead of the shrub, shall come up the fir tree, and instead of the nettle, shall come up the myrtle tree.[43]

In this context of resurrection appears the figure of the Servant of Yahweh. He too succumbs, "cut off out of the land of the living,"[44] but it is not, like Israel, for His sins. It is, on the contrary, because "the Lord hath laid on him the iniquity of us all."[45] He dies a tragic death, incomprehensible and scandalous, but one which is freely accepted. And God raises Him up and exalts Him from this humiliation, giving Him length of days

178

and a spiritual fecundity unique in mankind. The resurrection is no longer only the renaissance of a vanished people. Promised to a being of flesh and blood, a specific person, one condemned to death, it signifies perforce, and in the strict sense, the triumph of life through death.[46]

These prophecies do not try to give precise visions of this new life but rather to evoke the atmosphere of it. It is an impenetrable world, which can only be described by contrasting it with the present world:

> For, behold, I create new heavens and a new earth: and the former things shall not be in remembrance, and they shall not come back upon the heart.[47] There shall be no more an infant of days there, nor an old man that shall not fill up his days: for the child shall die a hundred years old. For as the days of a tree, so shall be the days of my people.[48]

There, the promises of Deuteronomy will be fulfilled:

> And they shall build houses and inhabit them: and they shall plant vineyards and eat the fruits of them.[49]

It will be the return to Paradise, closed since Adam:

> The wolf and the lamb shall feed together; the lion and the ox shall eat straw; and dust shall be the serpent's food.[50]

Still, this Eden is located in Israel, "in my holy mountain."[51] Jerusalem becomes Paradise, the center of the new world.

Habacuc lacks the religious profundity of Isaias, but he is, like all the prophets, witness to the disasters which are falling upon his people, and, for him also, life consists in escaping this ruination. While he has not grasped, in using the formula "the just shall live in his faith," the fulness of meaning which St. Paul gives it,[52] he is faithful to the prophetic tradition which sees salvation only in adherence to Yahweh.

The meaning of the word "life" seems much more limited in Jeremias than in Osee or Isaias. It seems to denote the present existence and to ignore any possibility of another world. To live or to die means, for Israel, to succumb to the threatening disaster or to escape it. No metaphors here. Nevertheless, the issue depends on the choice between good and evil, or more precisely, on obedience to God's warning:

Behold, I set before you the way of life and the way of death.
He that shall abide in this city shall die by the sword and by the famine and by the pestilence: but he that shall go out and flee over to the Chaldeans, that beseige you, shall live.[53]

The fact is that Jeremias is too profoundly upset by the spectacle he has before his eyes to put together the features of another world. His visions of the future seem without highlights and without color. The future, for him, is the gathering together of the exiles,[54] their return to the homeland.[55] The images are those which speak to the heart because they express the simple realities of daily life. Yahweh will "gather his flock,"[56] will "close up thy scar and will heal thee of thy wounds,"[57] will "have pity on his houses,"[58] "will yet plant vineyards,"[59] restore the festivals,[60] "will comfort them and make them joyful."[61]

Is not this return to the land a step backward, after the grandiose dreams of an Osee and an Isaias? In neglecting eschatological expectations, did Jeremias not put an end to the expectation of another world, of a new life, and shut up Israel's hopes within purely earthly horizons?

Perhaps we must, on the contrary, be grateful to the prophet for his discretion. We search in vain in his work for the radiant visions of a transfigured world. But the real transfiguration of the world is but the visible radiating of the transformation of hearts. Jeremias is the prophet of this interior renewal, of the law written in hearts.[62] If, moreover, he conjures up no new world, in marvelous colors, what he does anticipate is no doubt purer than such expectations. He announces the resurrection of Israel. Now in the concrete situation in which the people— which, humanly speaking, had no chance of survival—found itself, it required more faith to believe that Yahweh, in the real

180

expectations. It is always hope of life, of a life which is primarily earthly existence, but which is also filled with new echoes. The formulas of the first collection of Proverbs, so profoundly permeated with the prophetic and deuteronomic teachings,[75] seem scarcely to differ from the maxims of natural human morality which fill other collections. Even where the parallelism with the expressions of Deuteronomy is most evident:

> My son, forget not my teaching,
>   keep in mind my commands;
> For many days, and years of life,
>   and peace, will they bring you,[76]

the reward of virtue remains this-worldly. The frequent appeals "Give me life,"[77] signify primarily happiness, or health. From one end to the other, the "land of the living" means primarily the earthly world and the present life.[78] Still, in the purity of heart and the divine familiarity which characterize this life, there is already evident a deeper meaning: life is the joy of being at ease before God. We must remember this if we wish to compare the expectations of Israel with those of its neighbors, the Egyptians especially, who were so preoccupied with the future life that we might think they were ahead of Israel.[79]

If we did think this, we would be mistaken. By itself, belief in an after-life, a belief which seems to arise quite spontaneously in mankind, has but a very ambiguous religious value. Even the hope of retribution involves an equivocation. A formula such as Bossuet's: "It is one of the characteristics of the new people to set as the foundation of religion faith in the future life; and this was to be the fruit of the coming of the Messias,"[80] calls for some clarification. Christianity does not rest on the expectation of any sort of after-life, but on the expectation of the definitive union with Christ in the life to come. For, to practice virtue in the hope of some day obtaining a better lot, in a world less deceptive than earth, is to demonstrate great strength of soul, but it is not necessarily to love God. To be able to sacrifice

183

immediate joys in the expectation of more noble joys, is the stuff of real greatness, but it is not of an order higher than natural human morality. The Egyptian beliefs attest to a very high morality, but they are not evidence of a religion superior to that of Israel's. Religious hope is not the hope of an after-life, but the hope of finding God. It is possible that the Egyptian representations of the other world at times nourished this pure hope.[81] It is a fact, at any rate, that the religion of Israel, without having known, for long centuries on end, how to provide itself with an encouraging representation of an after-life, gave it, as soon as it had to express that life, features that were purely religious.

It took the trial of martyrdom for Israel to become aware of the nature of the life which its traditions promised it. Faced, through the prosecutions of Antiochus Epiphanes, with the decisive choice between death and the rejection of his God, the faithful Israelite then grasped the real significance of the promise with which Yahweh had sanctioned the observance of His commandments: "Keep ... my statutes and ... find life through them."[82] There could no longer be any question of natural life, since, on the contrary, that had to be sacrificed. It had to be, then, a life beyond death, a resurrection. The Book of Daniel proclaims this faith in categorical terms:

At that time shall thy people be saved, every one that shall be found written in the book.
    And many of those that sleep in the dust of the earth shall awake: some unto life everlasting, and others unto reproach, to see it always.[83]

A new belief assuredly, but one which has continuity with the ancient hopes. The saved are those "that shall be found written in the book," "the holy ones,"[84] like those whom Isaias could see crossing the flame of divine wrath, who "shall be called holy; every one that is written in life in Jerusalem."[85]

Moreover, the Book of Daniel sees in the destiny of the people of God, miraculously saved from destruction, the sign of the triumph over death which God reserves to those who will have

184

loved Him above all things. The whole book is an exhortation to martyrdom. It is entirely constructed on one major theme: God snatching His own from the death prepared by men. Susanna miraculously delivered from the hatred of the old men, through having hoped in God,[86] Daniel delivered from the lion's den,[87] the three young men spared in the furnace[88]—all are images of the eternal life promised to martyrs. But all these episodes take place in the period of Israel's great trial, at the time when, between Yahweh and the seductions of Babylon and its paganism, Israel had played out its existence and had experienced, "hoping against hope,"[89] the fidelity of God. A small detail is to be noted here, that the first canticle of the young men in the furnace is but a prayer asking for the salvation of the people. There is no allusion to the flames. It is clear that Sidrach, Misach, and Abdenago represent all Israel.

The clearer the affirmation of eternal life, the vaguer are the characteristics which constitute it. More than vague, they are completely lacking. There is not one description of the after-life, even beneath apocalyptic images. Still, the Book of Daniel is full of these strange and grandiose images; all of them denote events and powers of the earth and of history. Only one image appears of this life beyond death: the unalterable splendor of the stars.[90] There is the same sobriety in the perspectives which animate the courage of the seven martyr-brothers in the Second Book of Maccabees.[91] None of them has to make up a tableau of the happiness which awaits him. They only know that some day they will find again these members they are sacrificing to torture.[92] But the important thing is that they will receive them from God, that they will be given life again by God. "Eternal life" is that which one receives from God.[93]

These convictions which seem to us to be without precedent did not seem so new to their contemporaries. They do not give the impression of making any discoveries. We might say that they find in the former tradition everything which they affirm so bravely. To justify their assurance, the seven brothers and their mother fall back upon the Canticle of Moses, which is found at the end of Deuteronomy. They quote only one phrase from it: "the LORD shall do justice for his people."[94] This isolated quotation could have had no meaning, but it is probably meant to evoke the whole Canticle. Foreseeing the disasters with which Israel was threatened, it taught the latter to see therein the punishment of its sins,[95] but ended in a cry of confidence and a challenge hurled to the false gods:

It is I who bring both death and life.[96]

The horizon of the Canticle was the destruction of Israel and its resurrection. The martyrs of Antiochus read therein their own resurrection. For, having been faithful to the end to the God of their fathers, they see the hopes of their people being fulfilled, and their eyes, even as they close, discover the true nature of the life promised to the just.

The Book of Wisdom does not go any further. Permeated with the Greek spirit, it calls the condition of the just man after death, immortality, ἀφθαρσία. But if it is no more explicit than its predecessors regarding the concrete conditions of after-life, so that, while it is legitimate to distinguish in the Bible both a Greek and a Jewish current in the representations of life after death, it is especially important to realize that both currents show the same reserve, the same soberness of the imagination. Only one point is really affirmed: "they . . . are in the hand of God,"[97] and "shall abide with him;"[98] "they shall receive the splendid crown, the beauteous diadem, from the hand of the Lord."[99] And, as in the Books of Daniel and of Maccabees, the affirmation of this life received from God is only born in the midst of tribulation, of persecution. Death is not necessarily bloody,[100] but it is bloody death which gives its meaning to the choice imposed on the just man, a choice which can be as cruel as any. It is a question of choosing an absurd life[101] against all human experience.[102] It is only through the folly of this choice,

186

through this apparent death to the instincts and calculations of nature that certitude is born. To understand that life consists in rediscovering God, it is necessary to have sacrificed all creatures to Him.

Thus, the hope of life in the Old Testament, whatever its foundations in some sort of natural belief, does not come from a progressive refining, but is rather the end product of a faith —the naive faith of the pious Israelite, convinced that, if every one did his duty, the people would live in happiness and peace; the purified faith of the prophets who, though they had plumbed the depths of sin, trust now only in God, and whom all deceptions confirm in their expectation of a world renewed by God; the enlightened faith of the martyrs who see their sacrifice opening the doors of this better world to them.

However pure it may be, the hope for life in the Old Testament remains threatened with deviations and degradations. Popular faith in the superiority of a good conscience does not exclude the temptations of a success-morality. The messianic hope of the prophets becomes, among the people, filled with human and nationalistic dreams. The expectation of eternal life by the just man who has been tried, is encumbered by a need for revenge against the persecutor. These worldly components are inevitable, since the life which is expected, which is affirmed, remains undecipherable, separated from man by a dark veil. The prophet, the martyr, at the apex of their experience, pass through this veil, but without being able to express the unutterable. In Jesus Christ alone is life revealed. Also, life assumes a new form in the New Testament.

In the Synoptics, life is still a purely eschatological grandeur. Moreover, the word is not very frequent in their pages, and it is almost always modified by a note which excludes all equivocation: "Eternal life."[103] In this way, it is distinguished from the present existence which is limited by death. Even where this distinction is not found, the opposition is clear.[104] This

187

"eternal" life is reserved for the future; it is acquired, one enters into it.[105] The description of the Last Judgment seems to place its coming at the end of time,[106] while the parable of the wicked rich man makes Lazarus, in the bosom of Abraham, the contemporary of men living on earth.[107] Perhaps we must not necessarily seek, in these representations adapted to Jewish visions of the time, the precise formulation which our imagination would prefer. Jesus' reserve is obvious. Eternal life is a revelation of life after death.

Jesus seems to add nothing to the certitude of Daniel or of the Book of Maccabees. There is no new feature in His description. Or, more precisely, Jesus does not describe eternal life any more clearly than did Daniel or the Book of Maccabees. The revelation of Jesus does not consist in describing, but in affirming. The prophets made affirmations themselves. It would be impossible to be more categorical than Daniel or the martyrs of Antiochus. But they affirmed as witnesses, as spokesmen, transported beyond themselves by a divine force. Jesus speaks without raising His voice, as of a familiar subject, of His own horizon. Eternal life is His personal kingdom;[108] He admits into it, those who, consciously or not, have loved Him on earth.[109] He speaks of it with the natural air of a man who knows He is destined to die and to rise again; He lives beyond death. He speaks of it from the inside, and that is why He reveals it in the proper sense. In His words, and even more in His actions, in His spontaneous reactions, we find ourselves in immediate contact with the world of life.

This certitude of having encountered life is one of the features which mark the physiognomy of St. Paul. The word is much more frequent in his writings than in the Synoptics. In the first Epistles, he concurs exactly with the usage of the Synoptics. Christian life is a watch in the night, until the time when Jesus shall come and when "we [shall] live together with him."[110] In the first letter to the Corinthians, the theologian who reflects on the Christian fact appears. The life promised to the believer is given him by Jesus Christ. It is an absolutely new reality in the world, without any common dimension with natural life. To express this divergence, Paul resorts to the comparison of the two Adams. To the first man, head of a mankind which is living but subject to failure, to corruption, to death, is opposed the second Adam, "a life-giving spirit," head of a glorious, immortal, spiritual, mankind.[111]

This certitude is better than a hope: it is an experience. In his daily life, and in particular, in his apostolate, in this effort which he carries on without pause, Paul feels himself transformed. Urged on by the charity of Christ, dead through love, his life no longer belongs to him, it belongs to Him who died for him.[112] In turn, this life becomes a death, a daily death.[113] The miracle is this, that this death suffered for Jesus is revealed to be a mysterious manifestation of the death of Jesus Himself,[114] but also is His risen life. In the impotence of the apostle is revealed the weakness of the crucified, incapable of escaping death, but through it, showing forth the sovereign power of God who draws forth life from death.[115]

The Epistle to the Romans is the most magnificent dogmatic commentary on this interior experience. What St. Paul lived in his flesh becomes the type of the Christian life. In the Epistles to the Corinthians, natural life, radically distinct from the new life in Christ, still appears as life. This is because it was always a question then of physical existence. Here, St. Paul envisages the moral life of man without Christ and names it death. This is because this life is under the sign of sin, because sin and death, those two sinister and conspiratorial forces, rule the world.[116]

Condemnation by the Law, and its sanction of death, make the whole tragedy of this situation burst forth, a situation which manifests God's judgment.[117] But God condemns only in order to save. Jesus dies for sinners, for the condemned.[118] He took upon Himself the condemnation of the sinner, but it was for the purpose of raising up and giving to the world, reconciled to God, a new life. The Christian participates in this activity of Christ's through Baptism. Dying to his old life, renouncing sin, he finds in the resurrection of Christ the divine strength to be born again to a new life.[119] Thus, "eternal" life is no longer just the life which the Christian expects along with the revelation of another world; it is, even in this world, a life in the Spirit, still hidden, and destined to blossom forth through the death of the body. Between the life of the Christian on earth and the life which awaits him beyond death, there is no separation, no obstacle which was not already surmounted from the moment he received the charity of Christ.[120]

When we go from St. Paul to St. John, we have the impression of going from a battlefield to a triumphant celebration. Life has conquered. The past tense is used: "The life was made known,"[121] "He who hears my word . . . has passed from death to life."[122] The prince of this world is cast out,[123] the new world is born. This difference is perhaps not the most profound. Paul, too, affirms that "the former things . . . are made new,"[124] and defies death ever to separate him from Jesus.[125] And John knows that, if he who eats the flesh of Christ receives life,[126] it is in order to rise on the last day.[127]

The real difference is therefore not in the doctrine. It is in the proper originality of two religious temperaments. For both, Jesus is life, victory over death and sin. But St. Paul writes: "Christ, your life,"[128] or else: "For to me to live is Christ,"[129] or again: "It is now no longer I that live, but Christ lives in me."[130] He lives "that the life also of Jesus may be made manifest in our mortal flesh."[131] Paul does not separate the life of Christ from the life of the Church, from his own existence. How could he? In his interior combats and his missionary labors, in his anguishes and his conquests, in the Christian communities which he established, he sees Christ growing, building His own body, manifesting the power of His life. He no longer

190

owns himself, the life of Jesus has swept away all barriers to itself in him.

St. John is no less close to Jesus, but His own person seems to disappear before the figure which he contemplates. Jesus is not his, John's life. He is, without any other qualification, life. Life has revealed itself. John has seen it, has touched it. He delivers this revelation to men. It is not enough to preserve the ineradicable remembrance of the Galilean days: it is necessary to penetrate the unfathomable mystery of the Lord. In calling Him life, John seeks to give Jesus His real dimensions. The source of all the forces of creation, the accomplishment of the expectation of Israel and of the supreme wish of man, His figure, the center of the world, rises up to an infinite degree above John, into the divine heights, out of the grasp of death. St. John, with fascinated eyes, sees the living waters, the unfailing source of all life, the inexhaustible fount offered to all those who are thirsty, flowing from the opened heart of his Lord.

2. TO POSSESS THE EARTH

Israel's experiences gradually gave very rich meaning to the words concerning life. Still, though it became broader and deeper, the idea of life did not change its meaning. Also, it was accessible to every man, on the condition that he felt within himself the action of an interior force which transformed him, the action of a life. In fact, to arrive at these affirmations of a life superior to ordinary existence, Israel had had to follow an exceptional itinerary. Life was, initially, for the Hebrew people, life in the Promised Land.

This life was its heritage. Around this theme there revolve a certain number of words and expressions, which present in a more concrete fashion than those concerning life, the people's own experiences and give its hopes a well-characterized appearance.

191

The first promises made to Abraham have as their object the possession of Palestine.[132] Originally, as St. Paul justly remarked, this promise is not linked with any commandment whose reward it would be. The reward is in the very faith which adheres to the word of Yahweh. The Book of Genesis, with its cycles of stories grouped around the places consecrated by the manifestations of Yahweh, was suitable for permeating the Hebrew people not only with a wondering desire for the land flowing with milk and honey, but especially with a sacred attraction for the Lord's own dwelling-place.[133] Alongside Adam, rebellious toward God, head of a race given over to sin, Genesis raises Abraham, the faithful servant, root of a blessed race. In place of paradise lost, it promises the patriarch, in a mysterious future time, possession of this blessed land. The idyllic tone of so many of these pages gives a presentiment of a land which, while not Eden, is still no longer the land given over to weeds and thorns. But Genesis is more than idyllic. It has a sacred grandeur. It aims to give the impression that, if the life of the patriarchs on this earth was filled with good things, this was because they had abandoned themselves to Yahweh, had believed in Him. Likewise, if the generation which came out of Egypt saw itself totally excluded from the Promised Land, it was because it doubted Yahweh.[134]

The history of the conquest, as the tradition of Israel handed it down, contributed also to anchor the people in their faith, to show them that a sovereign initiative by God had placed them in possession of their country without any help on their part. Such is the meaning of the miracles of the Book of Josue. The taking of Jericho, of Hai, the marvelous victory of Gabaon, attest to the fact that Yahweh truly "delivered into the hands of his people,"[135] the land which they occupy. In its traditions Israel keeps,[136] along with the memory of fabulous exploits, the feeling of the gratuitous nature of its destiny.

Awareness of this gratuitousness persists throughout the entire Old Testament. The word set aside to denote it is the verb *yarach*, which denotes not a conquest by arms, but a taking possession, even, oftentimes, of the dispossession of the former proprietor to his successor's benefit, and almost always of the entering into possession of a good over which one had no title at all. If Eliezar is to inherit from Abraham, it is only because of the absence of a legitimate heir;[137] a chastisement from God is needed before the thistle takes possession of the territory of Israel,[138] the pelican and the hedgehog the ruins of Edom.[139] This aspect of intrusion is generally hidden by the ordinary translation of the Septuagint, χληρονομεῖν, and its Latin equivalent, *hereditare*, one of the characteristic words of the old Psalter.[140] Besides, and this is a curious detail, apart from in the psalms, Ecclesiasticus, and Isaias,[141] the word is missing from the Vulgate. Perhaps St. Jerome rejected this word, which evokes a legal and statutory inheritance, because he was in the presence of examples of expropriation. In general, he translates *yarach* by *possideo*,[142] which has the awkward feature of erasing the aspect of coming into possession,[143] and especially obscures the essentially free nature of this taking possession.

Deuteronomy consecrated this usage of *yarach* to denote the taking possession of Palestine by Israel;[144] it underscores an idea which is dear to it: Palestine is the country where everything is free, where one finds, all prepared to receive everyone:

> . . . a land with fine, large cities that you did not build, with houses full of goods of all sorts that you did not garner, with cisterns that you did not dig, with vineyards and olive groves that you did not plant.[145]

A land so different from Egypt, that had to be watered by hand,[146] where one was obliged to work hours on end at the waterwheel, whereas this land "drinks in rain from the heavens,"[147] and irrigation depends only on the grace of God. The fervor of the praise may seem naive to one who compares the abundant harvests of Egypt with the poor fields of Judea, but it can help us to understand why Israel, comparing the climate of Palestine with the immutable floods of the Nile, should have had such a vivid image of a God, sovereign master over His gifts.

Moreover, Deuteronomy is not the inventor of these perspectives. Long before it, one of the ancient accounts of the history of Abraham is built up on the word *yarach*. It is repeated five times in four verses, and has the precise sense of "heir."[148] Abraham is growing old without children; his inheritance will pass to a stranger; is it to be he who will gain the inheritance promised by God? Without going into details, Yahweh is content to confirm that the inheritance is indeed intended for Abraham and his race. All thought of conquest, or even of personal initiative, is set aside here. More than a gratuitous gift, it is the pure expectation of divine action.

There is another word frequently associated with *yarach*, a word which underscores even more clearly the gratuitous nature of the conquest. Both as a verb, under the form *nahal*, and as a feminine noun, *nahalah*, this word denotes the action by which one grants to someone his portion. It is a word from the vocabulary of inheritance, and *nahalah* is the proper word to signify inheritance. It is the word used by Naboth to Achab who covets his vineyard: "[May] the Lord . . . not let me give thee the inheritance of my fathers."[149] Since this inheritance is often the result of an apportionment, the word *heleq* is often joined with *nahalah*, which indicates the portion distributed to each one of the heirs. Lea and Rachel, on the day when they break with their father in order to link their destinies with that of Jacob, declare to him: "Have we any share or heritage left in our father's house?"[150]

Like *yarach*, *nahal* is almost exclusively a word of the promised land; like it, too, it constitutes one of the key words of Deuteronomy.[151] It is not, however, of the latter's invention. Already in two ancient passages of Exodus, *nahal* signifies to enter into possession of the land given by God.[152] From that point on, the expression is fixed, and it is to make common cause

194

with one or the other of the two verbs, but especially with *yarach*, to enter into possession of the land (*'eres*), that is, of the country.

Among the prophets, the theme is missing in Isaias. We have noted that, for the prophet of Jerusalem, the great man in the history of Israel is David much more than Moses. His thought does not stray from the streets and heights of Sion, his hopes are centered in "the mountain of the house of the Lord,"[153] of God "whose fire is in Sion, and his furnace in Jerusalem,"[154] who, from its high places, "as a torrent overflowing,"[155] submerges sinners and purifies Jerusalem from the "filth of the daughters of Sion . . . and the blood," while spreading over it a "cloud by day and a smoke and the brightness of a flaming fire in the night."[156] When Isaias, in the face of the luxury of the boisterous capital, dreams of Yahweh's designs, all images seem to disappear before the consuming splendor of this glory.

One of them, however, persists: that of Paradise. Vision of peace, glimpsed by the glow of lightning, it brings us back to the days of Eden, into a creation which is all goodness. On two occasions, this paradisiacal theme is linked with that of the holy mountain of God:

And in the last days the mountain of the house of the Lord shall be prepared on the top of mountains, and it shall be exalted above the hills: and all nations shall flow unto it.
. . . .
. . . and they shall turn their swords into ploughshares and their spears into sickles. Nation shall not lift up sword against nation: neither shall they be exercised any more to war.[157]

The wolf shall dwell with the lamb: and the leopard shall lie down with the kid.
. . . .
. . . and the lion shall eat straw like the ox. And the sucking child shall play on the hole of the asp; and the weaned child shall thrust his hand into the den of the basilisk.
They shall not hurt, nor shall they kill in all my holy mountain.[158]

There is no question that it would be possible to take possession of these splendors, both fabulously far away and terribly near at the same time. They can only be waited for, in trembling and in faith. The theme of the promised land disappears in favor of that of Paradise, and the latter becomes more and more that of access to the glory of Yahweh.

New perspectives fill the last chapters, with their concern for the exiles. In the poem whose superb beginning—"Give praise, O thou barren, that bearest not"[159]—inspired St. Paul, the prophet, evoking the promises made of yore to Abraham and to his posterity, sets up, as the heritage of the new community, the entire world:

> For thou shalt pass on to the right hand and to the left: And thy seed shall inherit the Gentiles.[160]

This is something quite different from the blessing formerly promised to Abraham, and from which the peoples could not benefit except in some mysterious manner. Even in giving to the promise its strongest sense: "All the nations shall be blessed in thee,"[161] the inheritance promised to the patriarch remains a limited region: he is to inherit a country. Here the heritage is the world, and Yahweh can give it, because "He is called the God of all the earth."[162] For the rest, the material features of this empire remain totally unspecified, while the finale of the poem, in associating the heritage with the gift of justice, places it in a spiritual framework:

> This is the inheritance of the servants of the Lord and their justice with me, saith the Lord.[163]

Elsewhere, the promised inheritance is no longer the prerogative of the people, but of a specific category, the just:

> But he that putteth his trust in me shall inherit [nahal] the land and shall possess [yarach] my holy mount.[164]

> And thy people shall be all just: they shall inherit [yarach] the land for ever.[165]

The just—representatives of Israel; we are entering into the

196

sapiential perspectives. The pious Israelite takes unto himself the threats and the promises addressed to the people by the prophets. This individual transposition explains how the just man can "enter into possession of the holy mountain" of Yahweh. This mountain is Mount Sion, the hill of the Temple. It is well known in the prophetic tradition. It is the formidable place where the thrice-holy God lives in His glory, the mysterious point through which man will one day re-enter the lost garden. But there had never been any talk about possessing it. In order for the connection with *yarach* to be possible, it was necessary for the theme of the revelation of God on His mountain to be linked with the theme of the entering into possession of the country. This link itself was only possible if the people had passed through God's judgment, if a small remnant had held fast in its faith. The more its situation is precarious, the more its faith needs to depend on the ancient oracles. These are, in fact, the perennial themes which keep coming back. Those of the inheritance:

And I will bring forth a seed out of Jacob, and out of Juda a possessor [*yarach*] of my mountains: and my elect shall inherit [*yarach*] it, and my servants shall dwell there;[166]

those of the country transformed by unheard-of fertility, as in Osee:

And the plains shall be turned to folds of flocks, and the valley of Achor into a place for the herds to lie down in.[167]

those of the holy mountain, the new Eden:

The wolf and the lamb shall feed together; the lion and the ox shall eat straw; and dust shall be the serpent's food. They shall not hurt nor kill in all my holy mountain.[168]

those of the gathering of all the nations around the glory of Yahweh:

And they shall bring all your brethren out of all nations for a gift to the Lord, upon horses and in chariots and in litters and on mules and in coaches, to my holy mountain Jerusalem, saith the Lord.[169]

Were these images taken literally? Undoubtedly, there was no giving up—never less than at this time of humiliations—of the old hope of a sovereign intervention by God coming to establish a new world. But there was visible a first fulfillment of this promise in the peace reserved for the just man faithful to Yahweh. One of the poems of the series, in fact, by a bold transposition, applies the predictions of the return from exile to individual destiny. If he observes Yahweh's commandments, the Israelite will enjoy all His promises:

> Then shalt thou be delighted in the Lord, and I will lift thee up above the high places of the earth and will feed thee with the inheritance [nahalah] of Jacob thy father.[170]

It is clear that the faithful soul could understand this promise only as a participation, on his own level, in the collective promise. As long as it was a question of material goods, it was easy to imagine. Every Israelite benefits from the prosperity of Palestine. But what can a portion of Yahweh's mountain signify? It is not a question of a plot on the slopes of Sion. This participation in the glory which radiates from the sanctuary, this mysterious access to Eden, transposed into an individual destiny, necessarily has an interior meaning. The heart of the just man learns to savor the blessings of God. Does he not read, in these same poems, that if Yahweh has His temple "in the high and holy place," the sanctuary of Sion, He also dwells with "a contrite and humble spirit."[171]

Osee and Jeremias, who live in the anguish of catastrophes and in a desolate land, return to the promises of the inheritance. Osee announces, after the pardon of Yahweh and the new betrothals, a second return from Egypt. Israel will rediscover its vineyards, but in an unrecognizable country. The valley of Achor, the pass which recalled the entry of Josue into Palestine,[172] losing its desolateness, shall be cheerful to the point where it will be called "an opening of hope."[173] The land will be changed into a paradise:

And in that day I will make a covenant with them, with the beasts of the field and with the fowls of the air and with the creeping things of the earth: and I will destroy the bow and the sword and war out of the land: and I will make them sleep secure.[174]

Jeremias seems scarcely to develop the theme of Eden; the miracle of God forgiving the sins of Israel and bringing it back into its own land, is itself quite striking. Rather than abandon himself to dreams of an upheaval in nature, the prophet dares, in the last hours of a hopeless siege, in the horror of the desolate city, to evoke the "voice of joy and the voice of gladness, the voice of the bridegroom and the voice of the bride,"[175] the simple joys of peace. On the other hand, the theme of inheritance is frequent in Jeremias. Palestine is the land given by Yahweh to His people,[176] the return from the exile is a re-entering into possession of the patrimony.[177]

Ezechiel is acquainted with the theme. He makes the mountains of Israel hear the voice of Yahweh:

And I will bring men upon you, my people Israel: and they shall possess [yarach] thee for their inheritance. And thou shalt be their inheritance [nahalah].[178]

The return from exile, moreover, is for him something other than a return to the past. It is the establishment of a purified people, consecrated to the glory of Yahweh. Ezechiel symbolizes this renewal by means of a new apportionment of the country, different from that of Josue. An altogether idealistic apportionment, in which all the tribes receive exactly the same share.[179] Thus the geographical features of the land are subordinated to its sacred, almost liturgical, character. Entirely consecrated to the service of Yahweh, it has the Temple as its center. The sanctuary itself becomes the new Eden. It is built on a high mountain, undoubtedly that of Isaias.[180] From under its threshold flows the river of life, whose waters, spreading over its banks a marvelous abundance, will finally go on to give life to the Dead Sea.[181] In this way, this sinister region will become "like the garden of Yahweh,"[182] just as Abraham saw it before the destruction of the guilty cities.

Another element contributes to reinforcing the religious aspect of the re-establishment of the people, and to making Palestine a land given by God. It is no longer the homeland of Israelites scattered by exile, but of those who have known total ruination. Jeremias already had written to the exiles, in Babylon, to make them understand that the hope of Israel did not reside in the survivors in Palestine, but in them, the captives.[183] Ezechiel pronounces the final sentence against those who, dwelling on the land which Abraham had inherited [yarach],[184] thought themselves the legitimate owners of this inheritance (morachah). Their claims are rejected by Yahweh. This is the situation in which Jesus will find the Jews, glorying in having Abraham as their father,[185] and He will, in His turn, condemn them: "The father from whom you are is the devil."[186] Blood serves for naught, since "from these stones, God can raise up sons to Abraham."[187] St. Paul, too, takes up this theme of inheritance, refused to the flesh and turned over to those who, renouncing human hopes, place their faith in God's promises. He traces this law of dispossession of the natural heir in favor of the children of promise as far back as Ismael, the normal heir who is supplanted by Isaac, the son of Abraham obtained from God through hoping against hope.[188] He sees in Sara the type of the Christian church, and in Agar the type of Synagogue. In placing their pride in their carnal ancestry, the Jews, renouncing Isaac's privilege, attached themselves to Ismael's lineage. The bonds of blood give them no other rights.[189] They misunderstand the entire point of Genesis and miss one of the major themes of the Old Testament.

This theme appears in the return from exile. Did St. Paul see this, when, unexpectedly, he associated the vision of the new Jerusalem descending from heaven with the figure of Sara? It is impossible to know. It is a fact, at any rate, at the time when

Jeremias and Ezechiel could only see Israel's future through the death and rupture of the exile, that there was being born in this people a new vision of the heritage which awaited it.

Three psalms, all three laden with promises, reflect this theme. Psalm 68, after a long cry of distress, ends on this vision of hope:

> For the LORD hears the poor,
>   and his own who are in bonds he spurns not.
> . . . .
> For God will save Sion
>   and rebuild the cities of Juda.
> They shall dwell in the land and own it [yarach],
>   and the descendants of his servants shall inherit it [nahal],
>   and those who love his name shall inhabit it.[190]

The perspectives are those of the end of captivity; the return from exile, the ruins rebuilt, the people restored in their inheritance. But this people is not the national community; they are composed of "the servants of Yahweh," of those "who love his name." A new feature of the psalm is the name, "the poor," that these believers give themselves. These poor people of Israel[191] have become aware that they are the heirs of the religion of Yahweh, and with it, of the promises of the land. In repeating them to themselves, what exactly did they expect? No doubt they did not lose hope of some day being masters of their homeland, but their sincere fidelity to God saw in this event, not so much the triumph of personal ambitions as the conversion of their people, and Palestine living under God's dominion.

Psalms 2 and 46 also take up the theme of the expectations which extended the heritage of Israel to the very dimensions of the world.[192] Psalm 2 puts the inheritance of the nations back into the hands of the Messias, established by Yahweh on the throne of His holy city, Sion:

> Ask of me and I will give you
>   the nations for an inheritance [nahalah]
>   and the ends of the earth for your possession.[193]

201

Psalm 46 also has Sion and its sanctuary as its central theme, but makes it the capital of the nations:

> He brings peoples under us;
> nations under our feet.
> He chooses for us our inheritance [*nahalah*],
> the glory of Jacob, whom he loves.[194]

Whether it be a question of receiving as inheritance a regenerated homeland or the entire world, prostrate before the glory of Yahweh, it is, in all these cases, the hope of Israel which is exalted. It could be engulfed by political and human ambitions, but it was also capable of entertaining the expectation of the kingdom of God. Everything depended on the choice that was made.

Certain sapiential texts show how this choice was determined. At times, the expected inheritance is truly interior. Naturally, we have to pick and choose among the texts. A certain number of them use the idea of inheritance only metaphorically:

> Honor is the portion [*nahalah*] of wise men,
> but fools inherit shame.[195]

Nachal and *yachar* may therefore designate any enjoyment at all, without any reference to Israel's own inheritance. In the Book of Job, for example, the reflection, repeated three times in almost identical terms:

This is the portion [*heleq*] of a wicked man from God,
the inheritance [*nahalah*] an oppressor receives from the Almighty,[196]

excludes all perspectives of the Promised Land. Likewise, the maxim:

> He who seduces the upright into an evil way
> will himself fall into his own pit.
> And blameless men will gain prosperity,[197]

remains at the level of the most pedestrian wisdom. After all, natural metaphors suffice to explain these expressions. This is not the case in the first collection of Proverbs, of the appeal of

202

Wisdom to her faithful. Her voice, which seems to be the interior echo in each Israelite of the word of Yahweh to His people in the Law and the prophets, proposes to them an inheritance which also has its place in the framework of the heritage of Israel:

> On the way of duty I walk,
>   along the paths of justice,
> Granting wealth [*nahal*] to those who love me,
>   and filling their treasuries.[198]

It is, in any event, impossible to hesitate any longer in recognizing a transposition of the promise when we see the formula "enter into possession of the earth" denoting the individual reward of the just man. The expression appears in two psalms, both of sapiential inspiration:

> When a man fears the LORD,
>   he shows him the way he should choose.
> He abides in prosperity,
>   and his descendants inherit [*yarach*] the land.[199]

While it is not certain that the mention of Yahweh's conduct is a harking back to Exodus, not certain even that "abides" is a conscious recalling of the theme of abiding in the promised land,[200] there can, at any rate, be no doubt that the posterity of the just is a reference to Abraham, and inheritance of the land the fulfillment of the promise made to the patriarch. His beneficiary has become the "man who fears the Lord." The same allusion to the descendants of the just man is found again on several occasions in Psalm 36.[201] The latter is, as it were, pervaded by the refrain: "[they] . . . shall possess the land."[202] Verse 11 presents the equivalent of the third beatitude according to St. Matthew: "the meek shall possess the land."[203]

What land is involved here? Is the individual transfer an interior transfer? It must be acknowledged that, if in Psalm 24 most of the space is taken up with the sentiment of sin and a docile and profound confidence in the goodness of God, Psalm 36, on the other hand, is filled with a candid assurance of an altogether material happiness, the unfailing lot of the just man, despite the passing triumphs of evil. The expectation here is certainly less pure than in the final chapters of the Book of Isaias. The concern for morality doubtless justifies these illusions, but it is rather quickly compromised by mixed motives. The Bible is not all on the same level. Psalm 118, for example, raises us up again:

"Your decrees are my inheritance forever [nahal]."[204] This is already "an eternal inheritance," and it is simply docility to God. Can we go further?

But have we not gotten completely away from the theme of the Promised Land? True, there is no longer any question here of the earth, but its image is not far off. It flowers under the form of the sharing among the tribes, in which the sons of Levi, deprived of geographical territory, received for their share Yahweh Himself: "I will be your portion and your heritage."[205] Of the Levites themselves, the formula was only relatively true, since they owned lands and houses among each of the tribes. But the formula seemed more than once to express quite accurately the desire of hearts directed exclusively toward God. The same Psalm 118, in its rather dull style, proclaims: "My part is to keep your words."[206] But Psalm 15 is more vibrant:

> O LORD, my allotted portion [heleq] and my cup,
> you it is who hold fast my lot.
> For me the measuring lines have fallen on pleasant sites;
> fair to me indeed is my inheritance [nahalah].[207]

But it is from a heart weighed down by suffering that the affirmation, the only one capable of turning aside the fascination of despair, burst forth:

> Whom else have I in heaven?
> And when I am with you, the earth delights me not.
> Though my flesh and my heart waste away,
> God is the rock of my heart and my portion [heleq] forever.[208]

It is certain that the hope expressed in the preceding verse: "You will receive me in glory,"[209] still remains obscure and groping. But that is not the important fact. The important thing is the affirmation, lucid and bold, that God is preferable to everything else on earth, and that the supreme happiness is to live with Him. The Christian heaven is nothing more than this. All the representations of an after-life may be faulty—this is unimportant. What matters is that heaven is not imagined, it is substantially affirmed.

The same religion could therefore promise to "possess the land" and to "possess God." This is because possession of the land was the object of a promise, not the fruit of a desire. Biblical tradition has multiplied the features which recalled to the people the gratuitousness and the precariousness of their establishment. Never did it condemn the spontaneous instinct of man to exploit the earth and to found his domain therein, to "plant and to build." But at all times it maintains that, while his existence is the normal destiny, it is only assured to those who do not make it their reason for living. This is already the spirit of the evangelical formula "Seek ye first the kingdom of God and his justice, and the rest shall be given you besides."[210]

To possess the land; if the promise echoes down to the final pages of the Old Testament, it is because it has not yet been fulfilled. It is because the wicked are still in the land, because peace does not as yet constitute its frontiers, because Yahweh has not yet exterminated all its enemies. The story of Jesus, in fact, shows clearly that the people of that time feverishly awaited the day when God would take His cause in hand and when, abolishing in the land and beyond, the power of the wicked, He would finally grant peace to His faithful people.

Jesus responds to this expectation by announcing the Kingdom of God. The theme of the Promised Land disappears almost entirely from the New Testament, at least in its consecrated form: to inherit the earth. More than any other, apparently, it was earthly, and even its spiritualization in the sapiential tradition remained equivocal, for it continuously directed hope toward a temporal reward. Nevertheless, the theme persists by transforming itself. While the word "land" disappears, the word "inherit" remains. The Christian formula is to "inherit the kingdom."[211]

This expresses the entire relationship between the two Testaments. Interpreting the expectation of a kingdom come down from heaven, independent of the powers of the earth, it infinitely surpasses all the perspectives of Israel. Presenting this gift of God as an inheritance, it shows the fulfillment therein of all the promises made to Israel from the time of the patriarchs. The Epistle to the Galatians,[212] the Epistle to the Hebrews,[213] show us the reflection working to justify this conviction, which is Christianity itself. Independent of these demonstrative arrays, the formula is simple: "to inherit the kingdom" is the living testimony of the common faith.

It finds itself fulfilling to the letter the most audacious expression of Israel's hope: "possess my holy mount."[214] Combining the themes of the promised land, the sanctuary of Sion, dwelling-place of the glory of Yahweh and the new Eden, this formula, unique in the Bible, had appeared in a poem which was already sapiential, in which the hopes of the people, having become personal hopes, tended to lose their concrete force. Still, everything was accomplished in Jesus Christ. The paradise which He opens unto His own is the very house of His Father, the glory of the living God. And those whom He introduces therein do not enter as strangers, but into their own inheritance, for they are sons.[215]

3. YAHWEH'S HERITAGE

One of the most ancient names given by Israel to its homeland is "inheritance of Yahweh." The expression is repeated four times in the Books of Kings,[216] and might date back as far as the text in which Palestine is called the inheritance of Israel.[217] The two formulas are not only akin, but complementary. Israel cannot claim its heritage unless there is someone from whom to receive it. It was aware at all times of having established itself by dispossessing the native occupants of its territory. In naming it the heritage of Yahweh, it legitimized its conquest, but affirmed very clearly its gratuitous nature.

At the same time, it distinguished Yahweh from all the other divinities of the earth. In the neighboring religions, the gods had their particular domains. Their names, *Ba'al, Ba'alat,* generally associated with a noticeable geographical feature, a spring, a forest, a city or a mountain, show precisely that they were the proprietors of these places. Calling Palestine the heritage of Yahweh, was, in one sense, to utilize the same concepts, but to interpret them in a contrary sense. It indicated that, amidst all regions, Yahweh had chosen a privileged area. This idea of preference, of choice, was unknown to the other gods who had, on the contrary, no existence except through the waters, the trees, or the temples which they animated.[218] The Lord who had chosen Palestine for His own heritage may have been as yet far from being called the only God, but His method of possessing the land was already unique. As soon as Yahwism is born, the attitude which it requires in man and the image which it implies of God, are those of the religion of the true God.

Thus we see David despairing at being obliged to flee the "inheritance of Yahweh." In his exile, his enemies wanted to force him to "serve strange gods." They may indeed cause him to tremble at perishing "far from the face of the Lord." They cannot prevent his heart, even in a pagan land, from placing this heritage above all goods, from remaining fixed on the true God.

The inheritance of Yahweh, moreover, soon ceases to be the land of Palestine. It becomes the people itself. It is so already in one of the passages of the Books of Kings: at the moment when Samuel, pouring on Saul the oil which consecrates him king, addresses to him the formula that we might consider liturgical—"The Lord hath anointed thee to be prince over his inheritance."[219] It is so in an ancient page of Exodus, where Moses, after the episode of the golden calf, beseeches the Lord on behalf of his people: "Pardon us our wickedness and sins, and receive us as your own."[220]

Only Jeremias continues to denote the country itself by means of the formula "Yahweh's inheritance." For him it is not a question at all of an inability to separate God from the soil. On the contrary, it is to inculcate in the people that their native land, before belonging to them, is Yahweh's own property and that it is defiled by idolatry:

. . . they have defiled my land with the carcasses of their idols, and they have filled my inheritance with their abominations.[221]

It is Jeremias who, in his struggle against the idols, identified the Promised Land with the holy land, the land that sin sullies, since it belongs to the Lord.[222]

Moreover, the people, as much as the land, are, for Jeremias, the inheritance of Yahweh. In this traditional theme, the prophet discovers the depths of kindness and tolerance which already are revealing a God whose heart is close to man's. He it is who complains:

I have forsaken my house, I have left my inheritance [*nahalah*], I have given my dear soul into the hand of her enemies. My inheritance [*nahalah*] is become to me as a lion in the wood.

. . . .

Many pastors have destroyed my vineyard: they have trodden my portion [*nahalah*] under foot, they have changed my delightful portion [*heleq*] into a desolate wilderness.[223]

The inheritance is also the devastated soil which the people ruined because of their leaders, the pastors to whom God had entrusted the care of His inheritance. The theme of the inheritance links up with that of the flock and gives it one of its fundamental traits: the flock of the Lord belongs to its shepherd because it has been chosen. People, inheritance, flock, these three words weave in and out throughout the Bible.

Feed thy people with thy rod, the flock of thy inheritance.[224]

The association is common enough to come into play even when the people is not Israel. Isaias, announcing the era of peace that Yahweh will introduce on earth, sees the reconciliation of Israel and its adversaries. The two ancient enemies come to take part in the blessing and the privilege of the chosen people:

Blessed be my people of Egypt, and the work of my hands to the Assyrian. But Israel is my inheritance.[225]

Deuteronomy, without matching Jeremias' depth, appeals, like him, to the sentiment of preference which made God choose His people, His inheritance.[226] The prophets take up the same theme, in the same images:

I was angry with my people, I have polluted my inheritance.[227]

Return for the sake of thy servants, the tribes of thy inheritance.[228]

And the Lord shall possess Juda his portion in the sanctified land; and he shall yet choose Jerusalem.[229]

The same image of the portion shared and chosen by Yahweh occurs in the Canticle of Moses, at the end of Deuteronomy:

> While the Lord's own portion was Jacob,
> his hereditary share was Israel.[230]

The psalms, too, in particular, associate the inheritance with the people. Though Psalm 78 sees therein the land, and in particular, Jerusalem—

> O God, the nations have come into your inheritance,
> they have defiled your holy temple,
> they have laid Jerusalem in ruins—[231]

the common association is that of the inheritance and the people.[232] Twice in this context, the theme of the shepherd comes up:

> Save your people, and bless your inheritance;
> feed them, and carry them forever![233]

209

And he chose David, his servant,
  and took him from the sheepfolds;
From following the ewes he brought him
  to shepherd Jacob, his people,
  and Israel, his inheritance.[234]

The shepherd of sheep becomes the shepherd of men, charged with a flock which does not belong to him, which is the inheritance of Yahweh. Thus Peter, the lake fisherman, becomes the fisher of men, charged with letting down a net which the angels of God must pull up. The constants in the biblical themes are the constants of God's ways.

The image of Yahweh's inheritance demonstrates in a striking way what we can already call the human traits of God. Like a shepherd or a vinetender, Yahweh concerns Himself with His inheritance. He has chosen a plot of land in this world where He takes up his work, and He repeats there, on His own account, the eternal action of man: to plant, to build, and to wed. It is in this domain that Israel lives. From this time on, its hopes have to be reoriented: its own grape-harvests, its houses, its loves, pass into the background. The soil of Palestine is destined to give God His harvest, His home, His bride.

These hopes are fraught with risk. God does not own His inheritance the way Baal reigns over his kingdom, without concern and without history. The only events which can animate the nature-divinities are the invariable succession of the seasons; and the imagination of the Egyptian and Canaanitic mythologies had exhausted its strength in introducing, in the legends of Osis or Adonis, some drama into these congealed divinities. In Yahweh, the drama is immediate, overwhelming. Not a mythology, a far-fetched evocation of a fabulous past, it is a continuing reality. It is the very history of the world which re-echoes in Him. This is an authentic preparation for the Incarnation. Not in the appearance of a figure from a literary creation with a more or less pronounced personality, but in the revelation of a God who lives in the world of men.

4. THE VINEYARD

The most precious of harvests is that of the vineyard. The vineyard is, in Israel, the type of that which attaches a man to the soil. The sin of David had been to take the wife of Urias, the sin of Achab is despoiling Naboth of his vineyard.[235] The sin of the rich is to deprive the poor man of this harvest:

For you have devoured the vineyard; and the spoil of the poor is in your house.[236]

When Amos imagines the splendor of a Palestine flourishing in the peace of God, he sees the harvests corresponding to the grape-gathering and succeeding one another without interruption:

Behold the days come, saith the Lord, when the ploughman shall overtake the reaper and the treader of grapes him that soweth seed.[237]

But the image of the vineyard is privileged:

And the mountains shall drop sweetness, and every hill shall be tilled.[238]

The vision of a land covered with magnificent vineyards calls forth another, more exalted vision: the entire country is transformed into an immense domain planted by Yahweh:

And I will plant them upon their own land; and I will no more pluck them out of their land.[239]

Osee is the first to give this plantation its name: it is a vineyard:

Israel, a vine full of branches, the fruit is agreeable to it.[240]

But the more God made His people prosper, the more it sinned:

According to the multitude of his fruit he hath multiplied altars; according to the plenty of his land he hath abounded with idols.[241]

And Yahweh finds Himself obliged to destroy what He has planted:

The bur and the thistle shall grow up over their altars; and they shall say to the mountains: Cover us; and to the hills: Fall upon us.[242]

Burs and thistles, the curse of this first sin, will fall upon the country. Still, God's love is stronger than sin. If Yahweh has made His people a vineyard, it is because His heart, once and for all, has surrendered itself. He cannot forget "the days of her youth"[243] and the betrothal, and this memory which He cannot erase has the taste of the vine:

> I found Israel like grapes in the desert.[244]

Also, when He considers going to take the unfaithful one back:

> Therefore . . . I will . . . lead her . . . and I will speak to her heart,[245]

the gift He plans to give her to seal this forgiveness consists of vineyards:

> And I will give her vinedressers.[246]

For Isaias also, the theme of the vineyard is a theme of love. In his burning work, seared by the breath of God, the poem of the vineyard, mysterious in title, overflows with the freshness of a spring:

> I will sing to my beloved the canticle of my cousin concerning his vineyard. My beloved had a vineyard on a hill in a fruitful place.
> And he fenced it in, and picked the stones out of it, and planted it with the choicest vines.[247]

So much care, so much love, all in vain:

> I looked that it should bring forth grapes, and it hath brought forth wild grapes. . . .[248]

Deceived, Yahweh's kindness turns into a curse:

> And I will make it desolate. It shall not be pruned and it shall not be digged: but briers and thorns shall come up.[249]

Eternal rejects of the accursed land,[250] the bur and the thistle seem to grow readily only on that soil whence God's love, having exhausted its resources, has had to retire. This feature was already noticeable in Osee.[251] It is very remarkable that in Isaias, the same plants grow up in the vineyard.[252]

The theme is less developed in Jeremias, but it is identical. Israel is the vineyard of the Lord, "my delightful portion."[253]

212

He has lavished every attention on it; He sees His care frustrated:

> Yet I planted thee a chosen vineyard, all true seed: how then art thou turned unto me into that which is good for nothing?[254]

For Ezechiel also, Israel is the vineyard of Yahweh, but the emphasis is no longer placed on God's kindness. It is on the superb vigor that this plant showed.[255] The punishment of the proud or sterile vine is new and more terrible than in Isaias. It will be handed over to the fire and consumed, for the whole value of the vine is in its fruit. Its wood is of no use.[256]

Psalm 79 is entirely built up on these themes,[257] that of the vigorous vine whose branches stretch far out, "to the Sea, its shoots as far as the River,"[258] even to covering the "cedars of God";[259] the theme of the punishment deserved: the broken-down walls,[260] the passers-by plucking the fruit,[261] the branches burned in the fire.[262] Of course, we must not exaggerate the scope of these comparisons. Many of them can be explained naturally by the similarity of situations. The images of a devastated vineyard are always the same. Without invoking literary reminiscences too readily, it is more important to set forth the permanent traits of the theme of the vineyard throughout the Old Testament. The vineyard is the symbol of God's hopes for the land: hopes born of a consuming love and pursued with an impassioned perseverance; hopes deceived, which take their vengeance in curses.[263]

By what metamorphosis does this theme, exposed from its birth to the most heady temptations of the nature cults, this theme of inebriation and of passion, come to express the formidable "seriousness of the divine love"?[264] This is the secret of the religion of Israel. It is the secret of the true God—an unfathomable secret. Still, the theme of the vineyard allows us to approach it, by bringing to light two aspects of Yahweh: the inflexible exigencies of His grandeur, and the altogether natural simplicity of His "humanity."

Behind these images of a vinedresser-God are automatically silhouetted the Canaanitic Baals whose amorphous figures long remained so seductive for the heart of the Israelites. These evoked in their eyes the forces of nature and their inexhaustible drive. Man is constantly tempted to ask these forces, which he deems maternal, for a supply of sap, for a new impulse to be given to his life, always frail and threatened. Yahweh has nothing in common with these Baals. Not that He ignores man's appeals to life, their violence and despair. But He alone intends to satisfy them. He it is who will make the rain fall on the parched soil, who will give vigor to men, beautiful children to women. He it is who will guarantee happiness to the home, justice and peace to the city. The God of Israel assumes all these responsibilities. He will give life to His people, but He sets a condition: fidelity to His will as expressed in the Law, exclusive faith in Him alone.

There is more than this in the religion of Yahweh. At this stage, it was approximately the same religion that Islam took as its deposit and whose existence it continues. Allah has no other concern in this world than to keep it in action and to observe the conduct of men up until the day when he is to judge them. Yahweh undertakes an altogether different enterprise. The Old Testament does not know where this will lead it, but it does know that God has willingly planted His foot on the earth, that He expects other harvests than the yearly crops, that He dreams of a different festival than that of the grape-gathering. Palestine is no longer simply the land where Yahweh makes His people happy, it is the land where He plans to find His joy.

The Gospels reveal to us what this dream had as its object— God comes in person to visit His harvest. Or rather, He sends the one He still had left, a "beloved son."[265] It was folly: all the servants He had sent to His vinekeepers had been beaten or killed. But by this madness He is simply remaining true to Himself; He is at all times the one who has done all that He could do for His vineyard. The prophets had multiplied the signs of this passion. The Gospels reveal the heart where the passion was born.

This supreme act of love at the end of its resources also indicates that, for Israel, the hour of decision had struck. Still in the perspectives of the biblical theme, the evoking of the vineyard is the announcement of the long-delayed and all the more pitiless chastisement. The parable of the vinedressers belongs naturally in the final moments of the life of Jesus, at the hour when His death is decided upon, determining the destiny of the people which rejects Him:

Therefore I say to you that the kingdom of God will be taken away from you and will be given to a people yielding its fruits.[266]

The first parables, the parables of the entrance into the kingdom, presented a God sowing His hopes, entrusting them to the world. Now that Jesus sees His hour approaching, the images which come to His mind are those of God the vinekeeper, visiting His harvest. The last days of Christ, therefore, see Him alternate between apocalyptic revelations, filled with the destruction of the worlds that are crumbling, and the familiar actions of the master who settles his accounts, the proprietor who tours his domain. Different images, stamped with the same gravity. If the sun dims, if the earth trembles, it is because creation trembles at God's coming, and if God comes near, it is because His interest in man has reached its peak. What fruit will He garner from so much effort? What will the world weigh in the face of His love?

As in the Old Testament, God's care for His vineyard ends up, in the Gospels, in a deception. The difference is that, out of this deception, God draws forth the triumph of His love. He sends His son, but not to demand a settling of accounts. Jesus, on the contrary, will pay Himself. He comes to substitute Himself for the guilty people. Put to death by His father's vinekeepers, He makes His death into the act of love that

215

Yahweh could not obtain from Israel. He becomes the vineyard of God.

The Synoptics, without being clearly aware of it, turn the theme of the vineyard in this new direction. In their account of the Last Supper, all three insist on reporting these mysterious words of Jesus: "I will not drink henceforth of this fruit of the vine, until that day when I shall drink it new with you in the kingdom of my Father."[267] The formula of the eucharistic consecration explains this sentence. Jesus transforms the wine of the meal into His blood. This blood is the wine of the New Covenant. That of the Old Covenant is out-dated, unusable. The authentic wine is that which Jesus has just consecrated. The feast which Yahweh had planned to celebrate with His people in planting it upon the land, He had not been able to celebrate: His vineyard had never given anything but wild grapes. Tonight, at last, the hour has come when He can taste His harvest and take His meal with His own. For centuries He had waited for this hour: "I have greatly desired to eat this passover with you."[268]

What was still obscure in the Synoptics becomes clear in St. John. The words of Jesus: "I am the true vine"[269] have an obvious connection with the Eucharist, but their scope is not immediately evident. If we place this statement in its place in the biblical perspectives of the theme of the vineyard, it is more clearly seen. In saying: "I am the true vine," Jesus is not comparing Himself directly with the vineyard of which Yahweh was the owner.[270] It was not so much the domain that God was interested in, but its fruit, the plant He had put there, the incomparable vine, chosen among thousands.[271] He is not deceived in finding nothing to harvest, but in harvesting a fruit from the finest of vines which puckers the mouth. The most beautiful promises have been betrayed.

Jesus puts an end to this perpetual disappointment of God. He is the "true vine." True in the most complete sense of the

216

word, combining the Hellenic sense of exemplary truth and the Hebraic meaning of substantial solidity.[272] The true vine is at the same time the one of which all the vineyards of Palestine, and that of Yahweh's own vineyard, the people of Israel, were but a figure, and the vineyard which does not deceive, whose fruit fulfills God's expectations and fills Him with joy.

The purpose of the Eucharist is to make God taste this joy. In the Synoptics, it was the joy of the feast consecrating the New Covenant where God united Himself with the new people. For John too, union is the last word of this repast which he assumes without mentioning it. "He who eats my flesh, and drinks my blood, abides in me and I in him,"[273] was the promise of the discourse on the bread of life. Here is the promise fulfilled: "Abide in me, and I in you."[274] This union itself is not its own end. That end is to enter into the fulness of God. Christ's embrace extends the love with which the Father surrounds Him: "As my Father has loved me, I also have loved you."[275] In return, the adherence of the disciples to their Master has as its supreme goal the glory of His father.[276]

The theme of the vineyard, in St. John, ends in a rigorous stripping away. No vistas on the slopes of Palestine, no echo of the chant of the grape-gatherers or the joys of the feast. God alone examines His creature and gathers the fruit of love. In the silence of the earth rises "The song of the Beloved concerning his vineyard."

NOTES

[1] Ps. 126; Ecclus. 4: 9; 9: 5.
[2] Cf. Jer. 31: 16.
[3] Ruth 2: 12.
[4] Gen. 15: 1.
[5] Is. 35: 4.
[6] Jer. 51: 56; cf. Is. 59: 18.
[7] Jer. 32: 18; cf. Ex. 20: 5; 34: 6.
[8] Prov. 10: 16.
[9] Prov. 10: 27.
[10] Prov. 11: 19.

[11] Cf. Prov. 10: 17, 28, 30; 11: 11, 17, 18, 25, 30; 12: 3; 12: 28; 13: 9, 21; 14: 27; 15: 24; 18: 21; 19: 23; 21: 21, etc.

[12] This is the sense of the protest of Ecclesiastes.

[13] J. Pederson has clearly set forth this fundamental aspect of the Israelite mentality, *Israel, its Life and Culture*, I-II, London-Copenhagen, 1926, pp. 430–431.

[14] This point is of some importance—Prov. 10: 27; 28: 16; Job 36: 11; 42: 16–17; Ps. 20: 5; 90: 16; Eccles. 1: 12; 23: 27—but it is not dominant.

[15] Prov. 10: 9, 25, 29, 30; 11: 5, 6, 8, 9, 11, 14, 28, 29; 12: 3, 6, 7; 13: 3, 6; 14: 11, 26, 32; 15: 6, 25, etc.

[16] A Babylonian text says: "Him whose sins condemned to death, the king our master made live"; quoted by R. Labat, *Le caractère religieux de la royauté assyro-babylonienne*, Paris, 1939, p. 296.

[17] Ex. 3: 8, 17; 13: 5; 33: 3; Num. 12: 27; 14: 8.

[18] Deut. 8: 7–9.

[19] In substance it is already in Ex. 20: 12. It returns with some variations in Deut. 4: 26, 40; 5: 16, 30; 6: 3, 18; 8: 1; 11: 9; 16: 20; 22: 7; 25: 15; 30: 16, 20. In 6: 24 and 30: 6, it lacks the qualification "in the land."

[20] Ex. 20: 12.

[21] Deut. 30: 19–20.

[22] Deut. 28: 30.

[23] Deut. 20: 5–7. Possibly there is in these prescriptions a trace of some ancient taboos designed to "keep away from the army those who are particularly threatened by the invisible powers." (A. Lods, *Israël, des Origines au VIIIe siècle*, Paris, 1930, p. 342.) Whatever one may think about these uncertain origins, Deuteronomy gives a new sense to these customs, and this is the important thing.

[24] Rom. 7: 7: "I did not know sin save through the Law."

[25] Amos 5: 14.

[26] Amos 5: 4–6.

[27] Amos 5: 11.

[28] Amos 9: 14.

[29] Osee 6: 1–2.

[30] Osee 13: 14.

[31] Osee 6: 3.

[32] Osee 14: 6–9.

[33] Gen. 2: 9.

[34] Is. 4: 2.

[35] Is. 4: 3.

[36] Ex. 32: 32–33; Ps. 68: 29; 138: 16.

[37] The only image he evokes is the sacred vision of the glory of Yahweh in verse 5.

[38] Cf. R. de Vaux, "Le 'Reste d'Israel' chez les Prophètes," in *Revue Biblique*, 1933, pp. 526–539.

[39] Is. 43: 1.

[40] Gen. 1: 1.

[41] Is. 40: 28; 42: 5; 45: 18; Ps. 147: 5. *Bara'*, which we translate "create," does not have, in Hebrew, the philosophical meaning of "to make from nothing." The philosophical notion of creation appears very late in Israel, in 2 Mac. 7: 28; but the fact that Hebrew set aside a word to denote the action of God on the world proves that it distinguished it completely from any other action. Cf. Jer. 31: 21–22.

[42] Is. 45: 8; cf. 41: 20; 43: 1, 7, 15.

[43] Is. 55: 13.

[44] Is. 53: 8.

[45] Is. 53: 6.

[46] Concerning the Servant of Yahweh, heir of the tragic destiny of the prophets, cf. A. Feuillet, "Le Messianisme du Livre d'Isaïe," in *Recherches de Science religieuse*, 1949, p. 221.

[47] Is. 65: 17.
[48] Is. 65: 20, 22.
[49] Is. 65: 21.
[50] Is. 65: 25. In Is. 11: 8, this serpent, now become inoffensive, is found again: "the sucking child shall play on the hole of the asp." Is this a reference to the serpent of Eden?
[51] Is. 65: 25.
[52] Hab. 2: 4; cf. 1: 12.
[53] Jer. 21: 8–9.
[54] Jer. 23: 3; 29: 14; 31: 8, 10; 32: 37.
[55] Jer. 23: 3, 8; 24: 6; 29: 10, 14; 30: 3; 31: 8, 9, 23; 32: 37, 44; 33: 11, 26.
[56] Jer. 31: 10.
[57] Jer. 30: 17.
[58] Jer. 30: 18; 31: 4.
[59] Jer. 31: 5.
[60] Jer. 31: 4, 13; 33: 11.
[61] Jer. 31: 13.
[62] Jer. 31: 31.
[63] Cf. L. Dürr, *Ursprung und Ausbau der israelitisch-jüdischen Heilandserwartung*, Berlin, 1925, pp. VII-XIV.
[64] Ezech. 37: 1-14.
[65] Ezech. 37: 14.
[66] Deut. 3: 20; Jos. 1: 13, 15; 22: 4; perhaps even Ex. 33: 14.
[67] Deut. 12: 10; Jos. 23: 1.
[68] Amos 5: 14.
[69] Lev. 18: 5.
[70] Ezech. 20: 11, 13, 21.
[71] Cf. Ezech. 33: 12, 15, 16, 19.
[72] Ezech. 3: 18; 13: 22; 18: 21, 23, 28, 32; 33: 11.
[73] Cf. J. Hempel, *Das Ethos des A.T.*, Berlin, 1938, p. 39.
[74] Rom. 7: 10: "when the commandment came, sin revived, and I died." Cf. Col. 2: 13–14, and the commentary of Fr. Benoit, "La Loi et la Croix selon saint Paul," in *Revue Biblique*, 1938, pp. 487–491.
[75] A. Robert, "Les attaches littéraires de Proverbes I-IX," in *Revue Biblique*, 1935, pp. 344–365.
[76] Prov. 3: 1-2. Cf. Prov. 3: 22; 4: 10, 13, 22; 5: 6; 6: 23; 8: 35.
[77] Ps. 40: 3; 70: 20; 79: 19; 84: 7; 118: 17, 25, 37, 40, 50, 88, 93, 107, 149, 154, 156, 159; 137: 7; 142: 11.
[78] Is. 38: 11; 53: 8; Jer. 11: 19; Ezech. 32: 23, 24, 26; Job 28: 13; Ps. 26: 13; 51: 7; 68: 29; 141: 6. The "light of the living" is also the light of our day: Job 33: 30; Ps. 55: 14.
[79] Regarding the Egyptian beliefs, cf. J. Vandier, *La religion égyptienne*, Paris, 1944, pp. 66–129.
[80] *Discours sur l'Histoire universelle*, Part II, chap. 19.
[81] By deceiving it most of the time by mythical hopes and magic rites. Cf. Fr. Lagrange, *Le Judaïsme avant Jésus-Christ*, Paris, 1931, p. 346, quoting G. F. Moore, *Judaism in the First Centuries of the Christian Era*, Cambridge (USA), 1927, II, p. 318.
[82] Lev. 18: 5; Deut. 4: 1; 5: 30, etc.
[83] Dan. 12: 1-2.
[84] *Ibid.*
[85] Is. 4: 3.
[86] Dan. 13: 60.
[87] Dan. 6: 23; 14: 42.
[88] Dan. 3: 94.
[89] Rom. 4: 18.
[90] Dan. 12: 3.

[91] 2 Mac. 7.

[92] 2 Mac. 7: 11.

[93] 2 Mac. 7: 9.

[94] Deut. 32: 36, according to the Septuagint.

[95] It is also one of the themes of the episode of the martyrdom. Cf. 2 Mac. 7: 18, 32.

[96] Deut. 32: 39.

[97] Wis. 3: 1.

[98] Wis. 3: 9.

[99] Wis. 5: 16.

[100] Wis. 2: 11, 20.

[101] Cf. Wis. 2: 20.

[102] Wis. 2: 1–9.

[103] Mark 10: 17, 30; Matt. 25: 46.

[104] Mark 9: 44; Matt. 18: 8.

[105] Matt. 7: 14; 18: 8–9; 19: 17, 29.

[106] Matt. 25: 46.

[107] Luke 16: 27–28.

[108] Matt. 25: 34.

[109] Matt. 25: 40.

[110] 1 Thess. 5: 10.

[111] 1 Cor. 15: 45.

[112] 2 Cor. 5: 14–15.

[113] 2 Cor. 4: 11.

[114] 2 Cor. 4: 10.

[115] 2 Cor. 13: 4.

[116] Rom. 5: 12.

[117] Rom. 7: 10.

[118] Rom. 5: 8; 8: 3–4.

[119] Rom. 6: 4.

[120] Rom. 8: 11, 35–39.

[121] 1 John 1: 2.

[122] John 5: 24. Cf. 1 John 3: 14.

[123] John 12: 31.

[124] 2 Cor. 5: 17.

[125] Rom. 8: 38–39.

[126] John 6: 54.

[127] *Ibid.*

[128] Col. 3: 4.

[129] Phil. 1: 21.

[130] Gal. 2: 20.

[131] 2 Cor. 4: 11.

[132] Gen. 12: 7; 15: 7; 28: 13; Ex. 3: 8, 17; 33: 1; Num. 14:23.

[133] Cf. R. Pautrel, *La Bible de la terre*, Le Puy, 1941, pp. 8–13. Milk and honey are doubtless an evocation of Paradise, if not of Eden itself, even though the biblical narrative does not mention this theme: cf. W. Eichrodt, *Theologie des A.T.*, 3rd ed., Berlin, 1948, p. 251, n. 1.

[134] Num. 14: 20–38; 20: 12.

[135] Jos. 6: 2; 8: 1; 10: 8.

[136] And embellishes. The text of the book of Josue utilized by the Septuagint is clearly more sober than the actual Hebrew text, and sometimes on important points, for example, the role of Rahab at the time of the capture of Jericho. Compare Jos. 2: 12 ff. in the two versions.

[137] Gen. 15: 3–4.

[138] Osee 9: 6.

[139] Is. 34: 11.

[140] Ps. 24: 13; 36: 9, 11, 22, 29; 81: 8.

[141] Ecclus. 4: 13, 16; 6: 1; 10: 11; 15: 6; 17: 11; 19: 3; 20: 25; 24: 12; 36: 10; 37: 26; 39: 23; 44: 23; 45: 25 (in every case, the meaning is precisely that of *yarach*). Is. 14: 21; 54: 3; 57: 13; 60: 21; 65: 9.

[142] This is the word of the beatitude of the meek (Matt. 5: 5); it is the word of the final entry into the kingdom in the scene of the last judgment (Matt. 25: 34). It is obviously not a question of conquering this kingdom, but rather of receiving it from God.

[143] A disadvantage the context itself often compensates for.

[144] Sometimes it comes back in every line: Deut. 1: 8, 21, 39; 2: 12, 21, 22, 24, 31; 3: 18, 20; 4: 1, 5, 26, 47, etc.

[145] Deut. 6: 10–11.

[146] Deut. 11: 10.

[147] Deut. 11: 11.

[148] Gen. 15: 1–17.

[149] 3 Kings 21: 3.

[150] Gen. 31: 14.

[151] Deut. 1: 38; 3: 28; 4: 20, 21; 10: 9; 12: 10; 15: 4; 19: 3, 10, 14; 20: 16; 24: 4; 25: 19; 26: 1; 31: 7, etc.

[152] Ex. 23: 30; 32: 13.

[153] Is. 2: 3; 30: 29; 31: 4; 33: 5.

[154] Is. 31: 9.

[155] Is. 30: 28.

[156] Is. 4: 4–5.

[157] Is. 2: 2–4.

[158] Is. 11: 6–8.

[159] Is. 54: 1=Gal. 4: 27.

[160] Is. 54: 3.

[161] On the precise meaning of the formula in Hebrew, see J. Chaine, *Le Livre de la Génese*, Paris, 1948, p. 181.

[162] Is. 54: 5.

[163] Is. 54: 17. It is true that, in these chapters, justice is often the equivalent of a salvation marked by the triumph over the enemy. Still, the original idea of innocence never disappears. See Ch. III, Sec. 5.

[164] Is. 57: 13.

[165] Is. 60: 21.

[166] Is. 65: 9.

[167] Is. 65: 10.

[168] Is. 65: 25; cf. 11: 9.

[169] Is. 66: 20.

[170] Is. 58: 14.

[171] Is. 57: 15.

[172] Jos. 7: 24.

[173] Osee 2: 15.

[174] Osee 2: 20.

[175] Jer. 33: 11.

[176] Jer. 3: 18, 19; 12: 14; 17: 4 (with *nahal*); 7: 7; 11: 5 (without *nahal*).

[177] Jer. 30: 3.

[178] Ezech. 36: 12.

[179] Ezech. 47: 14.

[180] Ezech. 40: 2.

[181] Ezech. 47: 8.

[182] Gen. 13: 10.

[183] Jer. 29.

[184] Ezech. 33: 24, 25–29.

[185] Matt. 3: 9; John 8: 33.

[186] John 8: 44.

[187] Matt. 3: 9.

[188] Rom. 4: 18.

[189] Gal. 4: 25–26.

[190] Ps. 68: 34, 36, 37.

[191] See A. Gelin, *Les pauvres de Jahweh,* Paris, 1954. It is they who become at once the poor, the meek and the suffering of the Beatitudes.

[192] These incidences do not suffice to determine whether there was any independence, even less to fix a date for these psalms. We must simply note here the agreement of the themes.

[193] Ps. 2: 8.

[194] Ps. 46: 4–5.

[195] Prov. 3: 35. In the second half of the verse, the correction of *merim* to *morichim* is tempting; it adds just one consonant, and can call on the frequent parallelism between *yachar* and *nahal.* The meaning remains the same.

[196] Job 27: 13; cf. 20: 29; 31: 2.

[197] Prov. 28: 10.

[198] Prov. 8: 20–21.

[199] Ps. 24: 12–13.

[200] Cf. Is. 14: 3; 63: 14; Ps. 94: 11.

[201] Ps. 36: 26, 37.

[202] Ps. 36: 9, 11, 22, 29, 34. Note also, in verse 18: "their inheritance [*nahalah*] lasts forever," and the formula "dwell in [*chakan*] the land," which occurs in verse 3 and undoubtedly in verse 27, where the Septuagint read it, and where, even according to the Hebrew, the verb *chakan* would suffice to indicate the image.

[203] Ps. 36: 11=Matt. 5: 5; the equivalence with the Septuagint is total. The latter translated as "meek" the Hebrew word *'anawim,* whose meaning is more general and specifically denotes the "poor."

[204] Ps. 118: 111.

[205] Num. 18: 20. Cf. Deut. 10: 9; 18: 2.

[206] Ps. 118: 57.

[207] Ps. 15: 5–6.

[208] Ps. 72: 25–26.

[209] Ps. 72: 24.

[210] Matt. 6: 33.

[211] Eph. 5: 5; Col. 3: 24; James 2: 5; cf. 1 Pet. 1: 4; 3: 22 (Vulg.).

[212] Gal. 3: 29; 4: 7.

[213] Heb. 4: 1–10; cf. 1: 14; 9: 15; 11: 8.

[214] Is. 57: 13.

[215] Rom. 8: 17.

[216] 1 Kings 10: 1; 26: 19; 2 Kings 20: 19; 21:3.

[217] Ex. 23: 30; 32: 13.

[218] The formula "the land of my inheritance," "the mountain of my inheritance," appears in several of the poems discovered at Ras Shamra (II AB VIII 14, in *Syria,* XIII, 1932, p. 159; I AB II 16, in *Syria,* XV: 1934, p. 314; V AB C 27 and V AB D 64, in C. Virolleaud, *La Déesse 'Anat,* Paris, 1938, pp. 36 and 41.) The context indicates that it is always a question of the personal residence of the god. In Israel this place is, on the contrary, the place in which Yahweh installs His people.

[219] 1 Kings 10: 1.

[220] Ex. 34: 9.

[221] Jer. 16: 18.

[222] Cf. Jer. 2: 7; 3: 1; 32: 34.

[223] Jer. 12: 7–8, 10. Replacing, in verse 10, *helqati* by *nahalati*, as in a considerable number of Hebrew and Greek manuscripts. Even without the correction, the meaning remains the same.

[224] Mich. 7: 14.

[225] Is. 19: 25.

[226] Deut. 9: 26, 29. The same formula, no doubt similarly inspired, in 3 Kings 8: 51.

[227] Is. 47: 6.

[228] Is. 63: 17.

[229] Zach. 2: 12; cf. 9: 16; Joel 4: 2.

[230] Deut. 32:9.

[231] Ps. 78: 1.

[232] Ps. 27: 9; 32: 12; 73: 2; 77: 62, 71; 93: 5; 105: 5, 40.

[233] Ps. 27: 9.

[234] Ps. 77: 70–71. In Is. 40: 10–11, the shepherd is the Lord Himself; He seems to substitute Himself for Jacob bringing back from Phaddan-Aram the flocks he had acquired as payment for his labors (Gen. 31: 18), and watching jealously over the ewes (Gen. 32: 13).

[235] 3 Kings 21: 1–24.

[236] Is. 3: 14.

[237] Amos 9: 13a.

[238] Amos 9: 13b.

[239] Amos 9: 15.

[240] Osee 10: 1.

[241] *Ibid.*

[242] Osee 10: 8.

[243] Osee 2: 15.

[244] Osee 9: 10.

[245] Osee 2: 14.

[246] Osee 2: 13.

[247] Is. 5: 1–2; cf. 27: 3. The vine symbolizes the beloved. Cf. Cant. 8: 11–12.

[248] Is. 5: 4.

[249] Is. 5: 6.

[250] Gen. 3: 17–18.

[251] Osee 10: 8, corresponding to 10: 1.

[252] Is. 5: 6; 7: 23; 27: 4.

[253] Jer. 12: 10.

[254] Jer. 2: 21.

[255] Ezech. 19: 10–11. See also the parable in Chapter 17, in which Sedecias is compared to a vine, issuing by metamorphosis from the top of a cedar. The images of Isaias and Jeremias were more natural. The Gospels will rediscover the simplicity of the original theme, and with it, its profound meaning: the hope of a passionate heart.

[256] Ezech. 19: 12; cf. 15: 4.

[257] God the vinedresser is at the same time God the shepherd. The psalm begins: "Shepherd of Israel," but there is no longer question of anything but the vine.

[258] Ps. 79: 12. Compare, in Is. 16: 8 and Jer. 48: 32, the vine of Sabama whose shoots "have reached even to Jazer . . . are gone over the sea." Cf. also Ezech. 19:11.

[259] Ps. 79: 11. Compare Ezech. 17: 3–9, 22–24.

[260] Ps. 79: 13. Compare Is. 5: 5.

[261] Ps. 79: 13. Compare Is. 5: 5 and Jer. 12: 10.

[262] Ps. 79: 17. Compare Exech. 15: 4; 19: 12.

[263] Gen. 3: 18.

[264] Cf. R. Guardini, *Dieu Vivant*, no. 11, pp. 17–26.

[265] Mark 12: 6.

[266] Matt. 21: 43.

[267] Matt. 26: 29; Mark 14: 25; Luke 22: 16. With regard to the different position of this

phrase in Luke and in the other two evangelists, cf. P. Benoit, "Le récit de la Céne dans Luc 22: 15-20," in *Revue Biblique*, 1939, pp. 357-393.

[268] Luke 22: 15.

[269] John 15: 1.

[270] With the domain, ἀμπελῶν, of Amos 9: 14; Is. 5: 1, 3, 4, 5, 6, 7; Jer. 12: 10.

[271] With the plant, ἄμπελος, of Osee 10: 1, Is. 5: 2; Jer. 2: 21.

[272] Cf. *supra*, Ch. III, Sec. 4.

[273] John 6: 56.

[274] John 15: 4.

[275] John 15: 9.

[276] John 15: 8.

Chapter VII

THE BREATH OF YAHWEH

1. THE WIND, THE BREATH OF YAHWEH

The wind, for the Hebrew poets, is "the breath of the nostrils" of Yahweh. The image is traditional with them: the canticle sung after the passage through the Red Sea says:

> At a breath of your anger the waters piled up,
>   the flowing waters stood like a mound.
> . . . .
> When your wind blew, the sea covered them.[1]

Psalm 17 repeats the theme:

> Then the bed of the sea appeared,
>   and the foundations of the world were laid bare,
> At the rebuke of the LORD,
>   at the blast of the wind of his wrath.[2]

This breath, which the nostrils can no longer hold in, is the breath of fury.[3] Also, it consumes sinners. Isaias describes its terrifying approach:

Behold the name of the Lord cometh from afar. His wrath burneth and is heavy to bear: his lips are filled with indignation, and his tongue as a devouring fire.

His breath as a torrent overflowing even to the midst of the neck.[4]

225

At this breath, the altar of Moloch will burst into flames like a brazier:

For Topheth is prepared from yesterday . . . deep and wide. The nourishment thereof is fire and much wood; the breath of the Lord as a torrent of brimstone kindling it.[5]

There is more than a grandiose image in this identification of the wind with the furious breath of Yahweh. There is a representation familiar to the ancient Hebrews. For them, the wind came directly from God. The poetical image of the Canticle of Exodus, which sees God piling up the waters with the breath from His nostrils,[6] is the scarcely changed rendering of the action described in the corresponding prose account:

Then Moses stretched out his hand over the sea, and the LORD swept the sea with a strong east wind throughout the night and so turned it into dry land.[7]

In all the ancient accounts of the events of the Exodus and the desert, the wind is produced immediately by the Lord.[8] The wind which God "sent over the earth" after the Deluge,[9] has the same source. The wind which, after three years of drought, brings the storm in answer to the prayer of Elias, is also a divine force, held in reserve in the regions of heaven. The only ancient text where the wind seems independent of Yahweh is that which describes the walk of Yahweh "walking in . . . the afternoon air."[10] It is not at all certain that Yahweh was borne on the wind. At least we must recognize that He takes pleasure in the wind.

For the prophets, the wind is the instrument of God's justice. The wind is, above all, the burning breath which comes from the desert across the Jordan to dry up the harvest of Palestine; it is the bearer of the divine wrath. Osee threatens the land of Israel:

The Lord will bring a burning wind that shall rise from the desert, and it shall dry up his springs and shall make his fountain desolate.[11]

In devastating the country, this wind strikes the inhabitants. Its irresistible force, its burning heat, make it formidable, but even more fearsome is the avenging mission with which it is charged: the chastisement of sinners. It is the great symbol of the sovereign power of God which laughs at human pretensions:

> The wind hath bound them up in its wings: and they shall be confounded because of their sacrifices.[12]

Carried along by the whirlwinds, the great empires, the most impressive religions, the most famous idols, tumble along like straws.[13] The pious men of Israel were to enjoy recalling these images, in which they saw the punishment of the sinner: "with the wind his blossoms shall disappear."[14]

In Ezechiel, the wind is never called "the wind of Yahweh," but it remains responsible for His vengeance. It is the wind from the east that dries up the vineyard of Israel,[15] which causes the proud vessel, symbol of Tyre and of its fleets,[16] to perish in the sea. It is a storm which breaks down the wall that Israel had thought of as its shelter.[17]

The expression "to the four winds," frequent in the texts of the exile period, especially in Ezechiel,[18] generally denotes more than just the main points of the compass.[19] It is a question either of the "winds of the heavens," the forces which are unleashed at God's call,[20] or of the extremities of the world, where God disperses His enemies;[21] in any event, of the confines of a world in which the whole divine power is unfurled.

In short, except for a characteristic usage in which it is the symbol of lack of solidity, of nothingness,[22] the wind, in the Bible, is normally associated in a more or less explicit manner with God. The wind, more than any other force in the world, is a divine force.

The wind owes this privilege to more than its strength. Of course, it is capable of overcoming all resistance. But besides strength, it has lightness and docility, it is from on high, from heaven. The sea also, is fearsome, but its power always appears savage and diabolical. The ancient myths of Babylonia gave it the figure of a monster: the goddess Tiamat. The poem *Enuma elish,* which describes the origin of the world, presents the combat in which Marduk, the god of intelligence and light, brings down the power of chaos:

> Tiamat and Marduk arise:
> He, the wise one among the gods,
> To the combat they march
> And approach for the battle.
> The Lord extended his net
> And enveloped him—
> The wicked wind which was behind him.
> In her face he let it go;
> She, Tiamat, opened her mouth
> So long as she could;
> He forced into it the wicked wind
> So that she could not close her lips:
> Terrible winds filled her belly,
> Her heart was seized,
> Her mouth remained wide open,
> He shot an arrow and pierced her belly.[23]

These wicked winds, these terrible winds can do great harm, but they are still at the service of the benevolent god.

The first chapter of Genesis, which eliminated all mythical elements, presupposes a similar view of the world. The *tehom* or abyss, the masculine equivalent of *tiamat,* may indeed have "lost all personality,"[24] but it has lost none of its fury, and the creative act consisted in setting between the waters and the dry land a boundary which no tempest could cross.[25] The poets unhesitatingly employ the same images. They celebrate the triumph of Yahweh over the monster, on the day when He crushed "Rahab with a mortal blow,"[26] when He "stirred up the sea by [his] might," and "smashed the heads of the dragons in the waters."[27] Conquered without any trace of effort, the sea remains the usual symbol of the forces hostile to God. The wind, on the contrary, is His instrument, forever docile. If the Lord, "by his power . . . stirs up the sea, and by his

228

might . . . crushes Rahab,"[28] it is because "his breath cleaves the waters."[29] When, renewing for His people the miracle of creation, He takes up arms against the sea and, "as in the days of old . . . struck the proud one [Rahab] and wounded the dragon . . . dried up the sea, the water of the mighty deep, who madest the depth of the sea a way, that the delivered might pass over."[30] He makes use of the wind, of the storm ever ready to "fulfill his word."[31] Does He not make "the winds his messengers, and flaming fire his ministers"?[32]

It is the wind which rushes to the ends of the earth to see that God's will is carried out, to impose His word. It is through its agency that God governs nature:

> He scatters his hail like crumbs;
>   before his cold the waters freeze.
> He sends his word and melts them;
>   he lets his breeze blow and the waters run.[33]

Indefatigable, invulnerable, incomprehensible, the wind dwells, along with the rain and the lightning, in the mysterious places where God alone rules. It belongs to the world of the heavens:

> Who has gone up to heaven and come down again—
>   who has cupped the wind in his hands?
> Who has bound up the waters in a cloak?[34]

Surely, only God:

> He has weighed out the wind,
>   and fixed the scope of the waters;
> . . . .
> When he made rules for the rain
>   and a path for the thunderbolts.[35]

For Yahweh, the wind is more than a trusted messenger. It belongs to His regular escort, it bears Him on its wings. Before the shaking of the earth, it forms the first defense with which Yahweh surrounds Himself. It is only after having crossed this double barrier that Elias, on Horeb, heard the murmuring of the wind, the sign of the divine presence.[36] Ezechiel, when he saw the glory of the Lord, saw first "a whirlwind . . . out of the north, and a great cloud and a fire infolding it! And brightness was about it, and out of the midst thereof . . . as it were the resemblance of amber."[37]

This heavenly, and, in a certain sense, divine, nature, no doubt explains the role which the wind plays in the account of the Creation, in the first chapter of Genesis. Above the abyss and the darkness hovers the *ruah* of Elohim. What is the nature of this *ruah*? Is it simply an element like the others, air or wind, different from the earth or the waters but of the same order as they?[38] Or is it, on the other hand, the spirit of God, a properly divine power, in which the creative force was somehow incarnate?

The answer is likely to be found between these two areas. This *ruah* is not that sovereign and pure force which transforms the prophets and puts them into immediate contact with God. For it remains material. It performs an action whose precise nature escapes us, but which is certainly of a tangible order, and is part of the immense spectacle of the visible world in the process of being born. Still, entirely different from the abyss and the darkness—these monstrous beings in the midst of which God will operate with an all-powerful hand, as in the midst of an inert, if not hostile, mass—the *ruah* belongs to God, it comes from Him, it is the *ruah* of Elohim.

The action which it performs is difficult to determine. The verb which describes it, *merahephet*, is very rare.[39] In the only other parallel passage,[40] it suggests the image of the fluttering of protective wings. The idea of movement which it seems to evoke, and which is also inseparable from *ruah*, forbids us from translating it "to nest," which would relate this passage to the cosmogonies in which the universe hatches out of a primordial egg.[41] It is probable that the verb denotes the squalls and gusts

230

of the wind "beating its wings"[42] above the chaos. *Ruah* is thus the wind, the breath of Elohim.

It therefore has a mission to fulfill. What is this mission? It is difficult to say specifically. Once the wind has been brought into the foreground, even before God begins His work, it is not mentioned again subsequently. One thing, therefore, is certain: it is not part of the work of the six days. It does not come from that side of the world which rises up at God's orders. It is, as its name indicates, from God's side. If it does play a role, it is not a passive role, but an active one.

Now it is likely that it does play a role. Otherwise, why mention its presence at all? And there is every likelihood that this role is linked to that of the word. Between the word and the breath there is a close relationship. There is no word without some letting out of breath: the breath carries the word, which, in turn, gives meaning to the breath. The Egyptian and Babylonian texts were very familiar with this theme, and the Bible repeats it.[43] All of creation is encompassed by the commandments of God: God speaks. Might not the breath of God be charged with bringing these words to the world? This is what is stated in one of the psalms which recalls the memory of the creation:

> By the word of the LORD the heavens were made;
> by the breath of his mouth all their host.[44]

Is there an explicit reference here to Genesis? Does "their host" refer to the verse in which "the heavens and the earth were finished and all their array"?[45] At any rate, we must note that the following verse:

> He gathers the waters of the sea as in a mound [*ned*];
> in cellars he confines the deep,[46]

assumes the intervention of the wind. For it is by Yahweh's breath that "the waters stood like a mound."[47] The role of the *ruah* is still a physical role.

It seems that it is necessary, in order to understand the role

231

of the *ruah* in creation, to remember two aspects. It is associated with the word of God, while still remaining a physical force, the wind. In fact, there is no opposition between these two elements. On the contrary, the wind, which carries the word of God to the hail in order to melt it,[48] is always ready to "fulfill his word,"[49] to rush to deliver His commands to the ends of the earth.[50] These are poetic images which express a representation that runs through the entire Old Testament and sees in the wind the privileged instrument of the divine power. If the wind of Elohim beats its wings above the chaos, it is because it is about to fulfill its mission. It is going to bear to those for whom they are destined, the orders given by God. Among the former are the living, and the spirit of God is therefore seen to raise up life in the world, to be the spirit of life. Still, it seems that, in this context, the *ruah* of Elohim is not evoked especially in order to bring forth life. However, its essentially mobile and dynamic character predisposed it in a particular way for this function.

The biblical text which sheds the most light on this account of the Creation is no doubt Psalm 103.[51] In this psalm, the *ruah* of Yahweh also plays a twofold role. In verses 3 and 4, it is the courier of the Lord, His faithful messenger, but it is also the rapid creature entrusted with bearing on its wings the person of the sovereign. This is the function of the wind throughout the biblical tradition. In verses 29 and 30, it is the very breath of Yahweh, the breath which comes forth from His mouth, by whose rhythm all creation lives. It is no longer the wind, but the spirit of life which animates every living thing. This representation is also common in the Old Testament, as we shall see. Do these two different missions presuppose two distinct beings? It does not seem so. It is probable that the author of the first chapter of Genesis was scarcely aware of our distinctions. For him, the *ruah* of Elohim which hovered over the waters at the beginning of the world was no doubt both the wind which rushes and the breath which comes from the mouth. These may well be distinct effects, but their origin is the same, the dynamism of the divine power.

Throughout all the texts of the Old Testament, the wind remains a creature apart. Nowhere does it appear that it is God. It even seems little by little, to lose the title of "wind of Yahweh," created by a naively anthropomorphic representation. But while Jeremias and Ezechiel no longer use it, they do preserve for it, in the apocalyptic images which they use, a role in keeping with the ancient tradition. In a world whose dimensions are no longer those of earth but of heaven, in a history of cosmic proportions, the wind remains the instrument of the power and of the mystery of God.

The Gospels complete the job of stripping the Old Testament of the last traces of naturalistic sentiment. Jesus savors intensely the beauty of creation, but He finds therein only His Father's image, and the forces of nature have no prestige as far as He is concerned. Heaven, which gives its name to the kingdom He announces, is no longer the mysterious region from which the life-giving light and the fecundating rain descend upon the earth. It is the Father's dwelling-place. The wind also loses its privileged position. Just as the sea ceases to be demoniacal, so the wind ceases to be the wind of God. "Who, then, is this, that even the wind and the sea obey him?" ask the disciples upon seeing Jesus command the unchained elements.[52]

If it is no longer anything more than a power of nature, the wind nevertheless does not stop speaking of God. No more does it bear Him on its wings, but it does remain His instrument, and it becomes the symbol of Him. On Pentecost morning, a violent wind, accompanied by tongues of fire, sweeps through the house where the Apostles are gathered.[53] The fire from heaven and the wind were, in the Old Testament, the messengers and the bearers of the Lord. The account in the Acts eliminates these images, but it still wants to show that the intervention of God upsets nature, and it sees in the appearance of the wind and the fire the sign of a conquest which transforms hearts. The wind is no longer the breath of Yahweh; it is the symbol of a breath proceeding from God Himself, from the center of His intimate self.

Was St. Luke aware of the place of Pentecost in world history? Did he notice the correspondence between the breath of Elohim which breathed on the waters when the world was created, and the breath of the Holy Spirit which came to give life to the new creation, the Church? The idea, at any rate, was known to St. John. After having, in his prologue, opposed to the creation described by Genesis the birth of the children of God through faith in the Incarnate Word, he reveals the principles of this new birth: "Unless a man be born again of water and the Spirit, he cannot enter into the kingdom of God."[54] When Nicodemus is astonished at this second birth, Jesus, in order to open his mind to the mystery, evokes the questions which are suggested to men by the passing wind: "The wind blows where it will, and thou hearest its sound but dost not know where it comes from or where it goes. So is everyone who is born of the Spirit."[55] The symbolism is over. The world described in Genesis was a material world, penetrated and animated by forces that were more or less divine. The world in which St. John lives is an invisible world, but it is also traversed by the breath of the Spirit of God.

2. THE BREATH OF LIFE, BREATH OF YAHWEH

If the breath of Yahweh had been but the wind, it would, of course, still have been the symbol of power and of mystery, but it would not have become the force which gives life to the world. However, it is also the breath of life. Psalm 103, after having sung of the grandeur of the wind, messenger of Yahweh and of His word, describes the ebb and flow of life on earth in terms of the rhythm of Yahweh's breathing:

234

If you hide your face, they are dismayed;
  if you take away their breath, they perish
  and return to their dust.
When you send forth your spirit, they are created,
  and you renew the face of the earth.[56]

Actually, this rhythm is not automatic, and the formula "you hide your face" shows that it depends solely on God's free choice. The vigor and vitality of the world depend directly upon the breath given forth by Yahweh. This breath has the same name as the wind, *ruah*. Still, the latter is distinct from it, but not completely, since both proceed from the breathing of Yahweh. It is difficult to categorize rigidly images which, while having a very precise traditional meaning, nevertheless bear the personal mark of the poet and of his freedom. Still, it seems that we can distinguish the breath of the nostrils and the breath of the mouth. The breath of the nostrils is normally that of God's wrath which descends as a storm on His enemies. The wind is, as we have seen, most often the bearer of the divine chastisement. The breath of the mouth, on the other hand, is a beneficent breath; from it emanates life in the world.[57]

In the ancient account of the second chapter of Genesis, Yahweh, after having fashioned man from the dust of the earth, breathes into his nostrils a breath *(nechamah)* of life, and the inert figure takes on life, becomes a living soul *(nephesh)*,[58] a person. The breath of God produces the life of man. The text does not call this breath the *ruah* of Yahweh, but the action which it depicts is, in its primitive naivete, the same as that presupposed by all the passages that attribute the breath of the living to the *ruah* of Yahweh.

Until the exile, no other text affirms this belief, but none contradicts it, either; and its presence throughout the ancient East leads us to assume that it was at all times a belief of the Hebrews. An oracle from the second part of Isaias speaks of Yahweh:

that created the heavens and stretched them out: that established the earth and the things that spring out of it; that giveth breath [*nechamah*] to the people upon it, and spirit [*ruah*] to them that tread thereon.[59]

Job acknowledged that

> . . . the spirit [*ruah*] of God has made me,
>   the breath [*nechamah*] of the Almighty keeps me alive.[60]

He is aware that he has, so long as he shall breathe, "the breath [*ruah*] of God . . . in [his] nostrils,"[61] but he knows that the day God

> . . . were to take back his spirit [*ruah*] to himself,
>   withdraw to himself his breath [*nechamah*],
>   All flesh would perish together,
>   and man would return to the dust.[62]

The only evolution which this belief underwent seems to be that, at the time of Ecclesiastes, no one dares send back to God the *ruah* of the beast, and that the latter is imagined, upon the death of the animal, to descend into oblivion in the earth, while the *ruah* of man ascends to God whence it comes.[63] The scepticism of Ecclesiastes—

Who knows if the life-breath of the children of men goes upward and the life-breath of beasts goes earthward?[64]—

seems, as a matter of fact, to indicate that people saw a difference of quality between the breath of the animal and that of man. But the account of Genesis had already underscored the superiority of man, animated directly by the breath of Yahweh. And Ecclesiastes himself is not obstinate in his doubt. In concluding his book, he returns to the traditional doctrine to evoke the inevitable hour when

. . . the dust returns to the earth as it once was, and the life-breath returns to God who gave it.[65]

The living creature, especially man, whose lot alone is worthy of interest, is made of dust and must return to dust. But there is in it, so long as it lives, a different element, a superior principle, which does not come from the earth and shall not be absorbed by it at death. This is not, properly speaking, the soul; it is the breath.

For the Hebrews, as for the Greeks and the Latins, the principle of life is in the breath. *Spiritus, animus,* πνεῦμα, ψυχή; all these words evoke a primitive representation, the most ancient perhaps, and one which, among all peoples, reveals the sacred respect, the trepidation man experiences in the presence of the "numinous," of forces which surpass him. For, man's breath does not have as its only distinguishing feature that it disappears at death; there are more mysterious properties which reveal a supernatural origin. In sleep, indeed, without consciousness and without motion, stripped of his personality, we might say, the sleeper continues to breathe, and therefore to live. This breath is therefore in him as something over which he is not master, and which comes from another. Thus man has, within himself, "the experience of a limitation," separating that on which he can act, the inert element, from the active element, of which he is but the receptacle, and which, for its part, animates and vivifies the inert part of his being.[66] This is, if you will, a distinction similar to that which we make between the body and the soul, excepting that the vital breath itself is also material. It is opposed by its dynamism to the body, which is passive and inert.

This body is called *basar* in Hebrew, and, through the Greek translation σάρξ and the Latin *caro,* it becomes "the flesh." The flesh without the breath which animates it would be just a cadaver. Still, it is not a cadaver, for it is the flesh animated by the vital breath; however, it is constantly threatened with becoming such:

All flesh is grass, and all the glory thereof as the flower of the field.[67]

To the weakness of the flesh is opposed the power and the permanence of the breath of God:

The grass is withered and the flower is fallen, because the spirit of the Lord hath blown upon it.[68]

But the breath of the Lord is not only the wind which, in the spring, consumes the green growth born of the winter rains. It is also the breath which, introduced into the very womb of the flesh, guarantees it life.[69] Still, the union of the two elements remains unstable. The breath of God could not remain indefinitely enclosed in such a fragile envelope:

My spirit [*ruah*] shall not remain in man forever, since he is flesh. His lifetime shall be one hundred and twenty years.[70]

From its Hebrew origins, before any transference of a moral or religious nature occurred, the idea of flesh contains an ambiguity. It denotes the living being, but a being already destined to death, a being which is basically corruptible.

Thus, the Hebrew conception of the living being fits in with its representation of the external world. In nature, the wind and its quasi-divine features—subtlety, rapidity, power, and docility—are opposed to the properly terrestrial elements, the earth and water, heavy and inert masses, born of chaos by a triumphant intervention of God. Likewise, in the living being, a force even more mysterious than the wind, but of a similar nature, an elusive breath, apparently fragile and vacillating, but, still, the only force capable of elevating the body and permeating it with life-energy, is opposed to the weakness and passivity of the flesh, destined for the corruption of the grave. Like the wind, but with an altogether different conviction and in more decisive terms, the Hebrew calls this breath a breath of God, the *ruah* of Yahweh.

This representation of the living being, divided between the inertia of the flesh and the dynamism of the vital spirit, directed thought into two quite different channels. One could, in fact, accentuate the difference between the two principles, or else stress their co-penetration. The first path caused God's transcendence to shine forth, the second uncovered the divine destiny

238

of the human soul. Both are found in the Old Testament. Both have their terminus in the New Testament.

In the first point of view, the flesh serves to define the world of the earth and of man, his impotence and sterility, as opposed to the fecund omnipotence of God:

Cursed be the man that trusteth in man and maketh flesh his arm, and whose heart departeth from the Lord![71]

More simply, flesh has the fatal mark of weakness:

> Have you eyes of flesh?
> Do you see as man sees?[72]

The fundamental undertone of impotence which is attached to flesh never disappears:

> In God I trust without fear;
> what can flesh do against me?[73]

It is this opposition of weakness to omnipotence which gives the word of Isaias its forcefulness:

Woe to them that go down to Egypt for help, trusting in horses . . .
. . . .
Egypt is man, and not God: and their horses, flesh, and not spirit.[74]

All the power of politics, the whole apparatus of empires and of their armies, are but flesh, nothingness, destined to death. God is spirit. Without being based on intellectual reflection, without expressing the results of a rational thought-process, this affirmation is nonetheless an authentic definition of God, because it expresses in precise terms an essential feature of His being, i.e., the radical difference which separates Him from all creation.

A common Hebraism associates the blood,[75] bearer of life, with the flesh. The formula "flesh and blood" therefore denotes the whole man. But it also denotes him in all his weakness, in all that distinguishes him from the world of the spirit. If at times this superior world is that of the "power of the air," "the world-rulers of this darkness,"[76] it is almost always the world of God Himself, to which "flesh and blood" cannot gain entrance, but which came to penetrate and transform flesh, just as the vital breath coming down from on high transforms a mass of inert flesh into a living being.

In this light, many texts of the New Testament become clear, texts which are easily disfigured by an idealism that robs them of their real scope. The declaration by Jesus to the Jews: "It is the spirit that gives life; the flesh profits nothing,"[77] is not an invitation to by-pass His teaching by some "interior" interpretation which would remove the scandal from it, but, on the contrary, it is a recalling of God's power which alone is capable of introducing man into a truth which goes beyond him.

Likewise, the opposition proclaimed by St. Paul between "the letter [which] kills" and the "spirit [which] gives life,"[78] is not an appeal to the independence of the human spirit liberated from the letter and made the master of its judgments. It is, on the contrary, the rejection of all human sufficiency, even that of the Law, and an appeal to the sovereign power of the Lord Jesus. He alone is the spirit,[79] that is, the strength to accomplish, in full liberty, what the Law could not obtain from its slaves, adherence to God.[80] The response of Jesus to the woman of Samaria: "God is spirit, and they who worship him must worship in spirit and in truth,"[81] is perhaps the Gospel phrase which has been "the most tortured, to the point where it has contradicted its own profound significance . . . in understanding by 'the spirit' a superior part of man, something human has been put in God's place. Under the guise of persecuting idolatry, we have consecrated the most pernicious form thereof—that which results in self-adoration."[82]

To adore God "in spirit and in truth" is not to build for oneself an interior sanctuary according to the pattern of one's religious principles or needs; it is, on the contrary, to renounce the temptation of a solitary cult, of efforts to approach God through personal ways. All these constructions by man are but an illusion, a lie in the biblical sense of the word. One must let oneself be carried away by the breath of God, which alone is capable of giving us access to the intimacy of God. The place in which man adores in spirit and in truth is the only place where the Spirit breathes, the Church of Jesus Christ.

To pursue in this way the identification of the vivifying spirit with God, it was necessary to strip it of all bonds which attached it to earth. But at the same time, it was also possible to bring out the personal nature of the breath of life, insofar as it animates the flesh. Breath of God, it is also the breath proper to everyone, one's most precious possession. Yahweh is not only the God who sends His spirit into all flesh, He is also the "God of the spirits of all mankind."[83] Every flesh therefore has its own spirit, which is what we call its soul.

There are many diverse, even contradictory, concepts in the idea which the Hebrews had of the soul. Rather than try to distinguish different, more or less spiritual, souls, it is better to accept this complexity.[84] If one insists on seeking in the soul a distinct, separable substance, one falsifies the Hebrew mentality, which is forever synthesizing, for which the soul is primarily the totality of the being—what we call the personality.[85] Observing the various elements which the Hebrew calls the soul, one constantly runs across a childish materialism. Consciousness itself, in which we see the sign of spirituality, is simply the life-giving breath. The modern Westerner spontaneously locates consciousness in the brain, the organ of perception of the external world, because the outstanding actions of his conscious life are based on the objective observation of facts and the calculations of reflection, operations dominated by cerebral activity. "The primitive peoples localize 'the soul,' or thought, sometimes in the head, or even more primitively, in the belly. This is because they are only led to awareness by things which 'move their bowels.'"[86] The Old Testament is completely permeated by this psychology. Seeing, which for us is an action of the eye, is for a Hebrew an action of the whole man, who can see equally heat,

241

misery, hunger, life or death.[87] The emotions which dominate conscious life for this kind of man are above all those which act upon the respiration. The Hebrew, to be sure, is not unaware of the profound emotions, those which affect his inner self, the type of which is the movement in the mother's womb, forever linked to the child which comes from thence. But the common emotions, especially in the man, do not reach these depths: fear, anger, sadness, joy, primarily affect the breathing, which they either constrict or overstimulate. Job's emotions can also be interpreted in terms of conscience:

> I will speak in the anguish of my spirit [*ruah*];
> I will complain in the bitterness of my soul [*nephesh*],[88]

or in physiological terminology:

> I will speak with halting breath,
> I will complain with bitter breath.

Out of context, both translations would be inaccurate. They have to be superimposed.

Man's *ruah*, the rhythm of breathing on which his life depends, is, therefore, more than the symbol or expression of consciousness. It is consciousness itself, now stirred by anxiety, like that of Pharaoh wakening from his dream,[89] now full of jealous bitterness, like that of Isaac and Rebecca in the face of Esau's marriages,[90] now full of joy, like that of Jacob learning that his son Joseph is alive.[91] But it is the moments of exaltation[92] and especially of anger[93] which reveal the true nature of the *ruah*, full of vigor and strength.

Until its contact with Hellenism, Hebrew thought never stopped representing the vital principle in man as a material force. Its naive realism gives it the appearance of materialism. Yet this mentality is at the very antipodes of modern materialism because, as far as it is concerned, matter is totally dependent on the divine action; for it, the breath of life which animates man puts him into immediate contact with God. It never came

242

to the point of thinking of a pure spirit, but it possesses a profound sense of the action of God in the world, and this action is purely spiritual. In the religious sphere, properly speaking, Greek thought—which was to be for Christianity an instrument of incomparable reflection—brings no new lights to Judaism. The Book of Wisdom, which affirms, as the final conquest of the Old Testament, the immortality of man, does not pretend to base its belief on the imperishable nature of the breath which animates him, any more than it has recourse to philosophical reflection on the spiritual essence of a being capable of thinking and willing.[94] It bases its affirmation on a purely religious conviction, namely, the impossibility of God's depriving those who loved Him above all things in the world, of His presence. For Wisdom, as for the entire biblical tradition, the breath of life is too essentially divine to remain full of man's personality once it has returned to its author. He who has made man, He who "breathed into him a quickening soul, and infused a vital spirit,"[95] simply grants a temporary loan to His creature, to this man who

> . . . shortly before was made from the earth
> And after a little, is to go whence he was taken,
> when the life that was lent him is demanded back.[96]

And St. Luke, repeating the same formula with reference to the foolish rich man:

> This night do they demand thy soul of thee,[97]

is rediscovering in its purity the Hebrew tradition in which there was no question even of use and loan, and in which the soul came directly from God.

It seems that the Old Testament comes to an impasse on this point. Permeated with the divine character which sets man apart, it makes, out of the breath of life which animates man and gives him consciousness, a force which has come from God and is destined to return to Him. However, this force is too frankly divine to be anything but a borrowed gift, a passing guest, in man. How could it be man himself, the individual of flesh and blood? It is unthinkable. Unthinkable, yet does it not have to be so? Man cannot dissociate himself from his life, from his soul. The parallelism which he sets up spontaneously between the *ruah* and the *nephesh*, between the divine principle, the spirit, and the earthly element, the soul, manifests this necessary unity. Divine soul or personal soul, how are we to choose if we cannot sacrifice anything?

In truth, the problem, posed in these terms, is of a speculative order and is not set forth in the Bible. The real problem, the practical problem of life after death was resolved by awaiting the Resurrection, which is the principal Christian dogma.[98] Still, it is not impossible that the Gospels, on this score, may have shed a decisive light on Christian thought.

As He was expiring, Jesus gave forth a cry borrowed from a psalm: "Father, into thy hands I commend my spirit."[99] But He gives this formula a meaning unknown to the entire Old Testament. To commend His breath into the hands of God was, in the proper sense, to die, to return to its author the breath which had come from Him and which had brought life. Job knew that God holds

> in his hand . . . the soul of every living thing,
> and the life breath of all mankind,[100]

and that, therefore, He does not abandon the breath which has come from His mouth. The suppliant in Psalm 30 gives an even deeper meaning to this already religious but still naturalistic belief. He sees in it the symbol and proof of a special protection, of a personal bond which ties him to God and guarantees that he will come forth out of the trials which are besetting him. To remit his breath into the hands of God no longer means, for Him, to die, but rather, as is borne out by the following verse—"You will redeem me, O Lord, O faithful God"—to be restored to a safe life and to peace. By means of this formula, the psalmist was attaching a very high religious value to the

244

common belief, but he could not go beyond the scope of the image. On His own account, at the moment when He was actually remitting to God the material breath which animated His body, Jesus, in stating that God would receive His breath and would give it back to Him (for the explicit quotation necessarily invokes its context in the psalm), was transforming the image into reality. He was pushing beyond death a hope which had served the psalmist only to turn death aside, and He fulfilled, while seeming to ruin it, mankind's hope and the promise of the Scriptures. He was also resolving the problem left unsolved in the Old Testament. In all biblical tradition the soul was a mysterious force in man, coming directly from God and destined to return to Him; however, it was also manifestly the most profound substance of man, his most personal being. To remit it to God, to lose it, was to find it again through death.[101] This is Christian immortality.

3. THE SPIRIT OF THE LORD

The fact that the mysteries of the wind or the vital breath manifest Yahweh's breath is the proof of a still-primitive anthropomorphism in Israel, but also of a profound sense of the divine power and of its presence in the world. We can also understand that these beliefs may reappear, transformed, in the revelation of Christ, along with the affirmation of a God who is at once spirit and life,[102] a power radically different from all flesh, and, yet, capable of transforming flesh and giving it eternal life.

However religious these representations may be in the Old Testament, they still do not go beyond the area of what we might call a naturalistic religion. Many of the biblical expressions which see in the wind or the respiration of the living being the breath of God, have their parallel in Babylon and Egypt.[103] Amon, Aton or Marduk are asked to send to their devotees "their good breath," in order to give them back health and life. The god of the air, Shou, gives life to men by an act identical with that of Yahweh creating Adam:

I make them subsist and keep them in life by the action of my mouth, I, the life which is found in their nostrils, I lead my breath into their throat.[104]

This representation is especially frequent in Egypt. So much so that it is quite tempting to believe that the Israelitic notion of the *ruah* of God, the vivifying power specially borne by favorable winds, was derived from imported ideas. Israel would then simply have purified these ideas by ridding them of their polytheistic context and concentrating in Yahweh, the unique God and the God of justice, all the mysterious forces felt in the world.

It is quite true, in fact, that Yahweh holds, in Israel, the place held by the various divinities of the surrounding paganisms. His role is to insure the harmonious march of the world, to keep evil, famine, and epidemics away, to give heat and rain in due season. Far from rejecting this role, Yahweh claims it and promises His faithful that He will put at their disposal the benefits of nature.[105] The God of Jesus Christ Himself is at all times the God who makes the sun shine and the rain fall.[106] The true God is also the God of the "nature" religions, those which expect from God the effects of which man feels himself incapable, but which yet do not transcend the normal course of human events.

Properly speaking, the representations of the *ruah* of God as the source of the wind and of the vital breath belong in this category. They give a religious explanation to natural phenomena. Profoundly permeated with the sentiment of human weakness and divine grandeur, they do not presuppose any interventions in the world other than His normal action on nature and on living things. They certainly ignore determinism and are not astonished by any sort of fantasy in God. But they do not envision the possibility that God could, throughout the normal development of the world, carry on a history other than that of

246

empires, spread into consciences forces other than the spontaneous drives of life.

Israel was the first to experience these interventions. Aware that it owed its birth to an unparalleled act of God, convinced of being promised a higher destiny, it sees repeated in its own midst some exceptional events. To whom to attribute these marvels, except to God? But men wanted to make this action of God more specific. They saw therein the work of His *ruah*. Two manifestations thereof were already known, the wind and the life-breath, in which were found the same mysterious power of acting at a distance and of entering into the very heart of things, of overcoming their inertia. The extraordinary actions which were multiplied in the history of the Hebrew people came, therefore, from a similar power, and were also attributed to the breath of God.

Although the wind and the life-breath remained entirely dependent on God, they progressively revealed the aspect of a natural phenomenon, for the former, and an ever-more individualized force, for the latter, and therefore ceased to be merely "the breath of Yahweh." Meanwhile the power which was manifested in Israel which was, more and more an interior one, more and more different from all natural forces, underwent an inverse evolution, constantly showing its divine traits and ending up by reserving to itself the name of "spirit of the Lord." A first series of phenomena is especially attributed to the spirit of the Lord. These are rapid or instantaneous movements. They are frequent in the story of Elias. One never knew when he might suddenly disappear: "the spirit of the Lord will carry thee into a place that I know not."[107] At times, these effects are not attributed to Yahweh's spirit but to His hand. Thus, on the day when Elias, on Carmel, having seen a light cloud coming up out of the sea, felt the hand of Yahweh upon himself, "he girded up his loins and ran," at one point in front of Achab's chariot, "till he came to Jezrahel."[108] Another series of texts gives an identical role to the spirit of Yahweh. These are the visions of Ezechiel. The spirit takes the prophet away and transports him to Tel-Abib,[109] or to Jerusalem,[110] and then returns him to Chaldea.[111] As in Elias, the spirit is often associated with the hand of Yahweh.[112] The spirit, blowing from the north in a storm, brings the celestial vision of the four living things which stand around Yahweh's glory, and sets in motion the wheels on which they are advancing.[113]

In all these texts, there are many instances where one might translate "wind" instead of "spirit." It is clear that, in these miraculous movements, the spirit of Yahweh is indeed a "wind of Yahweh," but a wind of quite a different sort from those which blow on earth, a wind charged with an exceptional mission, and bearer of the glory of Yahweh Himself. In these visions are fulfilled the images of the biblical poets. None of these texts makes a personal being out of the spirit; it is at all times a force similar to the wind, but in immediate contact with the Lord.

This aspect of the spirit is found even in the New Testament. When Philip had baptized the eunuch of the Queen of Ethiopia, and when they "came up out of the water, the Spirit of the Lord took Philip away, and the eunuch saw him no more."[114] For St. Luke, the Holy Spirit is the great artisan of the infant Church. He can still act in the manner of an all-powerful wind. Even when these violent manifestations are lacking, the ministry of the Apostles is determined by the impulses of the Holy Spirit. It is He who sends Paul and Barnabas to Seleucia from Cyprus,[115] who forbids entrance into Asia.[116] Throughout the Acts, the Pentecostal wind never stops blowing. In the Gospels, the account of the temptation of Jesus in the desert opens with a word which, especially in Mark, recalls the irresistible force of Yahweh's Spirit: "And immediately the Spirit drove him forth into the desert."[117]

The difference between the material wind and the spirit of

248

God as these texts present it is not that between an impersonal force and an individual being. It is primarily the difference between a mysterious though natural force and another force, incomparably more powerful, and, above all, productive of results foreign to the normal order of the world, attesting to the special intentions of God.

Only by way of exception is the role of Yahweh's spirit this still semi-external role. Most of the time, it is interior. The spirit of God acts on the spirit of man.

At the origin of these representations are no doubt found those conditions in which man seems no longer to belong to himself. The spirit which ordinarily animates him—which, of course, comes from God but over which he still feels himself the master—disappears under pressure from a violent force which takes possession of his consciousness and which can only be a more vigorous consciousness than his own, another spirit. Jealousy, for example, proceeds from a "spirit which passes over man";[118] it is also a wicked spirit which unleashes in Saul the fits of jealousy against David,[119] or which comes to sow discord between Abimelech and the people of Sichem.[120] It is a "spirit of fornication" which establishes itself "in the midst of Israel," so that they "have not known the Lord."[121] For the normal awareness, another force has been substituted, a force which comes from elsewhere, from the regions of the spirit.

It is possible that, in many cases, these spirits are truly personal beings, "demons" circulating in the world. Since, moreover, the passages in which the personal character of these spirits seems clearest are also those in which their dependence upon the Lord is most obvious,[122] there is no affront to monotheism. However, it is important to note that the texts in question are of popular origin or tone, that they are dominated by the always concrete tendency of the popular account in regard to the setting, and that the personal nature of these spirits may at times be no more than a device required to point the moral of the story.

Moreover, even where the personal traits of this spirit are least contestable, e.g., in the vision of the prophet Micheas, son of Jimla, who, in the midst of the heavenly army, sees a spirit begin to speak in the presence of Yahweh, this spirit, once it has come down to earth "into the mouth of the prophets," does not act in them like a ventriloquist might, a talking spirit which would make use of their voices; it comes to blind their spirit by establishing itself in them as a new personality.[123]

In the majority of cases, the spirit which takes possession in this way, by doing violence to the human consciousness, comes from God, even if its immediate action seems harmful.[124] Often it is called "the spirit of Elohim," on one occasion, "the evil spirit of Yahweh,"[125] but never simply the "spirit of Yahweh."

The spirit of Yahweh, in fact, does not demonstrate these wicked features. It is a spirit of good. Not that its primary role is to effect a moral transformation in those whom it surrounds. It puts them in a position to fulfill the extraordinary missions to which Yahweh destines them. These missions are of two kinds, one of liberation, the other of prophecy. They both seem about equally ancient and go back to the first recollections of the settlement in Palestine.

The exploits of the Judges are attributed to a sudden incursion of the spirit of the Lord which "was upon Othoniel,"[126] or upon Jephte[127] like a force coming from on high, which "came," like a wild beast upon its prey, over Samson,[128] or Saul,[129] which "enveloped Gedeon" like a garment,[130] to make them all capable of unheard-of feats of boldness. All these expressions, often picturesque and popular, which perhaps do not exclude the image of a personal being, bring out in a forcible manner, both the brusque change which transforms men who seem in no way prepared for it and have no presentiment of it, into heroes, and the "supernatural," divine, origin of this transformation.

These actions are not simply marvelous feats; they are all liberating actions. Isolated exploits of local heroes, scarcely going beyond the boundaries of one tribe and occasionally of its neighbors, they nevertheless are part of the same history, and mark stages in the progressive march which led Israel to independence. It is this liberating movement which constitutes their unity. The interventions of Yahweh's spirit at these different stages underscores one of the focal points of the divine action in the Old Testament. The spirit of God is at the source of the national community of Israel.

The Judges are still only temporary liberators, and the spirit which animates them leaves them once their mission is accomplished. But they have as their heir the king, who is entrusted on a permanent basis with securing the independence and existence of the people. Also, the spirit of the Lord remains with them in a continuous way. As soon as Samuel had poured over David his horn of oil, "the spirit of the Lord came upon David," but, adds the text, "from that day forward."[131] The expression is awkward; it juxtaposes a lasting formula and an instantaneous action. This is because it combines two different representations: the old image of the spirit coming upon Samson or Saul, for some unusual action, and the new idea of the king, definitively entrusted with a divine power.[132] It can be said of David, according to the subsequent expression of the prophets, that the spirit "rests" on him, consecrating him irrevocably to the salvation of his people.

Such is the vision which Isaias sets before Israel. On the Messias whom he announces—the ideal king of a regenerated people—the spirit of Yahweh will rest permanently, consecrating him for his supernatural mission:

> The spirit of wisdom and of understanding,
> The spirit of counsel and of fortitude,
> The spirit of knowledge and of godliness.[133]

Here, the spirit is no longer coming down only to insure the liberty or the normal government of Israel. It is coming in order to establish it in the joy of a new Eden, where harmony, rediscovered by nature, is the fruit of the transformation of hearts, where peace is the "work of justice."[134] The spirit of the Lord keeps the role it played among the first heroes of independence; however, the religious experiences of Isaias, by raising this liberation onto a higher level, give an incomparably more profound role to the spirit of Yahweh. Passionately concerned with justice, aware that the independence of his people requires the renunciation of the calculations of human policies, the prophet also sees that this work goes beyond the strength of the best ruler, that a force from on high is needed, the coming of the spirit of Yahweh.

In Israel, at the same time as the Judges, there lived prophets, the *nabis*. Grouped into communities, they constituted, as it were, "professionals in religious exaltation."[135] Their transports, at all times mixed with a large portion of human actions, dances, music, were to seem rather suspect to the great prophets to come.[136] While the religion of the *nabis* was too receptive to the impulses of popular piety, it was nonetheless faithful to the religion of Yahweh. Ecstasy, the characteristic phenomenon of this prophetism, is attributed to the spirit of Yahweh. The action of this spirit is described by the same terms as the action He exercises on the Judges. The "consecration" of Saul does not take effect until the new king, on Samuel's suggestion, joins a band of prophets, and, until, through contact with their exaltation, the spirit of Yahweh which possesses the group "comes upon" the new recruit and changes him into a different man, making him "prophesy," that is, go into trances, exactly like the other prophets.[137]

Tradition also placed the *nabis* in the circle around Moses. His sister Miriam was a prophetess.[138] The seventy elders grouped around him were prophets whenever Yahweh's spirit came over them.[139] Far from deprecating these transports, the narrator sees in them a precious gift of the Lord:

> Would that all the people of the Lord were prophets!
> Would that the Lord might bestow his spirit on them all![140]

These extraordinary manifestations of the spirit in prophetic phenomena are therefore considered at this time as one of the living forces of the religion of Israel, and that is why people see therein the authentic spirit of Yahweh. But the later prophets, those whose works have been preserved for us in the Old Testament, were hardly inclined to develop this tendency. Generally eager to differentiate their action from the tumultuous manifestations of the *nabis*,[141] preoccupied with giving lessons to their hearers, they present themselves as the bearers of Yahweh's word more than of His spirit. The conflict of Micheas, son of Jimla, with the prophets of the court of Samaria, demonstrates how the prophetic manifestations could, without ceasing to be considered authentic, appear wicked to a servant of God. In the eyes of Micheas, that which is speaking in the court prophets is indeed a spirit of Yahweh, but not *the* spirit of Yahweh. Also, Micheas is confident, not that he possesses a spirit, but that he speaks "whatsoever the Lord shall say to me."[142]

If the great prophets of Israel, Amos, Osee, Isaias, Jeremias, do not claim to have the spirit of Yahweh,[143] it is not because they are not aware of possessing it, it is because they realize that they possess it in a different way than do the *nabis* who came before them or the false prophets who are their rivals. They do not dispute the existence of a supernatural exaltation in the latter, they do not question that it may come from Yahweh, but they consider these manifestations without importance and sometimes misleading. God does not truly reveal Himself through these. He does act, of course, and pursues His designs, but His intention remains hidden. The secrets of Yahweh are found in His word and the true prophets are the confidants of this word:

For the Lord God doth nothing without revealing his secret to his servants the prophets.[144]

Jeremias defies the false prophets who speak without having received this word:

For who hath stood in the counsel of the Lord and hath seen and heard his word?[145]

It seems that Elias on Horeb already had experienced the superiority of the word of Yahweh over the tumultuous manifestations which are still only external signs of His presence. The scene in the Book of Kings evidently refers to the former manifestations of Yahweh, in the chaos of the unleashed thunderstorms.[146] This time, the Lord is neither in the wind, nor in the earthquake, nor in the fire.[147] He is in the faint murmuring which permits the ear to hear a "voice," Yahweh confiding in His prophet.[148]

The prophet is not an inert depository of this word: it works in him and transforms him. Isaias cannot carry the message of Yahweh until his lips have been purified by contact with the divine fire itself.[149] The moment of his calling is the moment when "he has taught me, with a strong arm."[150] To be grasped by the hand of God is at the same time to be possessed by His spirit.[151] The two actions have the same significance, the surrounding of man by the divine power. When Yahweh puts His words into the mouth of Jeremias before sending him to preach, He "put forth his hand and touched [the] mouth" of the prophet.[152] Therefore, Jeremias no longer belongs to himself; he is dominated by a force which leads him. He feels his being rebelling against it; it is a real agony, but God is the stronger:

Thou hast deceived me, O Lord, and I am deceived; thou hast been stronger than I, and thou hast prevailed.[153]

The word spirit may not be pronounced, yet the experiences of the great prophets, upset by an intervention of God which reaches into the very core of their beings, and entrusted with a mission which opposes them to an entire people, reproduce, on an altogether different, incomparably more spiritual, level, the marvels of the spirit of Yahweh in regard to the Judges and the *nabis*.

The extraordinary phenomena of the primitive prophetism reappear, moreover, with an exceptional power, in the ecstasies and visions of Ezechiel. Also, Ezechiel always attributes these ecstasies to the spirit.[154] Still, there are many points of difference between the effects of the spirit in him and in the *nabis*. The spirit which took these early prophets out of themselves and led them to extraordinary acts of strength or of penetration, made its effects felt in the natural world. The spirit which inspires Ezechiel transports him into a higher world, the world of heavenly visions, symbolizing the interior world, the action of God on hearts. The spirit of Yahweh is, in him, something quite other than an ecstatic force overwhelming the consciousness; it is the instrument of a divine providence.

The spirit which rests on the person of the Servant of Yahweh is stripped of all external features, and purely destined to consecrate for an exceptional mission the heart of the chosen one of God:

Behold my servant: I will uphold him. My elect: my soul delighteth in him. I have given my spirit upon him; he shall bring forth judgment to the Gentiles.[155]

The role of the spirit recalls both the role it played in the case of the prophet Micheas,[156] and that which it played in the case of the king-messias of Isaias.[157] The chosen one of God is to promote the coming of justice, and this mission goes beyond human strength. The word of the prophet, the action of the king, take their strength from the spirit of the Lord. The action of the Servant of Yahweh is of a still more mysterious order than that of the prophet or of the king.[158] His destiny seems impossible to decipher and remains an enigma even to the prophet who announces it. One point, at any rate, is sure: his mission will be a divine one and the spirit of Yahweh will be His strength. Thus, as Israel sees higher callings born in her womb, the power of the spirit who calls them forth grows greater. Its role becomes more mysterious and more divine each time.

Another divine mission, a mission which sums up and fulfills the mission of all the prophets, is that of the herald whose job it is to announce the "good news" to Jerusalem: God Himself will come to deliver it and to unite Himself to it in eternal nuptials:

The spirit of the Lord is upon me, because the Lord hath anointed me. He hath sent me to preach to the meek, to heal the contrite of heart.[159]

This text has often been compared with the passages concerning the Servant of Yahweh.[160] However, nothing in these chapters seems to presuppose a mission similar to that which the chants of the Servant outline. The herald who speaks is presented as a prophet. However, the news which he brings is so beautiful that he needs an exceptional gift of the spirit in order to be equal to his message; he needs an anointing which would permeate him definitively, not just in a passing way. Thus he is the type of the prophet par excellence, a type of Jesus,[161] of Him whom the spirit will not seize merely for a few hours and for this or that message, but will lead throughout His life, because His entire existence is to be the message of God, and each one of His actions the Good News, the Gospel.

Jewish tradition after the exile, for which the great figures of Israel are always the prophets, dwells upon the action of the spirit upon these prophets. In the later Judaism, at the time of Jesus, the Holy Spirit is above all the spirit who has spoken through the mouth of the prophets.[162] Such is still the formula of the Christian Creed: "*Qui locutus est per prophetas . . .*," a formula which summarizes and sheds light upon the meaning of the entire Old Testament. Entirely prophetic, entirely announcing Christ,[163] Scripture is completely animated by the breath which brought forth these inspired men and revealed in them its own power. Zacharias is aware of this continuity of the divine action:

And they made their heart as the adamant stone, lest they should hear the law and the words which the Lord of hosts sent in his spirit by the hand of the former prophets.[164]

The Book of Esdras repeats the same idea in the same terms:

[Thou didst] testify against them by thy spirit, by the hand of thy prophets.[165]

For the first time, the spirit of Yahweh is here called a witness. Its entire action in the Old Testament, through the prophets, was therefore a witness rendered to God. Witness is also the word constantly associated with the Holy Spirit by the New Testament. In the Synoptics, the spirit speaks for the disciples accused before the tribunals "to give witness" to Jesus,[166] that is, the witness given by the disciples is precisely that of the spirit. Also, Jesus, renewing before His Ascension the promise of the Spirit, links it with the testimony which they shall have to give: "But you shall receive power when the Holy Spirit comes upon you, and you shall be witnesses for me."[167] In St. John too, the promise of the spirit is the promise of assistance in their mission, and the role of the spirit will be that of giving witness:

But when the Advocate has come, whom I will send you from the Father, the Spirit of truth who proceeds from the Father, he will bear witness concerning me. And you also bear witness.[168]

This witness "will convict the world of sin, and of justice, and of judgment."[169] According to St. Paul, this Spirit, living in us, "gives testimony to our spirit that we are sons of God."[170]

From the time when it came down upon a Samson or a David, in order to show the Philistines the power of the God of Israel, the spirit of Yahweh had never ceased bearing witness to Him who sent it. Nevertheless, this witness remained obscure for a long time. Of course, it showed that God can give other forces than the breath of earthly life, and that He has other designs than the fecundity of nature. But what were these designs? As long as they remained hidden, one could not really speak of testimony. The first ones in whom the manifestations of the spirit are a witness, are the prophets. The superhuman power which fills them comes to them from the fact that they are the confidants of Yahweh. They have heard His word and they are the bearers thereof. They reveal to Israel the meaning of the adventure to which God has committed it. Their testimony is always overwhelming: the prophets cannot show to the people the ways of Yahweh except by convicting it of sin.

The testimony which the spirit gives to Jesus among His own has many traits in common with that of the prophets. It is a testimony given face to face with the adversary, a light which lays bare sin.[171] But it is above all the witness of a possession. The prophets perceived in flashes the word of God; the disciples saw it and touched it. The spirit does not come as a passing shower but remains "forever"[172] among His own in order to "bring to your mind whatever [Jesus] . . . said,"[173] to put them into permanent contact with the Word which God has given to the world and which will never cease belonging to it. In this familiarity with the Son in which the spirit establishes them, Christians, in their turn, discover themselves to be children of the Father, capable of speaking with Him.[174] The witness of the spirit is fulfilled in an inexhaustible intimacy.

4. THE OUTPOURING OF THE SPIRIT

Through those it inspired, particularly the prophets, the spirit of Yahweh designated a succession of witnesses in Israel. They were witnesses to God's power, witnesses to a power which had to extend beyond them to the whole people. Thus, the prophets are the representatives of a new era, and the spirit which possesses them is the guarantee of this future. In this way is established a twofold tradition concerning the spirit of Yahweh. It descends, like a special anointing, onto certain privileged ones—and this coming down is itself the harbinger of an outpouring which will spread this spirit over the entire community.[175] These two missions remain separate throughout the entire Old Testament. Perhaps they are found again in the New Testament, the one in the form of charisms—individual graces designed for the good of the community[176]—the other in the effusion into the heart of every Christian of charity and a filial spirit.[177]

This twofold tradition goes back to Isaias. In Chapter 21, he sees the spirit of Yahweh resting on the king-messias. All Israel is transformed by it, since this king is to establish a kingdom of justice, and the prophet turns the country into a paradisiac tableau. However, in a passage which undoubtedly dates back to the same epoch,[178] Isaias shows the spirit coming down on all the people:

Until the spirit be poured upon us from on high. And the desert shall be as a Charmel; and Charmel shall be counted for a forest.

And judgment shall dwell in the wilderness; and justice shall sit in Charmel.[179]

Along with a new idea, this text establishes a new image, one which is to become traditional, that of the spirit "poured out" upon the people, like a rain which comes to moisten and fecundate the parched earth.[180] Moreover, to describe the action of a wicked spirit, sent by God to cause the destruction of those whom He is punishing, Isaias uses similar images. To confound the rulers of Egypt,

The Lord has mingled in the midst thereof the spirit of giddiness; and they have caused Egypt to err in all its works, as a drunken man staggereth and vomiteth.[181]

Yahweh has poured forth on the false prophets a "spirit of a deep sleep,"[182] as one would pour a liquid. Still, in these images, it is not so much a question of an outpouring which covers an entire country but of a liquid prepared in advance that God gives to drink to those whom He wants to destroy. But Jeremias does not hesitate to say that Yahweh will "pour out their own wickedness upon them,"[183] like a hateful rain.

259

For the ancient images which suggested the abrupt seizure of a man by the spirit—a springing animal, bodies all contorted into strange gestures—are substituted images of a different order. These evoke the fluidity of the liquid which seeps into the most recessed depths and which gradually permeates the hardest substances. This liquid always comes from on high, from a higher power. It is the prophets who associated the gift of Yahweh's spirit with the trickling of rain escaping from the heavenly reservoirs. Free like the rain, depending only on Yahweh's good pleasure, it falls like the rain onto arid terrain in order to pour forth upon it renewal and life.

Rain or wind, it is remarkable that heaven, the image of the spirit, part of the divine region of the world, should return here. But it is not a natural association that has linked the rain with the wind. It is the religious experience of Israel, particularly that of the prophets, which perceived transformations more profound and more definitive than the outbursts of religious exaltation of the Judges or of the *nabis*. Typical of this is Jeremias, who seems not to know the spirit of Yahweh on his own account, yet is without any doubt one of the decisive agents of this evolution. It is Jeremias who, amid the catastrophe which engulfed Jerusalem, had the clearest awareness of what the restoration of the people would be, namely a transformation of hearts:

And I will give them a heart to know me, that I am the Lord. And they shall be my people, and I will be their God.[184]

But this shall be the covenant that I will make with the house of Israel after those days, saith the Lord: I will give my law in their bowels and I will write it in their heart: and I will be their God, and they shall be my people.[185]

Linking the images created by Isaias, of the messianic renovation under the outpouring of the spirit, with those of the renewal of hearts foretold by Jeremias, Ezechiel consecrates the interior role of the spirit of Yahweh:

> And I will pour upon you clean water and you shall be cleansed from all your filthiness: and I will cleanse you from all your idols.
>
> And I will give you a new heart and put a new spirit within you: and I will take away the stony heart out of your flesh and will give you a heart of flesh.
>
> And I will put my spirit in the midst of you: and I will cause you to walk in my commandments and to keep my judgments and do them.[186]

Here the spirit of Yahweh is like a new spirit of man, a new awareness, a new principle of action, producing a new existence. The influence of Jeremias is obvious, and literal. But we must note the presence of water. Elsewhere, Ezechiel repeats, if not the word itself, at least the image of Isaias, in order to announce the hour of the renovation:

> And I will hide my face no more from them, for I have poured out my spirit upon all the house of Israel.[187]

This is not an image of the rain, or rather, it is the image of a sacred rain, a ritual libation. Ezechiel is a priest: the actions of God, exalted though they may be, cannot, to his eyes, be other than liturgical actions. This libation of water poured forth on a whole people is the liturgical equivalent of Isaias' cosmic vision of a divine rain fecundating the earth for a springtime without precedent.

This combination of cosmic and liturgical themes, which makes Ezechiel one of the forerunners of the Apocalypse, is for him the means of representing the new world, the idea of which he found in his predecessors, particularly Jeremias. In a series of visions, he uncovers a world with horizons unknown to earth, where, however, a story unfolds which is the very story of his people. Thus, he reconstitutes the experiences lived by Jeremias in the turmoil of his heart.

It is thus that the wind of Yahweh, a material but divine force, had become in him an apocalyptic power. The famous vision of the dry bones,[188] synthesizes quite accurately the complex features of the spirit of Yahweh in Ezechiel. In the breath of the wind on the plain are found the old representations of the wind of Yahweh, messenger of His orders and chariot of His glory; however, the plain no longer belongs to earth and its dimensions are those of heaven. In the life-giving action of this breath permeating the corpses, is expressed the common belief in the presence of God's breath in the respiration of the living person. However, the dead involved are not human corpses, but rather the hopes of Israel; the very life of the people has gone out, and Yahweh will make it shine forth again. If, in the mixture of traditional images and visions of a new type, the spirit of Yahweh assumes traits which are clearly more personal, its role remains, in sum, the one which it had in Isaias.

The second part of the Book of Isaias repeats the promise of a new existence to the people awaiting the end of the exile. Like his predecessors, Isaias associates the spirit with the water which fecundates the earth:

> For I will pour out waters upon the thirsty ground and streams upon the dry land: I will pour out my spirit upon thy seed and my blessing upon thy stock.[189]

The theme of water here is enriched by new images. The verb "to pour out" still evokes the gift of rain; but now, it is the earth itself, the desert, which will give rise to the streams and the springs.[190] Not that they have changed their nature: they remain what they are; the power of the spirit which "pours out" these streams is that it makes these living waters spring forth out of arid and barren soil. Here is a miracle impossible to man, a transformation which is not just a simply renovation but a new creation.

One of the last chapters of the Book of Isaias shows the entire people become prophet and bearer of Yahweh's word. This word is not an extraordinary revelation: it is merely the Law:

> This is my covenant with them, saith the Lord: My spirit that is in thee and my words that I have put in thy mouth shall not depart out of thy mouth, nor out of the mouth of thy seed, nor out of the mouth of thy seed's seed, saith the Lord, from henceforth and for ever.[191]

262

The text is quite obscure, all the more so because it is difficult to see its connection with its context. Still, one point seems sure, the reference to the provisions of Deuteronomy. It is Deuteronomy which sees, in the law of Israel, a "word" placed by God "in your mouths and in your hearts,"[192] a word to be transmitted faithfully "to your children and to your children's children."[193] What was, in Deuteronomy, a commandment imposed, here becomes a promise of God. The covenant imposed on Israel terms which it continually failed to meet. Here God promises the new covenant, which will not depend on the ever-deficient forces of the flesh, but on the power of the spirit poured forth upon the people. This is precisely the teaching of Jeremias and Ezechiel. This text is also remarkable because it continues to associate the spirit with the word. Just as the breath of the spirit was necessary to the prophets, in order to render them capable of perceiving and announcing the word of Yahweh, so now the new people will need the gift of the spirit in order to make them adhere to God's word.

The last of the promises of the spirit in the prophets, that of Joel, the one which Peter and the Apostles will see fulfilled on Pentecost day, is in the same vein. It links water and the spirit, the people and the prophets:

> And it shall come to pass after this, that I will pour out my spirit upon all flesh: and your sons and your daughters shall prophesy; your old men shall dream dreams, your young men shall see visions.
> Moreover upon my servants and handmaids in those days I will pour forth my spirit.[194]

All prophets, all possessed by the spirit. It is, in apocalyptic terms, the promise of the former prophets; it is the coming of the day when the entire people is to be transformed by the force which was acting in Moses or David, Isaias or Ezechiel.[195]

The Christians had the experience of what this promise meant. They felt themselves engulfed beneath a heavenly flood. Of course, they did not invent the word "baptism." John the

Baptist, calling the Jews unto this immersion, announced to them that, after him, another, greater than he, would "baptize them in the spirit."[196] This formula continued to associate water and the spirit. After the departure of Jesus, the disciples live in the expectation of this baptism,[197] and Pentecost, though the exterior signs thereof are the wind and the fire, seems to them to be this outpouring of heaven.[198] St. Paul, speaking of baptism in the spirit—"for in one spirit we were all baptized into one body"—is caught up in this image of the quenching and life-giving water: "and we were all given to drink of one Spirit."[199]

In the same vein, but in his unique manner, St. John gathers into one statement a whole series of images. The spirit, for him, is "the living water":

> If anyone thirst, let him come to me and drink. He who believes in me, as the Scripture says: "From within him there shall flow rivers of living water." He said this, however, of the Spirit.[200]

By himself, man is but a barren land, incapable of producing anything. Let the spirit come, like a shower from on high, and from this inert flesh, from this dried-up heart, there will flow springs and life itself. Living water: the adjective is chosen purposely, for life is one of the essential traits of the spirit. The words of Jesus are "spirit and life."[201] Thus, all the biblical themes of the spirit are brought together. This convergence which seems so natural in St. John, is a perfectly conscious one. When Jesus promises "living water"[202] to the Samaritan woman, he adds that this water will become, in him who believes, "a fountain of water, springing up unto life everlasting."[203] The verb he uses, ἅλλομαι, does not usually mean the bubbling up of a spring but rather the leaping of a living being. In the Septuagint translation, it appears only in order to denote the rising up of the spirit which comes down upon Samson, Saul, or David.[204]

5. THE HOLY SPIRIT

None of the texts we have encountered so far in the Old Testament lets us see a person in the spirit of Yahweh. It is not the most "spiritual" passages, those richest in scope, which give us a glimpse, as it were, of the person of the Holy Spirit. It is, rather, the most primitive pages, those of naive and popular aspect, or else the visions of Ezechiel, which give the spirit of Yahweh personal characteristics. The case of Ezechiel must be considered separately: his visions are a representation of the divine world, obtained by means of a transposition into symbols of the interior world of Jeremias; and it is difficult to determine the nature of these heavenly personages. It seems, in short, that the spirit of Yahweh is all the more powerful, all the more mysterious, all the more "spirit," when he is less personal.

Still, some texts give this spirit, not features which are more personal, but a new name which will endure: the Holy Spirit. A chapter of Isaias evokes the passage through the Red Sea:

In all their affliction he was not troubled; and the angel of his presence saved them. In his love, and in his mercy he redeemed them: and he carried them and lifted them up all the days of old.
But they provoked to wrath and afflicted the spirit of his Holy One: and he was turned to be their enemy, and he fought against them.
And he remembered the days of old, of Moses and of his people: Where is he that brought them up out of the sea, with the shepherds of his flock? Where is he that put in the midst of them the spirit of his Holy One?
He that brought out Moses by the right hand, by the arm of his majesty: that divided the waters before them, to make himself an everlasting name.
He that led them out through the deep, as a horse in the wilderness that stumbleth not:
As a beast that goeth down in the field. The spirit of the Lord was their leader.[205]

Here the Holy Spirit does not merely assume a new name, but an unknown role. Up to now, present among the prophets, He was promised to the people for the day of the restoration, in the messianic future which God was reserving for Israel. He

265

is here revealed as already present in the past, and, in a specific way, during the sacred period of the Exodus. The prophet discovers the divine reality which manifested itself amid miracles of which the people's traditions keep an exalting memory: "it was the holy spirit. He was the ark which God placed in the midst of the waters"; He was the column of cloud which divided the sea, defended the camp against the Egyptian army and guided the march through the desert; He was also the mighty arm which gave the actions of Moses their miraculous power. From the Red Sea to the Promised Land, the Holy Spirit never stopped being in the midst of His people, and it is His presence which made of these forty years the divine period in the people's life, the period of the great miracles and great punishments, that in which Israel lived in immediate contact with its God, His jealousy and His kindness.

For, if the Holy Spirit seems in this context more completely "given" to men than elsewhere, present in their midst, moving about with His people, linking His existence, so to speak, to their fortunes, He is also closer than ever to Yahweh. He is "holy," that is, He belongs to the Holy One, to God. He is, indeed, "more than a messenger, more than an angel," as He had perhaps been thought of; He is "his very face," the very person of God, and it is God Himself that the rebellion and ingratitude of the people attacked. Thus, the more breadth and scope the role of the Spirit of God has in the world and in history, the more His features are delineated, so to speak, and the less they appear to be separate from those of God. It is not by revealing features that are progressively more individual that the Spirit of God becomes the Holy Spirit; it is rather by revealing new aspects of the power of God and of His presence in His creation.

Chapter 63 of Isaias revealed such wealth in the action of the spirit of Yahweh in Israel that it profoundly inspired subsequent piety. Nehemias, causing the Levites to recapitulate the

266

history of Israel in the presence of the assembled people, sums up the Exodus in these terms:

> Thou gavest them thy good Spirit to teach them: and thy manna thou didst not withhold from their mouth; and thou gavest them water for their thirst.[206]

The association of water, manna, and the spirit gives us a glimpse of the sacramental character which St. Paul was to find in these episodes.[207]

The psalms transpose this theme into personal piety. The spirit which led Israel, defended it against its enemies and caused it to live under God's regard, keeps its role, but now it is present in every just person:

> Teach me to do your will,
>> for you are my God.
> May your good spirit guide me
>> on level ground.[208]

The level ground is no longer the road traced out by the cloud for Israel in the desert: it is the way which man must follow, through temptations and struggles, to remain faithful to Yahweh. This is a requirement beyond man's strength, did not God put into his heart His spirit as a guide and defender, as an Ark and a cloud.

The psalm Miserere makes the same prayer:

> A clean heart create for me, O God,
>> and a steadfast spirit renew within me.
> Cast me not out from your presence,
>> and your holy spirit take not from me.
> Give me back the joy of your salvation
>> and a willing spirit sustain in me.[209]

One of the surprising beauties of this unique prayer is the transformation which occurs therein of the primitive representations and the liturgical or historical references into the most personal and spontaneous burst of sentiment. The call for a renewal, for a new spirit, issues from the cosmic images of the breath of God whose rhythm regulates the seasons:

267

When you send forth your spirit, they are created,
and you renew the face of the earth.[210]

Here is the heart saturated with its filthiness and its inability
to free itself from it, crying out to God its thirst for innocence
and purity. The fear of being rejected far from the face of God,
deprived of His spirit, comes also from the naive idea that man,
so long as he lives, remains animated by the breath which the
face of God breathes into him.[211] The fear of losing the presence
that God gave us as a gift to His people, and which He continues to grant to His chosen ones, contact with His holiness,
His "Holy Spirit," is substituted here for the fear of losing
natural life.

Of course, the revelation of Christ and the gift to the Church
of the Holy Spirit will be needed, so that Christians, discovering
that they have really entered into a new era, that "the former
things have passed away; behold they are made new . . . through
Christ,"[212] might dare to give an integrally spiritual sense to the
old beliefs of the naturalistic religion and call on the Holy Spirit
in terms which used to serve to evoke the renewal of springtime:

*Emitte Spiritum tuum et creabuntur,
Et renovabis faciem terrae!*[213]

This spiritual sense is authentic because, throughout the Old
Testament itself, the primitive images of the wind and the
breath of respiration were gradually stripped of their material
aspect, and because their divine nature finally predominated.
The mystery which they manifest was revealed more and more
as a mystery of God, less and less as a power of flesh and obscurity.

This is why, no doubt, the Christians adopted without difficulty the word of the Old Testament: they were convinced
that they were dealing with the same divine power. In fact, we
see the Gospels, especially the Synoptics, speak of the spirit in
exactly the same style as the older Scriptures, without indicating
clearly that they are speaking about a distinct person. The

268

spirit which fills Elizabeth when Mary greets her,[214] or Zacharias intoning his canticle,[215] the spirit which rests on Simeon and impels him to the Temple,[216] the very spirit which produces in Mary the miraculous conception[217] is scarcely different from that which animated the prophets. These resemblances are pursued beyond the accounts of the Infancy. The spirit which draws Jesus into the desert,[218] makes Him exult with joy,[219] gives Him power over devils,[220] has the same features. Even the final promise of Jesus, on the point of leaving His own, at the moment of the Ascension:

But you shall receive power when the Holy Spirit comes upon you, and you shall be witnesses for me in Jerusalem and in all Judea and Samaria and even to the very ends of the earth,[221]

did not necessarily mean anything more than an extraordinary manifestation of God.

In receiving this gift, the Christians were given the revelation of its unique nature. First of all, they experienced its absolute newness. John, like Paul, sees in the possession of the spirit the sign that the old economy has been abolished, that a world is born.[222]

They also become aware that they had been put by the spirit into immediate contact with God.[223] This contact is continuous. It has been remarked,[224] that, for John as for Paul, the spirit is a reality so familiar and concrete that they have no need to add any details to His name. If at times, for some particular reason, they call Him the Spirit of God, the Spirit of Christ, the Holy Spirit, most of the time they speak of the Spirit simply as of a well-known person, often even without the article, like a proper noun.

Conscious of having received the Holy Spirit as a personal possession, the Christians still were in no way embarrassed at seeing this name appear in so many texts of the Old Testament. Up to that time, His miraculous power had always been manifested in sudden and temporary interventions. They now lived in the permanent possession of this power. They felt that their existence was perpetually animated by this inexhaustible source. They could see this irresistible force building the Church. The miracles of the past seemed to them like the initial actions of God preparing His work. It was the same hand, and it was also the same Spirit.

6. THE WORD AND THE SPIRIT

The Spirit remains the most mysterious of realities. He is everywhere in the Church; He is at the source of the humblest of Christian actions as of the most exalted; He lives in the heart of every Christian, carrying on with the spirit of each one the dialogue which makes it live before God. How could He not be a person? Paul adores Him alongside the Father and the Son, and the Church baptizes in the name of the Three Persons. Yet He has no proper face, no apparent personal function which sets its mark on Him. The Word has an unforgettable physiognomy, His own speech, inimitable in its accent. The Father is visible in His Son. His name alone, on the lips of Jesus, suffices to give us an inkling of the depths of which He is the father. The Spirit has no role which determines His traits. He has no face. He does not even have His own name. As intangible as the wind, is He not even more evanescent?

He would be, were He not the Spirit of Jesus. There, for us, is the secret of His being. The New Testament reveals it to us. Perhaps a look back at the Old has helped us understand this revelation better.

True, it is going beyond the letter of many of our texts— though it is not false to the perspectives of the Bible—to read into them a constant correspondence between the Spirit and the Word. In the area of natural phenomena, the wind carries God's orders to the very ends of the world, just as the whispered breath of the sovereign goes forth to express his will to his subjects. At an altogether different level, that of the miraculous

270

and the special interventions of God in the world, the history of Israel involves a similar parallelism. It brings to light a succession of inspired men, of various types. Warriors, kings, prophets, they feel themselves roughly seized from on high, torn from their familiar dreams and thrown into some action which should crush them but which they dominate with ease. For a Gedeon or a David, this action means a specific mission: a campaign of liberation, a kingdom to be founded. For the prophets, the task is just as imperative: it is the Word of Yahweh which must be announced—not the holding of pious conversations, but the giving, in the immediate situation, of the most concrete and often the most portentous message, to the people and its rulers. For each of these particular missions, God sends His Spirit. It is always the Spirit of Yahweh: His name does not change. Still, it is a different action every time, each time marvelously adapted to the mission in view. No matter how far above the sphere of nature we may be, the same constants seem to be present. The Word of Yahweh, which comes down from heaven to His people and never returns to Him without having fulfilled its mission and produced its effect,[225] seems borne on the wings of the Spirit of Yahweh. The two forces are inseparable.

Nevertheless, they have traits which are quite distinct. The Word is imposed as from the outside. Of course it penetrates "even to the division of soul and spirit, of joints also and marrow,"[226] but its blade is steel, it lays all things bare. The Spirit however, is fluid, it infiltrates without being seen. The Word is heard and known,[227] no one knows the ways of the Spirit. The Word is revelation,[228] the Spirit, interior transformation. The Word stands up, tall, enduring,[229] the Spirit falls, spreads, is submerged. All these images reveal two quite different attitudes, two distinct actions, two ways which God has of reaching men.[230] By His Word, Yahweh lighted the way for His people, marked out their path, indicated His Will to them,

271

gave them the meaning of their past history and set the direction for the future. By His Spirit, of which certain chosen ones benefited as signs and witnesses, He infiltrated hearts in order to transform them, to open them up to His word, to make them His bearers and His martyrs.

This division of roles is also found in the New Testament. The mission of Jesus was to speak, to guide, to announce the future, to reveal the Father. His mission fulfilled, once the name of His Father has been manifested to men,[231] He must disappear. He cannot go any further; He must go away, He has to be lifted up on the Cross to fulfill all the words of the Scripture by showing to the world the extent to which the Father has loved it. Then the Spirit can come, and the Word will in the end penetrate hearts. This will not be a new revelation; the Spirit has nothing more to say than what Jesus has said.[232] But, so long as He has not come, the words of Jesus fall on deaf ears: only the Spirit speaks to the spirit.[233]

The Spirit who speaks in this way speaks but of one thing: Jesus. He has but one movement: toward the Father. This is the secret which He whispers, in ineffable confidences. The Old Testament was acquainted with some of His unheard-of actions, it awaited Him with all its desire. To children alone is given the secret of this presence without name and without face. The living water proceeds only from the pierced side.

NOTES

[1] Ex. 15: 8, 10. The date of this canticle is difficult to determine, but there is nothing that compels us to believe it is recent. Cf. H. Schmidt, "Das Meerlied," in *Zeitschrift für die altestamentaliche Wissenschaft*, 1931, pp. 59–66.

[2] Ps. 17: 16, with the corrections made by P. Dhorme, *Les Livres de Samuel*, Paris, 1910, p. 427.

[3] Cf. P. Dhorme, "L'emploi métaphorique des noms de parties du corps en hébreu et en akkadien," in *Revue Biblique*, 1921, pp. 530–531.

[4] Is. 30: 27–28.

[5] Is. 30: 33. Cf. Job 4: 9; 15: 30.

[6] Ex. 15: 8.

[7] Ex. 14: 21.

[8] Ex. 10: 13–19; 14: 21; Num. 11: 31, where it is said that a wind from Yahweh blew.

[9] Gen. 8: 1.

[10] Gen. 3: 8.

[11] Osee 13: 15.

[12] Osee 4: 19.

[13] Is. 17: 13; 40: 24; 41: 2, 16; 57: 13; Jer. 13: 24; 22: 22.

[14] Job 15: 30; cf. 21: 18; Ps. 1: 4; 17: 43; 34: 5; 82: 14.

[15] Ezech. 17: 10; 19: 12.

[16] Ezech. 27: 26.

[17] Ezech. 13: 11, 13.

[18] Ezech. 5: 10, 12; 12: 14; 17: 21.

[19] It has the strict sense of these points only in Ezech. 42: 16–20 (in a vision!), 1 Par. 9: 24 and, probably, Jer. 52: 23.

[20] Jer. 49: 36; Ezech. 37: 9; Zach. 6: 5.

[21] Jer. 49: 36; Zach. 2: 10; Dan. 11: 4; cf. Dan. 7: 2; 8: 8.

[22] Osee 12: 2; Is. 26: 18; 41: 29; Jer. 5: 13; Job. 7: 7; 15: 2; Prov. 11: 29; 25: 14; 27: 16; Ps. 77: 39; Eccles. 1: 14, 17; 2: 11, 17, 26; 4: 4, 6, 16; 5: 15; 5: 9.

[23] P. Dhorme, *Choix de textes religieux assyro-babyloniens*, Paris, 1907, p. 53.

[24] J. Chaine, *Le Livre de la Genèse*, Paris, 1948, p. 58.

[25] Gen. 1: 9.

[26] Ps. 88: 11.

[27] Ps. 75: 13.

[28] Job 26: 12.

[29] Job 26: 13.

[30] Is. 51: 9–10.

[31] Ps. 148: 8.

[32] Ps. 103: 4.

[33] Ps. 146: 17–18, with the correction of Gunkel adopted in the new Latin Psalter.

[34] Prov. 30: 4.

[35] Job 28: 25, 26.

[36] 3 Kings 19: 11–12.

[37] Ezech. 1: 4.

[38] This is the solution of Fr. Joüon: "Quelques remarques sur Gen. 1: 2," in *Recherches de Science religieuse*, 1926, p. 307. It is also the solution of Fr. Heinisch, *Das Buch Genesis*, Bonn, 1930, p. 96.

[39] Among the numerous studies on this verse, see, for example: W. H. McClellan, "The meaning of ruah Elohim in Gen. 1: 2," in *Biblica*, 1934, pp. 517–527; Fr. Van Imschoot, "L'esprit de Yahweh, source de vie dans l'A.T.," in *Revue Biblique*, 1935, pp. 488–491. The question was discussed further by O. Eissfeldt, "Das Chaos in der biblischen und in der phönizischen Kosmogonie," in *Forsuchungen und Fortschritte*, 1940, pp. 1–3; cf. S. Moscati, "The Wind in Biblical and Phoenician Cosmogony" in *Journal of Biblical Literature*, 1947, pp. 305–310.

[40] Deut. 32: 11. In Jer. 23: 9, the verb signifies the trembling of fear. Again, it involves a sort of vibrating movement. One of the poems discovered at Ras Shamra furnishes several very clear examples of the verb *rhp*. It designates the flight of circling eagles, ready to swoop down upon their prey. See the text in C. Virolleaud, *La légende phénicienne de Danel*, Paris, 1936, text III D I, 20, 21, 29, 30, 32, p. 218, and the translation by C. H. Gordon, *Ugaritic Literature*, Rome, 1949, p. 93.

[41] As H. Gunkel thinks, *Genesis*, Gottingen, 1915, p. 104.

[42] Cf. Ps. 17: 11.

[43] Is. 11: 4; Ps. 146: 18. Cf. J. Hehn, "Zum Problem des Geistes im Alten Orient und im A.T.," in *Zeitschrift für die alttestamentliche Wissenschaft*, 1925, pp. 218–220.

[44] Ps. 32: 6. The hymn of Judith's epilogue also sings: "thou didst send forth thy spirit, and they were created" (Judith 16: 14, according to the Septuagint).

[45] Gen. 2: 1.

273

[46] Ps. 32: 7.

[47] Ex. 15: 8.

[48] Ps. 146: 18.

[49] Ps. 147:8.

[50] Ps. 103: 4.

[51] The points of contact have long been indicated. Cf. H. Gunkel, *Genesis*, Gottingen, 1910, p. 121; *Die Psalmen*, Gottingen, 1926, p. 453; Fr. Humbert, "La relation de Genése 1: 2 et du Psaume CIV avec la liturgie du Nouvel An israélite," in *Revue d'Histoire et de Philosophie religieuses*, 1935, pp. 1–27.

[52] Mark 4: 40.

[53] Acts 2: 2–3.

[54] John 3: 5.

[55] John 3: 8.

[56] Ps. 103: 29–30.

[57] The breath of the mouth can also be formidable. The Messias expected by Isaias, "with the breath of his lips . . . shall slay the wicked" (Is. 11: 4). The fact is that the breath of the mouth is the bearer of the word and the word here is the means of justice and vengeance. But other texts (Is. 30: 27–28, for example) show that the difference between the breath from the nostrils and that of the mouth is not absolute. What is certain is that the breath from the nostrils always denotes wrath.

[58] Gen. 2: 7.

[59] Is. 42: 5.

[60] Job 33: 4.

[61] Job. 27: 3.

[62] Job. 34: 14–15.

[63] Cf. E. Podechard, *L'Ecclésiaste*, Paris, 1912, p. 315.

[64] Eccles. 3: 21.

[65] Eccles. 12: 7. Cf. Wis. 15: 11.

[66] Cf. G. van der Leeuw, "Phénomenologie de l'âme," in *Revue d'Histoire et de Philosophie religieuses*, 1930, p. 20.

[67] Is. 40: 6.

[68] Is. 40: 7.

[69] Gen. 6: 17; 7: 22.

[70] Gen. 6: 3.

[71] Jer. 17: 5.

[72] Job. 10: 4.

[73] Ps. 55: 5.

[74] Is. 31: 1, 3. Cf. Zach. 4: 6; 2 Par. 32: 8.

[75] P. Dhorme, "L'emploi métaphorique . . .," in *Revue Biblique*, 1920, pp. 471–474.

[76] Eph. 2: 2; 6: 12.

[77] John 6: 63.

[78] 2 Cor. 3: 6.

[79] 2 Cor. 3: 17. This is the interpretation of Fr. Prat, *Le Théologie de saint Paul*, Paris, 4th ed., 1925, pp. 522–529, and Fr. Allo, *IIe Épître aux Corinthiens*, Paris, 1937, pp. 93–96 and 103–111.

[80] Cf. Rom. 8: 2–4; Matt. 16: 17; John 1: 13; 1 Cor. 15: 50.

[81] John 4: 24.

[82] L. Bouyer, *Le quatriéme Évangile*, Paris, 1938, pp. 113–114.

[83] Num. 16: 22; 27: 16.

[84] Regarding the Hebrew concept of the soul, M. Dussaud developed his own theory in a series of studies, *Introduction a l'histoire des religions*, Paris, 1914, pp. 46–47, 200; *Les origines cananéennes du sacrifice israélite*, Paris, 2nd ed., 1941, pp. 83–84; *La notion d'âme chez les Israélites et les Phéniciens*, Syria, 1935, pp. 267–277; "La nephesh et la rouah dans le Livre de Job," in *Revue de l'Histoire des Religions*, 1945, pp. 17–30. M. Dussaud distinguishes

two souls, the *ruah*, the spiritual soul, seat of the intellect, localized in the heart, and the *nephesh*, the vegetative soul, seated in the fat of the intestines, the loins, the membrane of the liver, in a word, the organs that our texts encompass under the name of fat. His conclusions did not convince everyone. M. Dussaud himself indicated the reservations of M. Lods (*Revue d'Histoire des Religions*, 1945, pp. 29–30). See also those of Fr. de Vaux in *Revue Biblique*, 1938, p. 637. The study by L. Durr, on the meaning of the Hebrew *nephesh* and the Akkadian *napishtu*, in *Zeitschrift für die alttestamentliche Wissenschaft*, 1925, pp. 262–269, based on etymological research, might perhaps make it possible to understand many of the particular items pointed out by M. Dussaud.

[85] Cf. J. Pedersen, *Israel, its Life and Culture*, London-Copenhagen, 1926, pp. 102–104.

[86] E. Mounier, *Traité du caractère*, Paris, 1946, p. 287.

[87] J. Pedersen, *op. cit.*, p. 100.

[88] Job 7: 11.

[89] Gen. 41: 8.

[90] Gen. 26: 35.

[91] Gen. 45: 27.

[92] Ex. 35: 21; Ezech. 11: 5; 20: 32.

[93] Judg. 8: 3; Prov. 29: 22.

[94] A.M. Dubarle, *Les Sages d'Israël*, Paris, 1946, p. 197.

[95] Wis. 15: 11.

[96] Wis. 15: 8.

[97] Luke 12: 20.

[98] It is the recurring formula of all the creeds: "Carnis resurrectionem."

[99] Luke 23: 46; Ps. 30: 6.

[100] Job 12: 10.

[101] Matt. 16: 25; John 12: 25.

[102] John 6: 63.

[103] J. Hehn, "Zum Problem des Geistes im Alten Orient und im A.T.," in *Zeitschrift für die alttestamentliche Wissenschaft*, 1925, pp. 210–225. The most characteristic of these texts were translated by Fr. van Imschoot in his article: "L'Esprit de Yahweh, source de vie dans l'Ancien Testament," in *Revue Biblique*, 1935, pp. 492–496.

[104] Quotation collected by A. de Buck, *Uitzicht*, December 1942–January 1943, p. 201, and translation by J. Sainte-Fare Garnot, *Revue de l'Histoire des Religions*, 1945, p. 108.

[105] Gen. 9: 12–17; Ex. 20: 12; Deut. 11: 13–15.

[106] Matt. 5: 45.

[107] 3 Kings 18: 12; 4 Kings 2: 16.

[108] 3 Kings 18: 46.

[109] Ezech. 3: 14.

[110] Ezech. 8: 3; 11: 1.

[111] Ezech. 11: 24.

[112] Ezech. 3: 14; 8: 3.

[113] Ezech. 1: 4, 20.

[114] Acts 8: 39.

[115] Acts 13: 4.

[116] Acts 16: 6.

[117] Mark 1: 12; Matt. 4: 1; Luke 4: 1.

[118] Num. 5: 14–30.

[119] 1 Kings 16: 14, 15, 16; 18: 10; 19: 9.

[120] Judg. 9: 23.

[121] Osee 4: 12; 5: 4.

[122] 1 Kings 16: 14; 3 Kings 22: 22. Cf. Fr. van Imschoot, "L'action de l'Esprit de Yahweh dans l'A.T.," in *Revue des Sciences philosophiques et théologiques*, 1934, pp. 553–587.

[123] 3 Kings 22: 23.

[124] Thus Judg. 9: 23. 1 Kings 16: 14, 15, 16; 18: 10; 19:9; 3 Kings 22: 22; 4 Kings

19: 7; Is. 19: 14; 29:10: In all these cases, a special intention of God seems indicated. This intention, on the contrary, does not appear where God is not mentioned, in Num. 5: 14–30; Osee 4: 12; 5: 4.

[125] 1 Kings 19: 9.

[126] Judg. 3: 10.

[127] Judg. 11: 29.

[128] Judg. 14: 6, 19; 15: 14.

[129] 1 Kings 11: 6.

[130] Judg. 6: 34.

[131] 1 Kings 16: 13.

[132] Still, there is a difference. Regarding the Judges, the spirit was said to *tislah 'al*, regarding David, *tislah 'el*. But the force of the expression is retained in the verb *tislah* and the nuance between the two prepositions seems negligible.

[133] Is. 11: 2.

[134] Is. 32: 17.

[135] P. Desnoyers, *Histoire du peuple hébreu*, I, Paris, 1922, p. 310.

[136] Cf. Amos 7: 10–17.

[137] 1 Kings 10: 6, 10.

[138] Ex. 15: 20.

[139] Num. 11: 17, 25.

[140] Num. 11: 29.

[141] Even Samuel and Elias, so close to these *nabis*, and in frequent contact with their confraternities, nevertheless do not seem to have belonged to them. Desnoyers, *op. cit.*, I, p. 223, n. 1.

[142] 3 Kings 22: 14.

[143] Regarding the reasons for this silence, see W. Eichrodt, *Theologie des A.T.*, II, Leipzig, 1935, p. 24, n. 13, and Fr. van Imschoot, "L'action de l'Esprit de Yahweh dans l'A.T.," in *Revue des Sciences philosophiques et théologiques*, 1934, pp. 570–573.

[144] Amos 3: 7.

[145] Jer. 23: 18. Several exegetes, among them Fr. Condamin, do not admit the authenticity of this verse. No doubt it is obscure and we must supply, along with Driver: "who, *therefore, among them. . . .*" But is this obscurity sufficient reason to reject it?

[146] Ex. 19: 10–20; 24: 15–18.

[147] 3 Kings 19: 12–13.

[148] W. Eichrodt, *op. cit.*, II, p. 3.

[149] Is. 6: 6.

[150] Is. 8: 11.

[151] Compares 3 Kings 18: 12 with 3 Kings 18: 46. Cf. Ezech. 3: 14; 8: 3. The touch of the hand has the same significance as the gift of the spirit: the outpouring in man of a divine power.

[152] Jer. 1: 9.

[153] Jer. 20: 7. Cf. 15: 17.

[154] Ezech. 3: 12–14; 8: 3; 11: 1, 24; 43: 5.

[155] Is. 42: 1.

[156] Mich. 3: 8. This text is difficult. For the meaning to be attributed to the word *michpat*, see *supra*, Ch. III, Sec. 1. With this slight difference, the meaning seems to be that of A. van Hoonacker, *Les douze petits prophètes*, Paris, 1908, p. 378. Many exegetes believe the intervention of the spirit to be a later interpolation, inspired by Is. 11: 2. The construction is indeed forced, but are we to reject all difficult texts? The borrowing from Isaias could not be explained unless this passage were messianic.

[157] Is. 11: 2.

[158] The Servant of Yahweh is above all the leader of a new people, a new Jacob, a new Moses. Cf. A. Feuillet, *Supplément au Dictionnaire de la Bible*, IV, 713; *idem*, "Le messianisme du Livre d'Isaïe," in *Recherches de Science religieuse*, 1949, p. 211.

[159] Is. 61: 1.

[160] For example, A. Condamin, *Le Livre d'Isaïe*, Paris, 1905, pp. 358–361. In an opposite sense, A. Vaccari, "I carmini del Servo di Jahwe," in *Miscellanea Biblica*, 1934, II, p. 216 ff. Cf. A. Feuillet, *Supplément au Dictionnaire de la Bible*, IV, 724.

[161] Cf. Luke 4: 21.

[162] Cf. J. Bonsirven, *Le Judaïsme palestinien au temps de Jésus-Christ*, Paris, 1935, I, p. 210.

[163] Matt. 17: 3; John 5: 39, 46.

[164] Zach. 7: 12.

[165] 2 Esd. 9: 30.

[166] Matt. 10: 18–20; Mark 13: 9–11.

[167] Acts 1: 8.

[168] John 15: 26–27.

[169] John 16: 8.

[170] Rom. 8: 16.

[171] Whence the gravity of the sin against the Spirit, committed in the light of this testimony: Matt. 12: 31–32; Mark 3: 28–30.

[172] John 14: 16.

[173] John 14: 26.

[174] Rom. 8: 15.

[175] To interpret this permanent possession of the spirit, the First Epistle of St. John (2: 20, 27) takes up the same biblical image of the anointing: "you have an anointing from the Holy One and . . . know all things. . . . the anointing which you have received from him, dwell[s] in you. . . . teaches you concerning all things." In the Old Testament, the theme of the anointing only coincides twice with that of the spirit, at the time of the consecration of David (1 Kings 16: 13), and the consecration of the prophet charged with announcing the good news, the coming of God (Is. 61: 1). At the time of the consecration of Saul (1 Kings 10: 1, 6), the two themes are quite close, but they are never brought together. It is natural that this connection should be rare in the Old Testament. The manifestations of the spirit are practically all exceptional and temporary, whereas the anointing with oil, which slowly seeps in and impregnates the hardest substances (cf. the anointing of the sacred pillars, Gen. 28: 18), endowed with permanent powers. The Messias is the Anointed, par excellence, who is filled with the power of God. Jesus knows that He is filled with this unction (Luke 4: 18). After Him, the Christians are impregnated for life by this unction, of ineradicable nature, from the moment the spirit "dwells with [them] forever" (John 14: 16, 17). In John, it is an anointing, in Paul, a seal (2 Cor. 1: 22; Eph. 1: 13); both themes express the permanent possession of the spirit.

[176] 1 Cor. 12: 7.

[177] Rom. 8: 11–15.

[178] Cf. A. Condamin, *Le Livre d'Isaïe*, Paris, 1905, pp. 99 and 204.

[179] Is. 32: 15–20.

[180] Is. 32: 15 has the verb 'arah. The word which Ezech. 39: 29, Zach. 12: 10 and Joel 3: 1, consecrate, is chaphak. The image is the same—that of a liquid poured out. Osee (10: 12, correcting weyoreh to yarwed) shows God irrigating the land of Israel with the waters of justice. This image is repeated in Is. 58: 11; Jer. 31: 12, 25.

[181] Is. 19: 14, according to the Septuagint.

[182] Is. 29: 10.

[183] Jer. 14: 16.

[184] Jer. 24: 7; cf. 32: 38.

[185] Jer. 31: 33.

[186] Ezech. 36: 25–27; cf. 11: 19.

[187] Ezech. 39: 29.

[188] Ezech. 37: 1–14.

[189] Is. 44: 3.

[190] Cf. Is. 41: 18; 43: 20.

[191] Is. 59: 21.

[192] Deut. 30: 14.

[193] Deut. 4: 9; 6: 6.

[194] Joel 2: 28-29.

[195] We should also quote the obscure text in Zacharias, which also announces a pouring out of the spirit. However, this spirit is not called the spirit of Yahweh, though this is almost the case: "I will pour forth upon the house of David and upon the inhabitant of Jerusalem, a spirit of goodness and supplication. They shall look upon him whom they have pierced, they shall make a lamentation over him as over an only son, they shall weep over him as one weeps over a first-born son" (Zach. 12: 10, according to the corrections and the translation by A. Gelin, *Aggée, Zacharie, Malachie*, in *La Sainte Bible*, Cerf, Paris, 1948). It seems that the following promise: "In that day there shall be a fountain open to the house of David and to the inhabitants of Jerusalem: for the . . . sinner and . . . the unclean . . ." (Zach. 13: 1), is the conclusion of the same poem and also confirms the relationship between the spirit and the water.

[196] Matt. 3: 11-12; Mark 1: 7-8; John 1: 33. Regarding the origins of Baptism and the use of the word, cf. M. J. Lagrange, *Évangile selon saint Marc*, 4th ed., Paris, 1929, p. 6; A. Oepke, in Kittel, *Theologisches Wörterbuch*, I, 535.

[197] Acts 1: 5.

[198] Acts. 2: 17-18.

[199] 1 Cor. 12: 13. It does not seem that this drink is a reference to the Eucharist. J. Huby, *Saint Paul, Ire Épître aux Corinthiens*, Paris, 1946, pp. 288-289. On this point Fr. Huby differs with M. Cerfaux, whose overall interpretation concerning the meaning of the word "body" he accepts. Cf. L. Cerfaux, *La théologie de l'Église suivant saint Paul*, 2nd ed., Paris, 1948, p. 207 and no. 1.

[200] John 7: 37-39. "We may punctuate Jesus' call another way and connect: 'He who believes in me' not to what goes before, but to what follows. In this event, the rivers of living water will flow from the bosom of the believer who has drunk at the source. This punctuation is in general use since Origen. But it runs up against the difficulty of identifying the Scriptural text to which it alludes and the unusual nature of the affirmation. On the other hand, the most ancient witnesses: Justin, Irenaeus, Hippolytus, the letter of the Church of Lyon, testify in favor of the punctuation adopted here. For them, the rivers of living water flow from Jesus." D. Mollat, "L'Évangile selon saint Jean," in *La Sainte Bible . . . de Jerusalem*, Paris 1953, p. 110. It is the most common interpretation nowadays, since the articles by R. H. Rahner, "Flumina de ventre Jesu, Die patristiche Auslegung von Johann, VII, 37-38," in *Biblica*, XXII (1941) pp. 269-302, 367-403. See also the arguments of E. Ruckstuhl, *Die literarische Einheit des Johannesevangelium*, Freiburg in der Schweiz, 1951, p. 250, note 2,—and those of F. M. Braun, "L'eau et l'esprit," *Revue Thomiste*, 1949, pp. 5-30.

[201] John 6: 63.

[202] John 4: 10.

[203] John 4: 14.

[204] Judg. 14: 6, 19; 15: 14, according to the *Vaticanus*. 1 Kings 10: 10; 16: 13. Cf. J. H. Bernard, *A Critical and Exegetical Commentary of the Gospel according to St. John*, Edinburg, 1928, I, p. 141.

[205] Is. 63: 9-14, according to the translation by P. Auvray and J. Steinmann in *La Sainte Bible . . . de Jerusalem*.

[206] 2 Esd. 9: 20.

[207] 1 Cor. 10: 1-4.

[208] Ps. 142: 10.

[209] Ps. 50: 12-14.

[210] Ps. 103: 30.

211 For the association face-spirit, cf. Ps. 138: 7: "Where can I go far from your face, where can I flee far from your spirit?" Cf. Is. 63: 9–10.

212 2 Cor. 5: 17.

213 Ps. 102: 30 (Vulgate).

214 Luke 1: 41.

215 Luke 1: 67.

216 Luke 2: 25–27.

217 Luke 1: 35.

218 Matt. 4: 1; Mark 1: 12; Luke 4: 1.

219 Luke 10: 21.

220 Matt. 12: 28.

221 Acts 1: 8.

222 2 Cor. 3: 6, 17; Gal. 3: 2; 4: 4–6; Rom. 8: 13, 15; John 3: 8; 7: 39; 14: 17.

223 1 Cor. 2: 10; 12: 3; 2 Cor. 1: 22; 3: 17; Gal. 4: 6; 5: 25; Rom. 8: 9, 14, 16; John 4: 24; 15: 26.

224 H. B. Swete, The Holy Spirit in the New Testament, London, 1909, p. 287.

225 Is. 55: 11. Cf. Zach. 1: 6; Ps. 146: 15.

226 Heb. 4: 12. Cf. Is. 49: 2.

227 Deut. 4: 36; Is. 1: 10; 28: 14; Jer. 5: 14, etc.

228 Ps. 146: 19.

229 2 Kings 7:28–29; Is. 40: 8; Ps. 118: 89; Wis. 18: 16.

230 For St. Irenaeus, the Son and the Spirit are the two hands with which God fashions the world and guides its history. Cf. Adversus Haereses, IV, preface, 4 (Harvey, II, p. 145); IV, 20, 1 (Harvey, II, p. 213); V, 1, 3 (Harvey, II, p. 317); V, 6, 1 (Harvey, II, p. 333); V, 28, 3 (Harvey, II p. 403).

231 John 17: 6.

232 John 14: 26; 15: 26; 16: 13.

233 Rom. 8: 16.